90 Days
Through the New Testament
IN CHRONOLOGICAL ORDER

RON RHODES

HARVEST HOUSE PUBLISHERS
EUGENE, OREGON

Cover by Dugan Design Group, Bloomington, Minnesota

Cover photos © AnnekaS / Bigstock; Volodymyr Horbovyy / Shutterstock

90 DAYS THROUGH THE NEW TESTAMENT IN CHRONOLOGICAL ORDER

Copyright © 2015 Ron Rhodes
Published by Harvest House Publishers
Eugene, Oregon 97402
www.harvesthousepublishers.com

Library of Congress Cataloging-in-Publication Data
    Rhodes, Ron.
    90 days through the New Testament in chronological order / Ron Rhodes.
        pages cm
    Includes bibliographical references.
    ISBN 978-0-7369-6431-9 (pbk.)
    ISBN 978-0-7369-6432-6 (eBook)
    1. Bible. New Testament—Criticism, interpretation, etc. I. Title. II. Title: Ninety days through the New Testament in chronological order.
    BS2361.3.R49 2015
    225.6—dc23
                                                                            2015000617

Printed in the United States of America

15 16 17 18 19 20 21 22 23 / BP-JH / 10 9 8 7 6 5 4 3 2 1

To Kerri, David, and Kylie

ACKNOWLEDGMENTS

Kerri, David, and Kylie—
>The sun seems to shine brighter with you in my world!
>What an awesome family the Lord has given us.

All my friends at Harvest House Publishers—
>Your collective efforts have spiritually enriched multitudes
>around the globe.
>I feel privileged to work with you!

CONTENTS

Introduction

Thank you for joining me on this exciting journey through the New Testament. You are in for a spiritually uplifting time! My hope and prayer is that as you read *90 Days Through the New Testament in Chronological Order*, you will…

- experience a growing love for the Word of God,
- grow in your knowledge of and appreciation for the wondrous salvation you have in Jesus Christ,
- experience more daily intimacy with Jesus than ever before,
- understand and experience God's incredible grace in your daily walk with Him,
- grow in your knowledge of the Holy Spirit and dependence on Him as He empowers you to live the Christian life,
- grow in your faith and trust in God in the midst of life's troubles, and
- gain an eternal perspective so that you see life's problems and difficulties from heaven's vantage point.

As we begin our journey together, I want to address a few things that will lay a foundation for better understanding the New Testament. Let's look at the big picture first and consider some preliminary matters about how this book is arranged. Then we will zero in on our chronological study of the New Testament.

The Significance of the New Testament

The New Testament is a collection of 27 writings composed over a 50-year period by nine different authors from various walks of life. The primary personality of the New Testament is Jesus Christ. The primary theme is salvation in Jesus Christ, based on the new covenant.

The word "testament" refers to a covenant or agreement. The Old Testament focuses on an old covenant between God and the Israelites. According to that covenant (the Sinai covenant), the Jews were to be God's people and render obedience to Him, and in return God would bless them (Exodus 19:3-25). Israel failed repeatedly and continually violated this covenant. So even in Old Testament times, the prophets began to speak of a new covenant that would focus not on keeping external laws but on an inner reality and change in the human heart (Jeremiah 31:31). Unlike the Sinai covenant, the new covenant was to make full provision for the forgiveness of sins.

When Jesus ate the Passover meal with the disciples in the upper room, He spoke of the cup as "the new covenant in my blood" (Luke 22:20; see also 1 Corinthians 11:25). Hebrews 7 demonstrates that Christ's priesthood is superior to the old priesthood, and it logically follows that such a superior priesthood would have a superior ministry. Such a ministry is provided for in the new covenant. Jesus has done all that is necessary for the forgiveness of sins by His once-for-all sacrifice on the cross. This new covenant is the basis for our relationship with God in the New Testament.

The Books of the New Testament

The first four books of the New Testament are the Gospels: Matthew, Mark, Luke, and John. Each of these contains an account of the life of Christ. None portrays all the details of His life, but taken together, they provide a full composite account.

Each Gospel author included different details, depending on his purpose for writing. For example, the Gospel of Matthew has more citations from the Old Testament than any other Gospel because Matthew sought to prove to the Jews that Jesus is the Messiah prophesied in the Old Testament. Mark, by contrast, had no such Jewish motivation, but instead sought to portray Jesus in action rather than as a teacher. Luke's Gospel stresses the wonderful blessings of salvation for all people. John's Gospel focuses heavily on the identity of Jesus and thoroughly demonstrates His deity.

Following the Gospels is the book of Acts, which traces the spread of Christianity following the death and resurrection of Christ. Though the book is traditionally understood as the acts of the apostles, it is probably more appropriately understood as the acts of the Holy Spirit, for truly it is the Holy Spirit who seems to be active in just about every chapter of the book.

Following the book of Acts are the epistles, or letters. The apostle Paul wrote 13 of these, and the rest were written by other followers of Jesus. Many of the New Testament epistles were written to brand-new churches that had certain issues that needed to be addressed (1 and 2 Thessalonians are examples). The apostle Paul often wrote letters to follow up his missionary visits to churches. (For example, Paul wrote Ephesians following his visit to the church at Ephesus.) Therefore, Paul's letters are often personal. In some cases, Paul gave advice to the leader of a particular church. (Such was the case when Paul wrote 1 Timothy.) Other times he addressed the church as a whole. (Philippians is a good example.)

Other New Testament epistles—the "general epistles"—were not directed at specific churches, but were circulated to a number of churches and dealt with general concerns. These are primarily the non-Pauline epistles, such as James; 1 and 2 Peter; and 1, 2, and 3 John.

Though the epistles were originally written for first-century Christians, they have tremendous relevance for Christians today. Indeed, the issues dealt with in the epistles are relevant to every generation. We need spiritual instruction just as the ancients did.

The final book of the New Testament is the book of Revelation, which is an apocalyptic book full of prophecy. This book was written to persecuted believers to give them hope, inspiration, and comfort so they could patiently endure the struggles they were facing. The book demonstrates that God wins in the end and that we will all live face-to-face with Him forever in new heavens and a new earth. The book also gives strong hope to current-day Christians who live in an increasingly troubled world.

The Inspiration of the New Testament Books

The biblical Greek word translated "inspired" literally means "Godbreathed." Biblical inspiration may be defined as God's superintending of the human authors so that, using their own individual personalities and writing styles, they composed and recorded without error His revelation to humankind in the words of the original autographs (handwritten manuscripts). In other words, the original documents of the Bible were written by men who, though permitted to exercise their own personalities and literary talents, wrote under the control and guidance of the Holy Spirit, the result being a perfect and errorless recording of the exact message God desired to give to man.

The writers of Scripture were thus not mere writing machines. God did not use them like keys on a typewriter to mechanically reproduce His message. Nor did He dictate the words, page by page. The biblical evidence shows that each writer had a style of his own. Matthew's writing had Jewish overtones, Mark's writing was action-oriented, Luke's style had medical overtones, John was very simple in his approach, and Paul had a theological style. The Holy Spirit infallibly worked through each of these writers, through their individual styles, to communicate His message without error to humankind. This means that you can trust your New Testament (and, of course, the Old Testament as well).

The New Testament Canon

The word "canon" comes from a Greek word that means "measuring stick." Over time, the word eventually came to be used metaphorically of books that were "measured" and thereby recognized as being God's Word. When we talk about the canon of Scripture today, we are referring to all the biblical books that collectively constitute God's Word.

Many books written during New Testament times were recognized as being the Word of God at that time. In 1 Timothy 5:18, for example, the apostle Paul joined an Old Testament reference and a

New Testament reference and called them both (collectively) Scripture (Deuteronomy 25:4 and Luke 10:7). It would not have been unusual in the context of first-century Judaism for an Old Testament passage to be called Scripture. But for a New Testament book to be referred to as Scripture so soon after it was written says volumes about Paul's view of the authority of contemporary New Testament books.

Only three years elapsed between the writing of the Gospel of Luke and the writing of 1 Timothy. (Luke was written around AD 60, and 1 Timothy was written around AD 63.) Despite this, Paul—himself a Jew, a "Hebrew of Hebrews"—does not hesitate to place Luke on the same level of authority as the Old Testament book of Deuteronomy.

Further, the writings of the apostle Paul were recognized as Scripture by the apostle Peter (see 2 Peter 3:16). Paul, too, understood that his own writings were inspired by God and therefore authoritative (1 Corinthians 14:37; 1 Thessalonians 2:13). Paul, of course, wrote about half the New Testament books.

When the church formally recognized which books belonged in the canon at the Council of Carthage in AD 397, five primary tests were applied.

Was the book written or backed by a prophet or apostle of God? The reasoning here is that the Word of God which is inspired by the Spirit of God for the people of God must be communicated through a man of God. Second Peter 1:20-21 assures us that Scripture is written only by men of God. In Galatians 1:1-24 the apostle Paul argued for support of the letter he was writing by appealing to the fact that he was an authorized messenger of God, an apostle.

Is the book authoritative? In other words, can it be said of this book as it was said of Jesus, "The people were amazed at his teaching, because he taught them as one who had authority, not as the teachers of the law" (Mark 1:22)? Put another way, does this book ring with a sense of "Thus saith the Lord"?

Does the book tell the truth about God as it has already been revealed? The Bereans searched the Old Testament Scriptures to see whether Paul's teaching was true (Acts 17:11). They knew that if Paul's teaching did not accord with the Old Testament canon, it could not be of God.

Agreement with all earlier revelation is essential. Paul certainly recognized this, for he said to the Galatians, "Even if we or an angel from heaven should preach to you a gospel contrary to the one we preached to you, let him be accursed" (Galatians 1:8).

Does the book give evidence of having the power of God? The reasoning here is that any writing that does not exhibit the transforming power of God in the lives of its readers could not have come from God. Scripture says that the Word of God is living and active (Hebrews 4:12). Second Timothy 3:15-17 indicates that God's Word has a transforming effect. If the book in question did not have the power to change lives, then the book could not have come from God.

Was the book accepted by the people of God? In the New Testament, Paul thanked the Thessalonians for receiving his message as the Word of God (1 Thessalonians 2:13). Paul's letters were circulated among the churches (Colossians 4:16; 1 Thessalonians 5:27). It is the norm that God's people—that is, the majority of them and not simply a faction—will initially receive God's Word as such.

Interestingly, in AD 367—some 30 years prior to the Council of Carthage—Athanasius (a bishop of Alexandria and a great champion of orthodoxy) wrote his Paschal Letter, in which he listed all the books of our present New Testament canon. So even before this definitive council met, the books that belonged in the New Testament were already known.

The bottom line is this: You can trust that the New Testament books are truly the Word of God.

The Reliability of the New Testament

The New Testament is not based on myth or hearsay. Rather, it is based on eyewitness testimony. John, who wrote the Gospel of John, said in his first epistle, "That which was from the beginning, which we have heard, which we have seen with our eyes, which we looked upon and have touched with our hands, concerning the word of life...we proclaim also to you" (1 John 1:1-3). Peter likewise wrote, "We did not follow cleverly devised myths when we made known to you the power and coming of our Lord Jesus Christ, but we were eyewitnesses of his majesty" (2 Peter 1:16).

The Bible writers gave up their lives defending what they wrote. No one gives up his or her life in defense of a lie! Further, manuscript evidence and archeological discoveries give a convincing stamp of approval to the reliability of the New Testament.

The Authority of the New Testament

Scripture alone is the supreme and infallible authority for the church and the individual believer (1 Corinthians 2:13; 1 Thessalonians 2:13; 2 Timothy 3:16-17; 2 Peter 1:21). Certainly Jesus and the apostles often gave testimony to the absolute authority of the Bible as the Word of God. Jesus affirmed the Bible's divine inspiration (Matthew 22:43), its indestructibility (Matthew 5:17-18), its infallibility (John 10:35), its final authority (Matthew 4:4,7,10), its historicity (Matthew 12:40; 24:37), and its factual inerrancy (Matthew 22:29; John 17:17).

Scripture has final authority because it is a direct revelation from God and carries the very authority of God Himself (Galatians 1:12). What the Bible says, God says. The Scriptures are the final court of appeal on all doctrinal and moral matters. We need no other source, and indeed no other source is authoritative and binding upon the Christian.

Jesus said, "Scripture cannot be broken" (John 10:35). He also said, "Until heaven and earth pass away, not an iota, not a dot, will pass from the Law until all is accomplished" (Matthew 5:18). He said, "It is easier for heaven and earth to pass away than for one dot of the Law to become void" (Luke 16:17). Jesus appealed to Scripture in every disputed matter. To the Sadducees He said, "You are wrong, because you know neither the Scriptures nor the power of God" (Matthew 22:29). He told some Pharisees that they invalidated the Word of God by their tradition that had been handed down (Mark 7:13). To the devil, Jesus consistently responded, "It is written..." (Matthew 4:4-10). Following Jesus's lead, we must conclude that Scripture alone is our supreme and final authority.

This means that as we read the New Testament, we are not to

consider it as merely the words of men. Let's recognize it for what it is—the very Word of God, which has authority over our lives.

The Challenges of a Chronological Approach

There are some definite challenges to taking a chronological approach to studying the New Testament. The foremost is that biblical scholars differ on the exact chronological order of events. This point has been recognized by all the chronological study Bibles in print. *The Chronological Life Application Study Bible* states, "Organizing the Bible into chronological order is sometimes tricky, and excellent Christian scholars do not always agree on the order of certain books or passages."[1] *The Chronological Study Bible: NIV* likewise affirms, "Rearranging the Bible is...a fallible human effort. Even those who have earned advanced degrees in the various fields of biblical studies would disagree on any particular rearrangement."[2] *The Chronological Study Bible: New King James Version* adds, "Rearranging the biblical books chronologically is by no means easily accomplished, since Bible scholars differ on almost every important point of chronology."[3] That means no biblical chronology—including the one suggested in this book—should be considered inspired or inerrant, as is the Word of God.

As I wrestled through the New Testament chronology, I discovered that chronological problems surface most in the four Gospels. To be fair, none of the Gospel writers set out to write a precise chronology of the teachings and events in the life of Christ. They could have done this, but that wasn't their purpose. Each of the writers had a unique purpose in writing his Gospel, and the varied purposes account for many of the differences in chronology.

There has also been significant debate over the varying details contained in the Gospel accounts. But I believe there are viable reasons for these differences. Foundationally, we know from human experience that different people will notice different things about the same event. Simply because there are different details reported does not mean any of the reports are wrong. Each report can be unique but nevertheless correct.

One must also keep in mind that Jesus's ministry spanned some three years—more than 1000 days. Many scholars believe it is extremely likely that He repeated the same teachings on many occasions. I am quite sure this is the case. This may account for some of the differences in the Gospel accounts on similar teachings of Christ. That is, Christ may have communicated the same truth on a number of different occasions, and on each occasion He may have communicated that truth in a slightly unique way. This has led some scholars to surmise that seemingly parallel accounts of a teaching may actually refer to two different teaching events. We can't be certain about such things, but I am convinced this is what happened. Of course, the important point is that Christ gave us these teachings, not the precise order in which He delivered them.

It is possible that some of the differences in the Gospel accounts are partly due to the reality that Jesus may have spoken three languages—Hebrew, Aramaic, and Greek. The New Testament, of course, was written in Greek. If Jesus gave a teaching to a Jewish audience in Hebrew or Aramaic, each Gospel writer's rendering of that teaching in Greek may have been slightly different from the others'.[4]

Further, we must note that unlike modern writers, the ancients were not overly fixated on verbal exactitude. They didn't use quotation marks in those days. Nor did they use ellipsis dots to note that words were deleted, or brackets to indicate clarifying insertions by the Gospel writers. These are all modern inventions, and we would be wrong to impose such writing protocols on the ancients. But the biblical writers were nevertheless trustworthy in all that they wrote.

Perhaps an illustration might help. Imagine three bystanders witnessing a car accident at a street intersection.

The first witness says, "The truck hit the car."

The second witness says, "The girl in that red truck hit the blue car."

The third witness says, "The blond girl in that red Ford F-150 hit the blue sedan, driven by a redheaded guy with freckles."

These are not contradictory accounts. They are partial, complementary descriptions of what happened. Taken together, we can reconstruct a trustworthy composite report.

Consider the death of Judas. In Matthew 27:5, we are told that

Judas died by hanging himself. In Acts 1:18 we are told that Judas burst open in the middle and all his entrails gushed out. These are both partial accounts. Neither account gives us the full picture. But taken together we can easily reconstruct how Judas died. He hanged himself first, and sometime later, the rope loosened and Judas fell to the rocks below, thereby causing his intestines to gush out.

Of course, the difference between the accident reports (in my illustration above) and the biblical writings is that the biblical writings were inspired by the Holy Spirit and therefore are inerrant. You can trust the biblical accounts despite their differences because God superintended each of the biblical authors as he wrote.

This means that apparent contradictions in the Gospels are not really contradictions. There are differences, yes, but not actual contradictions. Certainly if all four Gospels were the same, with no differences, critics would be accusing the writers of collusion. The differences in the Gospels show that there was no collusion and that the Gospels represent four unique (but inspired) accounts of the same events.

As we probe into alleged contradictions in the Gospel accounts, we consistently see that they are all explainable in a reasonable way. Those who wish to study the issue of alleged contradictions in more detail may wish to consult my book *The Big Book of Bible Answers* (Harvest House Publishers, 2013).

How to Use This Book

As you begin each chapter, consider using this prayer.

> *Lord, I ask You to open my eyes and enhance my understanding so that I can grasp what You want me to learn today* [Psalm 119:18]. *I also ask You to enable me, by Your Spirit, to apply the truths I learn to my daily life and to be guided moment by moment by Your Word* [Psalm 119:105; 2 Timothy 3:15-17]. *I thank You in Jesus's name. Amen.*

Because this book goes through the New Testament in chronological order, each day's reading includes a number of Bible passages to read. In some cases, they are parallel passages covering the same event (as in the

Gospels). In other cases, each passage covers a different New Testament event in a suggested chronological order. Reading the New Testament in chronological order will help you to see how all the New Testament books relate to each other in the unfolding drama of human redemption.

Because we are covering the entire New Testament in just 90 days, some of the reading assignments may seem a little long. But trust me—you'll be able to read through each day's assignment just fine. Just remember that there are rich spiritual dividends in spending time in God's Word!

I must also tell you that I'll give your thumb a good workout, especially on the chapters dealing with the Gospels' parallel accounts of the same events. Again, however, it will be worth your time and effort—and you might even burn a few extra calories!

Here is what you will find in each chapter.

Introduction. Each chapter that contains the first Scripture reading from a particular New Testament book will contain a brief introduction to that book, including information on the author, readers, and purpose for writing. In the case of the four Gospels, the first four chapters of the book contain one Gospel introduction each.

Overview of Today's Scripture Reading. For each passage, I provide a brief contextual overview that will help you grasp exactly what's going on. This is not a verse-by-verse commentary, but it will help you to see the big picture of the biblical text.

Today's Big Ideas. This section contains a short list of big ideas in the assigned reading, along with Scripture references. This, too, will help you quickly see the big picture.

Insights on Difficult Verses. Hard-to-understand verses are briefly explained.

Major Themes. These are topical summaries of important themes in the text of Scripture.

Digging Deeper with Cross-References. These cross-references will help you discover relevant insights from other Bible verses.

Life Lessons. These are personal, life-changing applications based on what you've read.

Verses to Remember. Here you will find a selection of a few verses from the assigned reading that are particularly relevant for your spiritual life.

Questions for Reflection and Discussion. The questions here are ideal for either personal reflection or group studies.

Prayer. Each chapter closes with a brief devotional prayer based on the daily reading assignment.

Each of these sections will necessarily be brief. After all, the book has 90 succinct chapters. But the short chapters are strategically designed to give you maximum benefit as you read Scripture and allow it to transform your life. So grab your favorite Bible, and let's begin our journey!

Lord, by the power of Your Spirit, please enable all who read this book to understand and apply important spiritual truths from each New Testament book. Please excite them with Your Word. Please instill in them a sense of awe for the person of our Lord Jesus Christ and the salvation He has provided for each of us. I thank You in Jesus's name. Amen.

CHAPTER 1

Jesus's Incarnation and Early Ministry

Day 1

Introducing Jesus Christ

We begin our journey through the New Testament with a focus on the Incarnation—that glorious event in which the eternal and divine Son of God became a human being. Begin by reading Matthew 1; Luke 1; 3:23-38; and John 1:1-5. Read with the anticipation that the Holy Spirit has something important to teach you today (see Psalm 119:105).

Chronological marker. Jesus was likely born in 6 BC, so Mary's pregnancy must have been in 7 BC. (The traditional birth date was a miscalculation by scholars about 500 years after Christ's death.)

Introduction to Matthew

Author: Matthew, one of the 12 apostles

Date: written between AD 50 and 60

Fast facts:

- Matthew, himself a Jew, wrote this Gospel to convince Jewish readers that Jesus is the promised Messiah. It contains about 130 Old Testament citations or allusions (for example, see 2:17-18; 4:13-15; 13:35; 21:4-5; 27:9-10).

- Though Matthew was writing to convince Jews that Jesus was the divine Messiah, he does not confine the good news to his own people, the Jews. Rather, he emphasizes that the gospel is for all people.

Key words in Matthew (and the number of times they occur):

Father (44)	righteous (17)
kingdom of heaven (32)	might be fulfilled (15)
kingdom (23)	worship (14)
which was spoken (20)	son of David (10)

(I will provide introductions to the Gospels of Mark, Luke, and John in the next three chapters.)

Overview of Today's Scripture Reading

John 1:1-5. Like Genesis 1, John 1 begins with an emphasis on life and light. Both are rooted in Jesus Christ. Jesus's light shines eternally.

Matthew 1:1-17; Luke 3:23-38. Jesus's arrival to earth in the Incarnation was not a quickly arranged event that God suddenly brought about. It involved God's sovereign and providential oversight over the messianic line for ages and ages.

Luke 1:1-4. Luke's Gospel is thoroughly researched and reliable.

Luke 1:5-25. God's children often tend to focus more on their own deficiencies and weaknesses than on the awesome power of our sovereign God. That was Zechariah's problem (see verse 18).

Luke 1:26-38. Mary was a God-honoring woman. She humbly submitted to the Lord's will despite the fact that it would bring her sorrow and suffering.

Luke 1:39-56. Notice that there are 15 distinct quotations from the Old Testament in Mary's poem. This shows that the Messiah was born into a home where God's Word was honored.

Matthew 1:18-25. Mary's was not a normal human pregnancy. The Holy Spirit overshadowed Mary to produce a human nature within her womb for Jesus, the eternal Son of God. Jesus was born as a human without a sin nature. He was "God with us."

Luke 1:57-80. John's name means "God is gracious"—appropriate because God graciously sent John the Baptist to prepare the way for the coming of the divine Messiah.

Today's Big Ideas

- Jesus is eternal deity (John 1:1-5).

- Jesus in the Incarnation had a human genealogy (Matthew 1:1-17; Luke 3:23-38).

- The angel Gabriel announced the upcoming birth of Jesus (Luke 1:26-38).

Insights on Difficult Verses

John 1:1-5. Contrary to what some cults claim, these verses prove Jesus is God! The same Greek words used to describe Jesus's deity here are used elsewhere to describe the Father's deity (Luke 20:38; see also John 8:58; 10:30; 20:28).

Matthew 1:1-17; Luke 3:23-38. Matthew's genealogy traces Joseph's line of descendants and deals with the passing of the legal title to the throne of David. Luke's genealogy traces Mary's lineage and goes all the way back to Adam and the commencement of the human race.

Major Themes

Jesus is the Word (John 1:1). The Word is portrayed as a living, divine being who is eternal, the Creator, and the source of life. John used the term because it was familiar to both Greeks and Jews.

Jesus saves His people (Matthew 1:21). "Jesus" means "the Lord saves" or "the Lord is salvation." It is a perfect name for our Savior.

Digging Deeper with Cross-References

Life is in Jesus (John 1:4)—John 3:15-16; 4:10-14; 5:21-26,39-40; 6:27-40,47-58,63; 7:37-38; 8:12; 10:10,27-28; 11:25-26; 12:49-50; 14:6; 17:2-3; 20:31

Jesus is God (John 1:1)—Isaiah 9:6; Matthew 1:23; Mark 2:5-12; John 8:58; 20:28; Philippians 2:6; Colossians 2:9; Titus 2:13; Hebrews 1:8; Revelation 1:8; 22:13,16

Life Lessons

We are responsible to the Creator (John 1:3). John says Jesus is the Creator of all that exists (see Colossians 1:16; Hebrews 1:2). Because we are creatures, we are responsible to submit ourselves to the Creator. Consider making Psalm 95:6-7 and Psalm 100:3 part of the daily fabric of your life.

God uses less-than-perfect people (Matthew 1:3,5-6). Notice that in Jesus's genealogies, less-than-perfect people are in the messianic line. For example, Tamar, Rahab, and Bathsheba were all involved in sexual sin (Genesis 38; Joshua 2; 2 Samuel 11:1–12:23). Yet all three were included in God's unfolding plan of salvation. God often does amazing things through people whom the world considers less than desirable (see 1 Corinthians 1:26-30).

Verses to Remember

- "In the beginning was the Word, and the Word was with God, and the Word was God" (John 1:1).

- "The angel said to her, 'Do not be afraid, Mary, for you have found favor with God. And behold, you will conceive in your womb and bear a son, and you shall call his name Jesus'" (Luke 1:30-31).

Questions for Reflection and Discussion

1. Why do you think John established the absolute deity of Christ at the very beginning of his Gospel (John 1:1)?

2. Does the fact that Jesus's name means "the Lord saves" cause you to look at Him any differently?

3. Have you ever thought about what might have happened had the Incarnation of Jesus never occurred?

My Father, how thankful I am that You sent Jesus into the world. As I ponder the meaning of His name—"the Lord saves"—I am filled with gratitude at the salvation I have in Him. May You ever be praised. In Jesus's name, amen.

Jesus's Boyhood

Yesterday we focused on the Incarnation—that glorious event in which the eternal and divine Son of God became a human being (Matthew 1; Luke 1; 3:23-38; John 1:1-5). Today we turn our attention to the circumstances surrounding the boyhood of Jesus.

Begin by reading Matthew 2 and Luke 2. As you read, remember that the Word of God is alive and working in you (Hebrews 4:12).

Chronological marker. Jesus was born in 6 BC, so His growth as a boy would have taken up till around AD 7. Two decades then passed. He grew into adulthood and began His ministry around AD 27.

Introduction to Luke

Author: Luke was a frequent companion of the apostle Paul.

Date: written in AD 60

Fast facts:

- Luke was a well-educated and cultured man.

- He wrote his Gospel based on reliable, firsthand sources (Luke 1:1-4).

- Luke, a medical doctor, expressed unflinching belief in Jesus's virgin birth (Luke 1:35) and many miracles (4:38-40; 5:15-25; 6:17-19; 7:11-15).

Key words in Luke (and the number of times they occur):

save (19)	grace (8)
sin/sinner (18)	salvation (6)
preach glad tidings/good news (10)	

Overview of Today's Scripture Reading

Luke 2:1-20. In stark contrast to Jesus's intrinsic glory and majesty, He was born in lowly conditions in a stable. Angels then appeared to shepherds in a field, announcing that "Christ the Lord" was born, not "Christ *your* Lord." Christ is sovereign over angels as well as humans.

Luke 2:21-38. When Jesus was presented in the temple by His parents, Simeon—a God-fearing man—recognized the babe as the One who would bring salvation to the world. Though Jesus wouldn't begin His public ministry for 30 years, Simeon knew this was the Christ, the Messiah. Now that he had witnessed the Savior, Simeon said he was ready to die peacefully.

Mary, Joseph, Jesus, and Simeon were then approached by the prophetess Anna. She had apparently been long awaiting the coming of the Messiah. When she heard Simeon speak, her spirit rejoiced, and she gave thanks to God.

Matthew 2; Luke 2:39-40. Back in Nazareth, Jesus was soon visited by Magi from the east. They followed a "star" to His house. When they beheld Jesus, they worshipped Him, presenting Him with gifts of gold, frankincense, and myrrh. These gifts were typically given to a king in biblical times.

Herod, meanwhile, was threatened with the possible prospect of a challenging king. He engaged in a failed plot to murder Jesus. There were many collateral casualties in this satanically driven plot (Revelation 12:4).

Luke 2:41-52. When Jesus was 12 years old, He accompanied His parents to Jerusalem to observe the Passover. While returning to Jerusalem, Joseph and Mary discovered that Jesus was missing. Families often traveled with other families in a caravan for safety purposes. Joseph and Mary apparently assumed Jesus was with other kids in the caravan. In reality, Jesus was still in Jerusalem, amazing learned interpreters of Scripture.

Today's Big Ideas

- Angels announced Christ's birth to some shepherds (Luke 2:1-20).

- Jesus was presented at the Jewish temple, where He was recognized as the Savior (Luke 2:21-38).

- Jesus was worshipped by wise men but hunted by Herod (Matthew 2; Luke 2:39-40).

Insights on Difficult Verses

Matthew 2:1-12. The fact that the Magi observed the unique star does not condone astrology, as some have claimed. This star existed to announce Christ's birth, not to foretell an event. Stars in the Bible point to God's glory (Psalm 19:1-6; Romans 1:18-20).

Matthew 2:23. No Old Testament verse calls Jesus a Nazarene. Nazareth was viewed as a city of vice, so being called a Nazarene was considered scornful. Matthew's point was that the prophets collectively foretold that Jesus would be a despised character (Psalm 69:8,20-21; Isaiah 11:1; 49:7; 53:2-8).

Major Themes

The kingship of Jesus (Matthew 2:2). Scripture reveals that the Messiah would reign as King (Genesis 49:10), have a dynasty (2 Samuel 7:16), and have everlasting dominion (Daniel 7:13-14).

The star of Bethlehem (Matthew 2:2). A normal star in interstellar space would be incapable of leading the wise men to an individual dwelling in Bethlehem. The "star" was likely a manifestation of God's Shekinah glory hovering in the atmosphere.

Digging Deeper with Cross-References

The necessity of Christ's birth as a human (Luke 2:7)—Luke 1:31-33; John 1:18; 1 Peter 2:21; Hebrews 5:1-2; 10:1-10; 1 John 3:8

Jesus, the divine shepherd (Matthew 2:6)—John 10:11; Hebrews 13:20; 1 Peter 2:25; see also Psalms 23; 78:52; Isaiah 40:11; Mark 14:27; Revelation 7:17

Life Lessons

Beware of selfishness, pride, and insecurity (Matthew 2:16-18). Herod was driven to horrific sin by these vices, and Christians must be on guard against them. It is much better to be self-giving and humble (1 Corinthians 10:24; 2 Corinthians 5:15; Galatians 6:2; Philippians 2:4).

Worship (Matthew 2:11). When the Magi saw Jesus, they "fell down and worshiped him." Falling down and worshipping Jesus will still be a common activity in heaven (Revelation 5:8,14; 19:4). Why not get into the habit now?

Verses to Remember

- "I bring you good news of great joy that will be for all the people. For unto you is born this day in the city of David a Savior, who is Christ the Lord" (Luke 2:10-11).

- "Jesus increased in wisdom and in stature and in favor with God and man" (Luke 2:52).

Questions for Reflection and Discussion

1. Why do you think God allowed Jesus to be born in humble circumstances instead of an environment fit for royalty?

2. Why do you think angels announced Christ's birth to shepherds and not to royalty or governmental officials?

3. What do you learn in Luke 2 about the nature of the good news announced by the angels?

My Father, truly the gospel of Jesus Christ is "good news of great joy." Like the wise men, I rejoice "exceedingly with great joy." I worship my Savior, "who is Christ the Lord." Praise be to Him. In His glorious name, amen.

John the Baptist Prepares the Way

In the previous lesson we explored circumstances surrounding Jesus's birth and boyhood (Matthew 2; Luke 2). Today we consider how John the Baptist prepared the way for Jesus's ministry.

Begin by reading Matthew 3; Mark 1:1-11; Luke 3:1-22; and John 1:6-34. As you read, remember that those who obey the Word of God are truly blessed (Psalm 119:2; Luke 11:28; Revelation 1:3).

Chronological marker. John the Baptist's ministry preceded the beginning of Christ's ministry. John engaged in his ministry in the winter and spring of AD 26.

Introduction to Mark

Author: Mark was a close companion of the apostle Peter.

Date: written around AD 55

Fast facts:

- Mark accompanied the apostle Paul and Barnabas on their first missionary tour (Acts 12:25; 13:5).

- Mark's Gospel is the shortest of the four Gospels. It is also the fastest paced.

- About one-third of Mark's Gospel focuses on the last week of Jesus's life on earth.

- Mark's Gospel targeted Gentile readers, so he was careful to explain Jewish customs.

Key words in Mark (and the number of times they appear):
    immediately (40)
    spirit (23)
    authority (10)

Overview of Today's Scripture Reading

Matthew 3:1-12; Mark 1:1-8; Luke 3:1-20; John 1:6-28. John called people to repent of their sin in preparation for the coming of the Messiah. Lip service was not enough. People needed to change their lives.

The response was mixed. Some repented and confessed their sins (Matthew 3:5-6). Others—the Pharisees and Sadducees—pretended to be righteous (verses 7-9).

Those who repented and turned to God became children of God. Jesus would later reveal that the unrepentant Jewish leaders were actually children of the devil (John 8:44).

Unlike the Jewish leaders, who were characterized by legalism and falsehood, Jesus was characterized by grace and truth (John 1:14). And unlike the Jewish leaders, who depended on the blood of lambs to cover their sins, Jesus Himself was the Lamb of God who would take away the sins of the world.

Matthew 3:13-17; Mark 1:9-11; Luke 3:21-22; John 1:29-34. Jesus was baptized by John the Baptist, not because He needed it, but in order to identify with those He came to save. God the Father declared His approval by affirming, "This is my beloved Son, with whom I am well pleased" (Matthew 3:17). At that moment, the Holy Spirit came upon Jesus to empower Him for His messianic ministry. All three persons of the Trinity were manifest at Jesus's baptism—the Father, the Son, and the Holy Spirit.

Today's Big Ideas

• John the Baptist prepared the way for Jesus's ministry (Matthew 3:1-12; Mark 1:1-8; Luke 3:1-20; John 1:6-28).

- Jesus was baptized, thereby identifying with the sinners He came to save (Matthew 3:13-17; Mark 1:9-11; Luke 3:21-22; John 1:29-34).

Insights on Difficult Verses

John 1:11. Jesus came initially to the Jewish people, but the Jewish people by and large did not accept Him.

John 1:30. Even though Christ in His humanity was born as a human being six months after John the Baptist, as the eternal Son of God He preceded John. Christ was both John's successor and predecessor. He was before John but also came after John.

Major Themes

Pharisees (Matthew 3:7). The word "Pharisee" comes from an Aramaic word meaning "separated." They separated from non-Pharisaic Jews, common people, and Gentiles. They were religious purists. However, they were more committed to external appearances than true inward purity. They constantly stood against Jesus during His three-year ministry.

Sadducees (Matthew 3:7). The Sadducees believed only in the Torah, the first five books of Moses (Genesis, Exodus, Leviticus, Numbers, and Deuteronomy). Most of the chief priests were Sadducees, and they were dominant in the Sanhedrin. They constantly opposed Jesus during His three-year ministry. Jesus warned His followers about the "leaven" of the Pharisees and the Sadducees (Matthew 16:1-12).

Digging Deeper with Cross-References

Jesus is the light of the world (John 1:9)—Matthew 4:16; 17:2; Luke 1:79; 2:32; John 1:4,9; 3:19; 8:12; 9:5; 12:35,46; Acts 22:6; 26:23; 1 John 1:5; 2:8; Revelation 1:16; 21:23

Spiritual adoption (John 1:12)—Romans 8:15; 9:4,8,25; 2 Corinthians 6:18; Galatians 3:26; 4:5-6; Ephesians 1:5; 2:19; Hebrews 2:13; 1 John 3:1

Life Lessons

Words are not enough (Matthew 3:8). John the Baptist urged, "Bear fruit in keeping with repentance." He said this to the Pharisees and Sadducees who gave lip-service to living for God but in reality were full of hypocrisy. They "talked the talk" but didn't "walk the walk." Christians can fall into the same deception. Let us resolve to always have fruitful repentance in our lives.

Confession of sin (Mark 1:5). Some who went to John the Baptist confessed their sins. You and I are called to confess our sins to God as well. "If we confess our sins, he is faithful and just to forgive us our sins and to cleanse us from all unrighteousness" (1 John 1:9). To confess means "to have the same mind." When we confess our sins, we agree with God that we did wrong and that we should turn from those sins. Confession restores our fellowship with God, which is broken by sin (1 John 1:6).

Verses to Remember

- "The Word became flesh and dwelt among us, and we have seen his glory, glory as of the only Son from the Father, full of grace and truth" (John 1:14).
- "Behold, the Lamb of God, who takes away the sin of the world!" (John 1:29).

Questions for Reflection and Discussion

1. Why do you think John calls Jesus the "true light" (John 1:9)?
2. How does John the Baptist's emphasis on repentance "prepare the way of the Lord" (Luke 3:4)?
3. How do you think people might respond today to John's message?

My Father, I rejoice that Jesus is the light of my world and that He is the true light that gives light to me personally. Please enable me to consistently walk in the light, as He is in the light, and allow my light to consistently shine before others. In Jesus's name, amen.

CHAPTER 2

Jesus's Ministry in Galilee, Perea, and Judea

Day 4

The Temptation of Jesus

Yesterday we considered how John the Baptist prepared the way for Jesus's ministry (Matthew 3; Mark 1:1-11; Luke 3:1-22; John 1:6-34). Today we will focus on Jesus's temptation and the beginning of His ministry.

Begin by reading Matthew 4:1-22; Mark 1:12-20; Luke 4:1-15; 5:1-11; and John 1:35–2:25. As you read, keep in mind that just as we eat food for physical nourishment, so we need the Word of God for spiritual nourishment (1 Corinthians 3:2; Hebrews 5:12; 1 Peter 2:2).

Chronological marker. Jesus began His ministry in AD 27.

Introduction to John

Author: The apostle John was a close companion of Jesus (John 13:23; 19:26-27).

Date: written between AD 85 and 90

Fast facts:

- This Gospel is evangelistic, seeking to persuade people to trust in Christ for salvation (John 20:31).

- The word "believe" occurs almost 100 times in this Gospel.

- John demonstrated that Jesus has the attributes of deity, including omniscience (4:29), omnipresence (14:23), and pre-existence (1:1; 8:58; 17:5).

- John also demonstrated that in the Incarnation, Jesus was fully human (John 1:14).

Key words in John (and the number of times they appear):

believe (97)	abide (41)
world (78)	life (36)
know (54)	judge/judgment (30)
love (44)	eternal (29)
glory (42)	light (23)

Overview of Today's Scripture Reading

Matthew 4:1-17; Luke 4:1-15. Jesus experienced Satan's temptation to prove He could not be made to sin. The devil waited 40 days until Jesus was at His weakest from hunger. It was to no avail. Jesus defeated the devil by means of the Word of God. Jesus also endured temptation so that He might personally know temptation and therefore be able to help us in our temptations (Hebrews 2:17-18; 4:15).

Matthew 4:18-22; Mark 1:16-20; Luke 5:1-11; John 1:35-51. Jesus now called His first disciples—Simon, Andrew, and James. There is a noticeable pattern—Jesus called them, and they immediately followed Him. Their purpose in following Him was evangelism ("fishers of men").

John 2:1-12. At a wedding banquet Jesus was invited to, He had servants fill six stone water jars—each holding 20 to 30 gallons—and He turned the water into wine. By a single word of command, Jesus, the divine Creator, instantly accomplished the transformation that a vine requires several months to produce.

John 2:13-25. Sometime later, Jesus engaged in His first cleansing of the temple. Pigeons and other animals were sold in the temple complex. The only coins allowable for buying and selling in the temple were ancient Hebrew shekels. Other coins had to be exchanged for shekels. The money-changers made a nice profit with each exchange. Jesus drove them out.

Today's Big Ideas

- Jesus was tempted by the devil but proved Himself incapable of sin (Matthew 4:1-17; Mark 1:12-15; Luke 4:1-15).

- Jesus performed a huge miracle that pointed to His divine nature (John 2:1-12).

Insights on Difficult Verses

Matthew 4:7. Christ could not have sinned because...

- In His divine nature, He is immutable and does not change.

- In His divine nature, He is all-knowing and fully aware of the consequences of sin.

- In His divine nature, He is all-powerful in His ability to resist sin.

- Hebrews 4:15 tells us that He was tempted yet was without sin.

- Unlike all other human beings, He had no sin nature (Luke 1:35).

John 1:5. John portrays Jesus as the revelatory link between heaven and earth. He is the One through whom the realities of heaven were to be brought down to earth (John 6:33,38,46,51-52).

Major Themes

The devil (Matthew 4:1). The word "devil" carries the idea of "adversary." The devil is the adversary of Christ and of all who follow Christ (see James 4:7; 1 Peter 5:8).

The kingdom of God is the kingdom of heaven (Mark 1:15). The Gospels of Mark, Luke, and John use "kingdom of God" (Luke 9:2). Matthew predominantly uses "kingdom of heaven" because he was a Jew writing to Jews, and Jews preferred not to use the divine name for fear of breaking the third commandment (Exodus 20:7).

Digging Deeper with Cross-References

Jesus, the Messiah (John 1:41)—Matthew 11:3; 12:23; 16:16; 26:63; Mark 8:29; 14:61; Luke 2:11,26; 4:41; 7:19; 9:20; 22:67; 24:21,26; John 1:41; 4:26; 6:14,69; 7:41; 8:24,28; 9:37; 11:27; 13:19; 20:31

Significant messianic prophecies (John 1:41)—Genesis 3:15; 12:3; 2 Samuel 7:12; Psalms 16:9-11; 22:18-31; 102:1-11; Isaiah 7:14; 9:6; 11:1-4; 53:1-12; Daniel 9:26; Micah 5:2; Zechariah 12:10

Life Lessons

Temptations (Matthew 4:1). Scripture warns that we are to beware of the reality of temptations (Galatians 6:1) and make every effort not to let evil get the best of us (Romans 12:21). We are not to let sin control us (Romans 6:12) but rather must be cautious not to lose our secure footing (2 Peter 3:17). When we are tempted, God will make a way of escape for us (1 Corinthians 10:13).

Dependence on the Word of God (Matthew 4:4). Like Jesus, we must depend on the Word of God. It is "profitable for teaching, for reproof, for correction, and for training in righteousness" (2 Timothy 3:16). Scripture helps us not to give in to sin (Psalm 119:9,11) and gives us comfort during affliction (Psalm 119:50).

Verses to Remember

- "Man shall not live by bread alone, but by every word that comes from the mouth of God" (Matthew 4:4).

- "Follow me, and I will make you fishers of men" (Matthew 4:19).

Questions for Reflection and Discussion

1. What does it mean to you personally that Jesus was tempted while He was on earth?

2. What do you learn from Matthew 4 regarding how Jesus defended Himself during the temptations?

3. What is the significance of the miracle Jesus performed at Cana (see John 2:11)?

My Father, I thank You for Your Word, which is the sword of the Spirit. Like Jesus, I want to learn to use Your Word as I battle temptations. Please help me become better at this. I'm grateful. In Jesus's name, amen.

For God So Loved the World...

In the previous lesson we discussed Jesus's temptation and the beginning of His ministry (Matthew 4:1-22; Mark 1:12-20; Luke 4:1-15; 5:1-11; John 1:35–2:25). Today we explore the wondrous salvation that is in Jesus Christ.

Begin by reading John 3. As you read, remember that storing God's Word in your heart can help you to avoid sinning (Psalm 119:9,11).

Chronological marker. The events in this lesson took place in late AD 27.

Overview of Today's Scripture Reading

John 3:1-21. Jesus spoke to Nicodemus about heavenly realities. He indicated that our earthly birth enables us to live on earth. The problem is, we eventually die. A second birth—being spiritually born again—enables us to go to heaven. The good news is that in heaven, we never die.

All this was made possible by the Savior, Jesus Christ. He came down from heaven and brought the gift of salvation with Him. This in response to the Father's great love for us ("For God so loved the world..."). We receive this wondrous gift of salvation by faith in Christ.

Notice that verse 16 cannot be divorced from the context of verses 14 and 15, where Christ alludes to Numbers 21. In this passage Moses sets up the bronze serpent in the camp of Israel so that anyone who looked at it experienced physical deliverance. In John 3:15, Christ applies the story spiritually when He says that whoever believes on the uplifted Son of Man may have eternal life.

John 3:22-36. Meanwhile, John the Baptist remained a humble man. His humility caused him to see that he had no intrinsic greatness. Rather, his ministry was given to him by heaven. John's entire purpose was to point people to Jesus, which necessitated pointing away from himself. He even verbalized that Jesus must increase while he must decrease. It is wise for each of us to adopt this mindset.

Today's Big Ideas

- Human beings must be spiritually born again by faith in order to enter the kingdom of God (3:1-15).
- God proved His love for humanity by sending Jesus (3:16-21).
- John the Baptist humbled himself and exalted Jesus, as we all should (3:22-36).

Insights on Difficult Verses

John 3:2. Nicodemus came to Jesus in the dark of night. Some commentators have speculated that this indicates the spiritual darkness in his heart. More likely he did so to avoid risking disfavor with his fellow Pharisees.

John 3:5. The reference to being "born of water" does not mean water baptism is necessary for salvation. Verses 5 and 6 contain parallel truths. "Born of...the Spirit" in verse 5 is parallel to "born of the Spirit" in verse 6. "Born of water" in verse 5 is parallel to "born of the flesh" in verse 6. These verses indicate that just as one has had a physical birth ("born of water") to live on earth, so one must also have a spiritual birth in order to enter the kingdom of God.

Major Themes

Born again (John 3:3). Being "born again"—literally, "born from above"—refers to God's act of giving eternal life to the one who believes in Christ (Titus 3:5). It places one into God's eternal family (1 Peter 1:23) and gives the believer a new capacity and desire to please the Father (2 Corinthians 5:17).

Jesus, the Son of God (John 3:16). Among the ancients, the term "son of" often carried the meaning "of the order of." "Sons of the prophets" meant "of the order of prophets" (1 Kings 20:35). "Sons of the singers" meant "of the order of singers" (Nehemiah 12:28). In contexts dealing with Jesus, "Son of God" means "of the order of God" (see John 19:7). Jesus, as the Son of God, *is God.*

Digging Deeper with Cross-References

Born again (John 3:3)—2 Corinthians 5:17; Titus 3:5; 1 Peter 1:3,23; 1 John 2:29; 3:9; 4:7; 5:1,18

God's love (John 3:16)—Matthew 18:14; 21:37; Mark 12:6; John 14:21; 16:27; 17:23; Romans 5:5,8; 8:32,39; 2 Corinthians 13:14; Ephesians 2:4-5; 2 Thessalonians 2:16; Titus 3:4; Hebrews 12:6; 1 John 3:1; 4:9,16,19

Life Lessons

Christians are given eternal life (John 3:16). God is the only being in the universe who is eternal, never having been created. He has always existed. He never came into being at a point in time. He is beyond time altogether (1 Timothy 1:17; 6:16). Those who trust in Christ are the recipients of eternal life, and they will live with Him forever in heaven (John 3:16-17). Revelation 21:4 assures us, "There will be no more death or mourning or crying or pain, for the old order of things has passed away." Eternal life is part of the new order of things.

Light has come into the world (John 3:19). Light has come into the world through Jesus, and this has profound implications for how you and I live. Walking in the light, biblically, involves living righteously. Walking in darkness, by contrast, involves living unrighteously. We have to make the choice every day to walk in the light, as Christ is in the light (see 1 John 1:5-10).

Verses to Remember

- "Truly, truly, I say to you, unless one is born again he cannot see the kingdom of God" (John 3:3).

- "For God so loved the world, that he gave his only Son, that whoever believes in him should not perish but have eternal life" (John 3:16).

Questions for Reflection and Discussion

1. Have you been born again? How do you know?

2. How is the Holy Spirit like the wind?

3. Can you come up with at least three character traits that show John the Baptist's deep spirituality (John 3:22-36)?

My Father, I keep repeating aloud the words "for God so loved the world." Your love is measureless. It is incomprehensible to me. That You love me so much that You sent Your Son to die for me confounds my understanding. I am thankful beyond words. You are worthy to be praised. In Jesus's name, amen.

DAY 6

Living Water

Yesterday we focused on the wondrous salvation that is in Jesus Christ (John 3). Today we zero in on Jesus as the source of living water (that is, new life through the Spirit).

Begin by reading John 4:4-42,46-54. As you read, remember that the Word of God teaches us, trains us, and corrects us (2 Timothy 3:15-17).

Chronological marker. This lesson considers events that occurred in late AD 27.

Overview of Today's Scripture Reading

John 4:4-26. Jesus, in His divine nature, was omniscient (John 2:24), omnipresent (John 1:48), and omnipotent (John 11). In His human nature, however, He knew hunger (Luke 4:2), weariness (John 4:6), and the need for sleep (Luke 8:23). Jesus asked the Samaritan woman for some water, for He thirsted as a man. But the thing He desired more than water was her salvation. He wanted to give her "living water." He told her, "Whoever drinks of the water that I will give him will never be thirsty again" (John 4:14).

The woman wanted the water. But before she could receive new life in the Spirit (the living water), she needed to be confronted about her sin. To help her see her sin, Jesus told her, "Call your husband." Once this point was made, Jesus revealed that He was the promised divine Messiah who could give her salvation.

John 4:27-42. The woman couldn't contain herself. She gave a powerful personal testimony to many Samaritans. She aroused their curiosity, and they checked out Jesus for themselves. Soon enough they told her, "It is no longer because of what you said that we believe, for we have heard for ourselves, and we know that this is indeed the Savior of the world" (John 4:42).

John 4:46-54. Soon after, an official asked Jesus to come heal his son. The man's faith was built on Jesus's signs and wonders, not on Jesus's divine person. Better to place faith in Him than merely in His divine abilities. Regardless, Jesus healed the man's son from a distance, without going to the man's house.

Today's Big Ideas

- Jesus offered living water to a Samaritan woman (John 4:1-42).
- Jesus healed an official's son, thereby pointing to His identity as the divine Messiah (John 4:46-54).

Insights on Difficult Verses

John 4:1-28. The Samaritans of New Testament times were considered half-breeds by mainstream Jews. Following the fall of Samaria in 722 BC, some Israelites from the tribes of Ephraim and Manasseh intermarried with Assyrians. Therefore, mainstream Jews considered the Samaritans to be racially unclean. When Jesus spoke to the Samaritan woman, He violated the cultural taboos of the day.

John 4:10. What is the living water? John's Gospel tells us: "Now this he said about the Spirit, whom those who believed in him were to receive, for as yet the Spirit had not been given, because Jesus was not yet glorified" (John 7:39). This brings to mind Jeremiah 2:13, where God is called "the fountain of living waters" (see also Zechariah 4:8).

Major Themes

Recognizing sin (John 4:16-18). The Lord helped the Samaritan woman understand her state of sin by noting that she was presently living in adultery. Jewish rabbis permitted two divorces, sometimes three. The woman had exceeded that and was unmarried to her present partner. Jesus allowed her to see her sinfulness so that He could bring her to salvation.

Jesus's miraculous signs (John 4:54). Jesus's miracles are often called "signs" (John 6:14; 9:16). As signs, they signified His true identity and glory as the divine Messiah (see Matthew 11:2-5; compare with Isaiah 29:18-21; 35:5-6; 61:1).

Digging Deeper with Cross-References

Signs (John 4:48)—Matthew 12:38; 16:1; 24:3; 27:42; Mark 8:11; 15:32,36; Luke 11:16,29; 21:7; 23:8; John 2:18; 6:30; 20:25

Great faith (John 4:50)—Matthew 8:2,10; 9:18,21,28; 14:36; 15:28; 20:33; Mark 1:40; 5:23,28; 6:55; 7:26; 10:51; Luke 1:48; 2:19; 5:12,20; 7:9; 8:41; 18:41; 23:42; John 1:49; 2:5; 4:50; 9:38; 11:3,21,32

Life Lessons

Worshipping Jesus (John 4:23). Jesus's instruction to worship the Father does not mean He Himself is not to be worshipped. Christ was worshipped as God many times and always accepted such worship as appropriate. He accepted worship from Thomas (John 20:28), the angels (Hebrews 1:6), the wise men (Matthew 2:11), a leper (Matthew 8:2), a ruler (Matthew 9:18), a blind man (John 9:38), an anonymous woman (Matthew 15:25), Mary Magdalene (Matthew 28:9), the disciples (Matthew 28:17), and others. Never hesitate to worship Jesus!

The invisibility of God (John 4:24). God is spirit, and a spirit does not have flesh and bones (Luke 24:39). Because God is spirit, He is invisible (John 1:18; Colossians 1:15; 1 Timothy 1:17). The good news, though, is that God—as an invisible Spirit—is also everywhere present (1 Kings 8:27; Psalm 139:2-12; Isaiah 66:1). That means He is always with you, despite the fact that you cannot see Him.

Verses to Remember

- "Whoever drinks of the water that I will give him will never be thirsty again. The water that I will give him will become in him a spring of water welling up to eternal life" (John 4:14).

- "God is spirit, and those who worship him must worship in spirit and truth" (John 4:24).

Questions for Reflection and Discussion

1. Just as Jesus omnisciently knew about the Samaritan woman's sin, so He omnisciently knows about everything in our lives too. How does that make you feel?

2. Are you experiencing any thirst in your spiritual life right now? What have you learned in this lesson that might help you?

3. Why do you think Jesus said worshippers should worship "in spirit and truth"?

My Father, John's Gospel is so rich in spiritual truths. I'm thankful that I've been born again and that my spiritual thirst can be quenched by living water. I'm thankful that You are always with me even though I don't see You. I'm also thankful for Your love for me. In Jesus's name, amen.

Jesus Exercises Divine Authority

In yesterday's lesson we explored Jesus as the source of living water (that is, new life through the Spirit) (John 4:4-42,46-54). Now we will consider Jesus's ministry of healing, casting out demons, and forgiving sins.

Begin by reading Matthew 4:23-25; 8:1-4,14-17; 9:1-8; Mark 1:21–2:12; and Luke 4:31-44; 5:12-26. As you read, never forget that you can trust everything that is recorded in the Word of God (Matthew 5:18; John 10:35).

Chronological marker. The events of our study today happened in early AD 28.

Overview of Today's Scripture Reading

Mark 1:21-28; Luke 4:31-37. Jesus did not teach the way the Jewish leaders did. He taught as one who had authority. And He proved His authority by commanding a spirit to come out of a man.

Matthew 8:14-17; Mark 1:29-34; Luke 4:38-41. Jesus continued to prove His authority as God by healing the sick and casting out demons. Many people were delivered.

Matthew 4:23-25; Mark 1:35-39; Luke 4:42-44. A defining aspect of Christ's purpose in coming into the world was bringing the good news of the kingdom of God to people. He wanted to reach everyone with this news. His miraculous works revealed His authority to share this good news.

Matthew 8:1-4; Mark 1:40-45; Luke 5:12-16. Jesus encountered a leper who knew Jesus could heal him but wasn't sure Jesus was willing to do so. Jesus was compassionately willing, and the man was healed.

Jesus told him to show himself to the priest so there would be public acknowledgment of his healing.

Matthew 9:1-8; Mark 2:1-12; Luke 5:17-26. Jesus pronounced a paralytic's sins forgiven. He then healed the paralytic to prove He had the authority (as God) to forgive sins.

Today's Big Ideas

- Jesus has authority over demonic spirits (Mark 1:21-28; Luke 4:31-44).

- Jesus has the divine authority to forgive sins (Mark 2:5-10; Matthew 9:2-6).

- Jesus can heal people of any disease (Matthew 4:23-25; 8:1-4,14-17; 9:1-8; Mark 1:29-34; 1:40–2:12; Luke 5:12-26).

Insights on Difficult Verses

Mark 1:44. Jesus instructed the man, "Say nothing to anyone." During those days, people were expecting a political messiah to deliverer them. At this early point in His ministry, news that He was the Messiah would immediately excite people's preconceived imaginations about what this Messiah was supposed to do. The Romans may very well subsequently mark Him as a rebel leader. So for now, Jesus told him to keep quiet about what He did.

Mark 1:22. Jesus's teachings were based on His own authority as the divine Messiah. This was in contrast to the scribes, who always quoted authoritative statements from their predecessors.

Major Themes

Demons forbidden to speak (Mark 1:34). The demons knew who Jesus was but were not allowed to speak of His identity (see Luke 4:41). Jesus did not want testimony about His identity from lying spirits (John 8:44). Besides, He did not want them revealing His identity as the Messiah because of the popular misconception that the Messiah would be a military leader who delivered the Jews from Roman domination.

Son of Man (Mark 2:10). This is a messianic title (Daniel 7:13) that appears often in the Gospels (see Matthew 8:20; 20:18; 24:30). At Christ's second coming, He will return as the Son of Man (Matthew 26:64).

Digging Deeper with Cross-References

Jesus's exorcisms (Mark 1:21-28)—Mark 1:12-13,34,39; 3:11-12,27; 5:1-20; 6:13; 7:24-30; 9:14-29

Jesus's authority (Mark 1:22)—Mark 1:27; 5:20; 6:2; 7:37; 10:24-32; 11:18; 15:5

Jesus's instruction not to reveal His identity (Mark 1:25)—Mark 1:34; 3:11-12; 8:30; 9:9

Life Lessons

Jesus forgives sin (Mark 2:1-12). Jesus healed the paralytic to prove He had the authority to forgive sins. Scripture also portrays Jesus as all-knowing (Matthew 11:27; 12:25; 22:18; Luke 6:8; John 1:48; 13:11; 16:30; 21:17). So when we became Christians, the Lord was fully aware of every sin we had ever committed and would ever commit in the future. He knows everything about us and accepts us anyway, and that should give every child of God a profound sense of security.

Jesus's example in prayer (Mark 1:35). Notice that Jesus always took time to pray, despite the fact that His ministry kept Him very busy. Jesus prayed for other people (Matthew 19:13), prayed by Himself (Luke 5:16), prayed with other people (Luke 9:28), prayed out in natural surroundings (on a mountainside) (Luke 6:12), and prayed regularly (Luke 5:16). Spend a few minutes meditating on Mark 6:46 and 14:32-39. Also check out Luke 3:21; 9:18; 11:1-4; 18:1; and 22:32.

Verses to Remember

- "'Which is easier, to say to the paralytic, "Your sins are forgiven," or to say, "Rise, take up your bed and walk"? But that you may know that the Son of Man has authority on earth to forgive sins'—he said to the paralytic—'I say to you, rise, pick up your bed, and go home'" (Mark 2:9-11).

- "They brought him all the sick, those afflicted with various diseases and pains, those oppressed by demons, epileptics, and paralytics, and he healed them" (Matthew 4:24).

Questions for Reflection and Discussion

1. Has Jesus's example of rising early in the morning for a time of prayer changed your view on the importance of prayer (Mark 1:35)?

2. Lepers were considered unclean, and yet Jesus touched one (Mark 1:41). Do you ever feel "unclean" and wonder whether the Lord would want to reach out to you? What have you learned in this lesson about the Lord's compassion toward the "unclean"?

3. What does it mean to you personally that Jesus, the divine Messiah, has intrinsic authority over all things?

My Father, if Jesus felt the need to pray, then how much more do I need to pray. Sometimes the tyranny of the urgent in my life crowds out my prayer time. Please help me to get my priorities right. Help me become a person of consistent prayer. In Jesus's name, amen.

DAY 8

Follow Me

Yesterday we considered Jesus's ministry of healing, casting out demons, and forgiving sins (Matthew 4:23-25; 8:1-4,14-17; 9:1-8; Mark 1:21–2:12; Luke 4:31-44; 5:12-26). Today we will focus on Jesus's calling of His disciples, a lesson on fasting, and some insights on Jesus's divine nature.

Begin by reading Matthew 9:9-17; Mark 2:13-22; Luke 5:27-39; and John 5. As you read, trust God to open your eyes so you can discover wondrous things from His Word (Psalm 119:18).

Chronological marker. Today's lesson features events that occurred in AD 28.

Overview of Today's Scripture Reading

Matthew 9:9-13; Mark 2:13-17; Luke 5:27-32. Notice that Jesus did not call the religious elite to join Him. Rather, He called such people as fishermen and a tax collector to join Him.

As Jesus sat at a table with tax collectors and sinners, some of the religious elite—the Pharisees—snubbed their noses at Him. Jesus was fellowshipping with people they considered to be lower-class, the dregs of society. Aware of their attitude, He affirmed that it is the sick who require a physician. He came not to call the righteous, but sinners.

Matthew 9:14-17; Mark 2:18-22; Luke 5:33-39. Jesus was asked why He and His disciples did not fast. He indicated that there is a time and a place for fasting, but this was neither the time nor the place. Jesus used an analogy of a wedding party to emphasize that fasting was inappropriate because the disciples were full of joy in the presence of the bridegroom. Why engage in fasting—a practice often associated with

48

seasons of sorrow and prayer—when the disciples were joyfully fellowshipping with the bridegroom? That wouldn't make sense. Fasting will come soon enough when the bridegroom (Jesus) is taken away from them.

John 5. A bit later, Jesus healed a lame man at a pool in Jerusalem called Bethesda. Jewish leaders criticized Jesus for doing this on the Sabbath. Jesus responded that He had been given all authority by the Father, and in fact, He was busy doing the work the Father sent Him to do. They didn't realize their inconsistency. In dishonoring the Son, they were dishonoring the Father who sent Him. Jesus made a forceful case, pointing to His many witnesses—John the Baptist, the miracles themselves, the Father, and the Scriptures.

Today's Big Ideas

- Jesus said, "Follow Me" (Matthew 9:9; Mark 2:14; Luke 5:27).
- The sick are the ones who need a physician, not the healthy (Matthew 9:12; Mark 2:17; Luke 5:31).
- There is a time and a place for fasting (Matthew 9:14-17; Mark 2:18-22; Luke 5:35-39).
- Jesus is God and has the authority of God (John 5:18-29).

Insights on Difficult Verses

Mark 2:21-22. The old wineskin of Judaism could not contain the dynamic new faith of Christianity. The grace teachings of Christ didn't fit in the legalistic wineskin of Judaism. Jesus was not offering a reformation of Judaism; He was offering something entirely new—Christianity.

John 5:19. Jesus is equal to the Father in His divine nature, but the Father is in authority over the Son. Jesus does not act independently of the Father but lives in perfect harmony with Him and submission to Him.

John 5:28-29. Salvation is solely by grace through faith (John 3:16-18; 5:24). The works in John 5:28-29 are those that take place *after* conversion (Ephesians 2:8-9). Authentic faith expresses itself in good works (Ephesians 2:10).

Major Themes

None are truly righteous (Mark 2:17). When Jesus said He came "not to call the righteous," He was not referring to those who were actually righteous in God's sight but rather those who were righteous in their own esteem, such as the scribes and Pharisees (Luke 16:14-15). Jesus came to minister to people who humbly acknowledged that they were sinners.

The resurrection of the wicked (John 5:28-29). Even the wicked will one day be resurrected. Then they will face Christ at the great white throne judgment and be cast alive into the lake of fire (see Revelation 20:11-15).

Digging Deeper with Cross-References

Fasting (Mark 2:18)—Leviticus 16:29-31; 1 Samuel 31:13; 2 Samuel 1:12; 12:21-23; Ezra 8:23; Esther 4:3; Matthew 6:16

Jesus as God (John 5:18)—John 1:1,18; 10:30,33; 20:28; Philippians 2:6; Titus 2:13; 2 Peter 1:1; 1 John 5:21

Life Lessons

Fasting (Matthew 9:14-15). The word "fast" is rooted in a Hebrew word that means "cover the mouth"—thus indicating abstinence from food and/or drink. During fasts, the people were supposed to humble their souls before God while abstaining from food. Unfortunately, the Jews of New Testament times made a show of their fasts with lots of external theatrics. Jesus made it clear that the most important thing was the internal change in a person's heart (Matthew 6:16-18).

Evangelize everyone (Mark 2:14-17). Levi invited his friends to his house so they could meet Jesus. They were sinners of such low caliber that the Jewish leaders were indignant. But many of them turned to Christ in salvation. Remember—God loves everyone. That means you and I should share the gospel with everyone (Matthew 28:19-20; 1 Peter 3:15; Jude 3).

Verses to Remember

- "Whoever hears my word and believes him who sent me has eternal life. He does not come into judgment, but has passed from death to life" (John 5:24).

- "Those who are well have no need of a physician, but those who are sick. I came not to call the righteous, but sinners" (Mark 2:17).

Questions for Reflection and Discussion

1. How is it possible that the Jewish leaders—supposed experts in interpreting Scripture—missed the reality that the Messiah was standing right in front of them (John 5:39-40)?

2. Why do you suppose so many people of ill repute decided to follow Jesus (Mark 2:15)?

3. What is your attitude toward fasting?

My Father, it is a comfort to me to know that You bring into fellowship any who are willing and not just super-saints. I count myself among those who need a physician—the Great Physician, Jesus Christ. Thank You for what You've done for me. In Jesus's name, amen.

Day 9

The Beatitudes

Yesterday we gave attention to Jesus's calling of disciples, a lesson on fasting, and some insights on Jesus's divine nature (Matthew 9:9-17; Mark 2:13-22; Luke 5:27-39; John 5:1-47). Today we turn our attention to the Beatitudes—the path to true happiness—and other key teachings of Christ.

Begin by reading Matthew 5:1-16; 12:1-21; Mark 2:23–3:19; and Luke 6:1-26. As you read, allow the Word of God to bring revival to your soul (Psalm 119:25,93,107).

Chronological marker. Our study today focuses on events that took place in AD 28.

Overview of Today's Scripture Reading

Matthew 12:1-8; Mark 2:23-28; Luke 6:1-5. The self-righteous Pharisees criticized Jesus and His hungry disciples for picking grain on the Sabbath day. They believed this violated God's command against working on the Sabbath. Jesus responded that meeting human needs (like hunger) trumped ritual laws. Jesus can authoritatively make this call because He is the Lord of the Sabbath.

Matthew 12:9-14; Mark 3:1-6; Luke 6:6-11. Jesus then healed a man's withered hand on the Sabbath day. This again brought an accusation by the Pharisees that He was doing work on the Sabbath. They pondered how to destroy Him.

Matthew 12:15-21; Mark 3:7-12; Luke 6:17-19. Jesus continued to heal people. As well, Matthew identifies Him with the suffering servant of whom Isaiah the prophet spoke (Isaiah 42:1-4). This is one in a long line of messianic prophecies that Jesus fulfilled.

The primary mission of the divine Messiah was to bring the message of salvation to people so they could come into a personal relationship with God. Jesus performed miracles primarily to confirm His divine identity. How unfortunate that many followed Him only to see miracles and not to receive the message of salvation.

Mark 3:13-19; Luke 6:12-16. Jesus commissioned, instructed, and supernaturally empowered 12 disciples to spread His message about the kingdom of God.

Matthew 5:1-12; Luke 6:20-26. Now, on a hillside near Capernaum, Jesus began His Sermon on the Mount. He demonstrated the character of the person who finds true happiness in life. For example, happy are those who are humble, patient, merciful, and pure. Happy are those who yearn for righteousness and make peace. What a contrast to modern formulas for happiness!

Matthew 5:13-16. Christians are called to be the salt and the light of the world. Though it may be politically incorrect, Christians must openly and proactively stand for Christ and Christian values in a secularized society. As one person put it, there is no need for secret-agent Christians who have never blown their cover!

Today's Big Ideas

- Jesus is the Lord of the Sabbath (Matthew 12:1-8; Mark 2:23-28; Luke 6:1-5).

- Jesus taught the Beatitudes—the path to true happiness (Matthew 5:1-12; Luke 6:20-26).

- Christians are to be salt and light in society (Matthew 5:13-16).

Insights on Difficult Verses

Mark 2:27-28. The Pharisees had twisted the teaching of the Sabbath into a legalistic burden, multiplying Sabbath requirements to such a degree that it became intolerable. Jesus corrected the Pharisees by saying that the Sabbath was made for human beings and was intended to bring them spiritual, mental, and physical refreshment, rest, and restoration.

Matthew 5–7. Jesus did not present the Sermon on the Mount as a means of attaining salvation by self-effort. Rather, the Sermon presents the way of righteous living for those who are *already* in the family of God. Much of what is in the Sermon contrasts true righteous living from the prideful self-righteousness of the scribes and Pharisees.

Major Themes

Humility and recognition of sin (Matthew 5:3). In contrast to the prideful and self-righteous scribes and Pharisees, the poor in spirit (humble) are truly blessed. These people recognize their spiritual bankruptcy apart from God. Instead of trusting in their own self-sufficiency, they depend on God for forgiveness. In receiving that forgiveness, there is great blessing.

Mourning over sin (Matthew 5:4). Also blessed are those who mourn over their sin, as opposed to those who are blind to their sin, like the scribes and Pharisees. Those who mourn over sin turn to God for salvation and experience the comfort of divine forgiveness and salvation (see 2 Corinthians 7:10).

Digging Deeper with Cross-References

Work on the Sabbath (Matthew 12:1)—Exodus 20:10; Deuteronomy 5:14; Luke 13:14; 14:3; John 5:10; 7:23; 9:16

The Lord desires mercy (Matthew 12:7)—Hosea 6:6; Micah 6:6-8; Matthew 9:13

Life Lessons

Jesus tells us how to be happy (Matthew 5:1-12). The word "blessed" literally means "happy," "fortunate," or "blissful." Blessing involves a divinely bestowed sense of well-being, which constitutes a little foretaste of heaven itself. In the Beatitudes, Jesus reveals how to receive from God a sense of well-being in daily life. Want to be happy? Make the Beatitudes your life philosophy.

Christians are the salt of the earth (Matthew 5:13). Just as salt is a preservative of food, so Christians ought to have a preserving effect on the world by influencing it for Christ, both spiritually and morally. Every

Christian can make a difference, just as a single pebble can cause many ripples in a pond.

Verses to Remember

- "Blessed are the poor in spirit, for theirs is the kingdom of heaven" (Matthew 5:3).

- "Let your light shine before others, so that they may see your good works and give glory to your Father who is in heaven" (Matthew 5:16).

Questions for Reflection and Discussion

1. Have you ever considered the reverse truths we learn from the Beatitudes? For example, "Unfortunate are the impure, for they will never see God." Try reversing a few more.

2. What are some practical ways you can be salt and light in society?

3. Even though most Christians worship on Sunday and not Saturday, do you think Christians need a day to rest and focus on God?

My Father, my perspectives are often out of focus, and my priorities are often misplaced. Please let the truths of the Beatitudes seep deep into my heart so that they are woven into the fabric of my daily life. I am appreciative. In Jesus's name, amen.

The Sermon on the Mount, Part 1

In the previous lesson we discussed the Beatitudes—the path to true happiness—and other key teachings of Christ (Matthew 5:1-16; 12:1-21; Mark 2:23–3:19; Luke 6:1-26). Today we explore more rich teachings of Christ.

Begin by reading Matthew 5:17–7:6 and Luke 6:27-42. As you read, never forget that God urges you to quickly obey His Word in all things (Psalm 119:60).

Chronological marker. The events in this lesson took place in AD 28.

Overview of Today's Scripture Reading

Matthew 5:17-20. Jesus did not come into the world to present a rival religious system to the Law of Moses. Rather, He came to fulfill the Law, which is a reflection of the holiness of God.

Matthew 5:21-26. Anger makes one feel bad, makes one do bad things, and hinders one's relationship with God. Be reconciled as quickly as possible.

Matthew 5:27-30. One should take drastic steps to avoid sin.

Matthew 5:31-32. God created the institution of marriage and intended it to be permanent (Genesis 2:18-25; Matthew 19:4-6). God hates divorce (Malachi 2:16). Marriage was originally to be dissolved only when one of the marriage partners died (Romans 7:1-4; 1 Corinthians 7:8-9; 1 Timothy 5:14). However, Jesus allowed for divorce if one's spouse engaged in sexual immorality.

Matthew 5:33-37. In Bible times, oaths were so common that people assumed that someone who did not take an oath might be lying. To counter this, Jesus said Christians should have no duplicity in their words.

Matthew 5:38-42. Jesus provided instructions for dealing with problem people. Don't retaliate. Be conciliatory. Be generous. Be radically benevolent.

Matthew 5:43-48; Luke 6:27-36. Jesus said we should love our enemies (see Luke 23:34; Acts 7:60; Galatians 5:22-23).

Matthew 6:1-4. We should give charitably, not to gain praise from people, but to please God.

Matthew 6:5-15. Prayer is for bringing personal petitions to God, not for gaining public praise.

Matthew 6:16-18. Don't use fasting to impress people, but to seek God.

Matthew 6:19-24. We ought to have a top-down perspective, seeking heavenly rewards instead of earthly rewards, which are temporal and will pass away. We must live with eternity's values in mind.

Matthew 6:25-34. Those who focus only on earthly values experience anxiety. Those who focus on eternity's values don't worry, for the Lord oversees everything.

Matthew 7:1-6; Luke 6:37-42. When we are busy judging others, we are blind to our own shortcomings. We are often guilty of the very sins we condemn in others. Jesus highlights the better policy—judge not.

Today's Big Ideas

- Seek reconciliation with others instead of remaining angry (Matthew 5:21-26).

- Take strong measures to avoid lust (Matthew 5:27-30).

- Telling the truth should not require oaths (Matthew 5:33-37).

- Love your enemies and pray for them (Matthew 5:43-48; 7:12; Luke 6:27-36).

- Build up treasures in heaven, not on earth (Matthew 6:19-21).

Insights on Difficult Verses

Matthew 5:22. The person who says "You fool" is demonstrating the anger that can lead to murder.

Matthew 5:29. Jesus was using a hyperbole—a figure of speech that purposefully exaggerates to make a powerful point. People must take drastic action in dealing with sin.

Matthew 6:13. We should ask God to order our lives and keep us from situations where we would be tempted to do evil.

Major Themes

Turning the other cheek (Matthew 5:38-42). The Jews considered it an insult to be hit in the face, much in the same way that we would interpret someone spitting in our face. Jesus thus taught that Christians should not retaliate when insulted or slandered (Romans 12:17-21). However, the verse is not prohibiting self-defense (see Luke 22:36).

Avoiding babbling prayers (Matthew 6:7). Prayer should not involve endless babbling, repeating the same request over and over again within the confines of a single prayer. God answers prayer not because of endless babbling but rather because He desires to do so as your heavenly Father.

Digging Deeper with Cross-References

Heavenly treasures (Matthew 6:19)—Matthew 13:44,46; 19:21; 25:17,22; Mark 10:21,29; Luke 12:33; 16:9,11; 18:22; 19:15; Philippians 3:8; 1 Timothy 6:19; Revelation 3:18

Judge not (Matthew 7:1)—Matthew 12:7; 26:8; Luke 6:37,41; John 8:7; Romans 2:1; 14:4,10,13; 1 Corinthians 4:5; 5:12; James 2:4; 4:12

Life Lessons

Christians ought to be perfectly loving (Matthew 5:48). The Jewish leaders of Jesus's day taught that we should love those who are near and dear to us (Leviticus 19:18) but hate our enemies. Jesus refuted this idea, instructing us to love even our enemies. We are to be "perfect" in loving, just as the Father is.

Give charitably, with no fanfare (Matthew 6:3-4). The Pharisees used opportunities of giving as a way of openly demonstrating their piety before people. Jesus said we should give quietly, with no fanfare to impress people. We should give so that our left hand does not know what our right hand is doing—that is, privately and in secret.

Verses to Remember

- "Do not lay up for yourselves treasures on earth, where moth and rust destroy and where thieves break in and steal, but lay up for yourselves treasures in heaven, where neither moth nor rust destroys and where thieves do not break in and steal" (Matthew 6:19-20).

- "Seek first the kingdom of God and his righteousness, and all these things will be added to you" (Matthew 6:33).

Questions for Reflection and Discussion

1. Do you think you focus more on building up heavenly riches or earthly riches?

2. Do you struggle with lust? Has this chapter helped strengthen your resolve in this area?

3. Do you need to reconcile with anyone?

My Father, what a rich collection of spiritual truths are found in this lesson, all of which resonate with me deeply. Perhaps most importantly, I want to build up treasures in heaven, not on earth. Please continue transforming me so that I can maintain a heavenly perspective. In Jesus's name, amen.

Day 11

The Sermon on the Mount, Part 2

Yesterday we focused on some rich teachings of Christ (Matthew 5:17–7:6; Luke 6:27-42). Today we zero in on building our lives on His teachings.

Begin by reading Matthew 7:7-29; 8:5-13; 11:1-19; and Luke 6:43–7:35. As you read, ask God to help you understand His Word (Psalm 119:73).

Chronological marker. This lesson considers events that occurred in AD 28.

Overview of Today's Scripture Reading

Matthew 7:7-11. The Greek tenses in Matthew 7:7-8 communicate the idea, "*Keep on* asking, and it will be given; *keep on* seeking, and you will find; *keep on* knocking, and the door will be opened." Don't give up on prayer!

Matthew 7:12. Jesus provides a guiding principle of life: Treat others as you would have them treat you.

Matthew 7:13-14. The way to eternal life is narrow and difficult. One should therefore be wary of claims that Christianity automatically includes everyone and is easy.

Matthew 7:15-29; Luke 6:43-49. The religious leaders of Jesus's day (scribes and Pharisees) made many boastful claims about their spirituality, but they bore no true fruit. Similarly, many people today make empty professions of faith. Jesus will one day say to them, "I never knew you."

We build our lives on Christ's words when we hear His words, understand them, and then choose to obey them (see James 1:22-25). We render complete obedience, not partial obedience.

Matthew 8:5-13; Luke 7:1-10. The centurion did not require that Jesus come to his home to heal his servant. He recognized Jesus had the authority to simply speak the word and heal his servant at a distance. Jesus was amazed at his faith.

Luke 7:11-17. Again we see that Jesus is a compassionate, divine Healer. He saw the widow grieving at the loss of her son, and as the Author of life (John 1:4; 14:6), He raised him from the dead.

Matthew 11:1-19; Luke 7:18-35. It was commonly believed that when the Messiah came, He would set up His glorious kingdom, which would be characterized by liberty and freedom. Because John was in jail (without liberty and freedom), he wondered if Jesus was truly the Messiah. Jesus responded that He performed all the signs of the Messiah. (Translation: Yes, I'm the One.)

Today's Big Ideas

- Keep on asking, and it will be given (Matthew 7:7-11).
- Treat others as you would have them treat you (Matthew 7:12-14).
- False prophets are recognized by their bad fruits (Matthew 7:15-20; Luke 6:43-45).
- Some who claim to be Christians will one day hear Christ say, "I never knew you" (Matthew 7:21-23).
- Build your life on Christ's words (Matthew 7:24-27; Luke 6:46-49).

Insights on Difficult Verses

Matthew 7:21-23. Jesus was referring to the Pharisees (Matthew 7:15). These individuals claimed to be God's representatives. In reality, they were full of hypocrisy and unrighteousness (Matthew 23:4-36).

Matthew 8:11-12. Jesus taught that many Jews who thought they'd be in God's kingdom because of ties to Abraham would in fact be denied entrance altogether. Many who do not have such blood ties (Gentiles) would be granted entrance.

Matthew 11:12. The kingdom of heaven forcefully advanced (see NIV footnote) through the miracles of Christ, pushing back demonic powers and current religious powers (the Pharisees and the Sadducees).

Luke 7:23. We might paraphrase Jesus, "Blessed is the man who recognizes me as the promised Messiah and does not fall away from believing in me simply because I do not fulfill popular misconceptions about the Messiah" (as a political deliverer).

Major Themes

The Golden Rule (Matthew 7:12). This is the most famous "rule" in the Bible: "Do to others what you would have them do to you." This verse summarizes God's requirements in the Law and the Prophets, so its relevance to daily living is obvious.

Hell's darkness (Matthew 8:12). Fire and darkness are powerful pictures of the unthinkable reality of hell. Fire points to eternal torment. Darkness points to ruination and eternal separation from the kingdom of light (heaven).

Digging Deeper with Cross-References

The saved are few (Matthew 7:14)—Matthew 19:25; 20:16; 22:14; Luke 13:24; 18:26; 1 Peter 3:20; Revelation 3:4-5

Bearing fruit (Matthew 7:16)—Matthew 3:8; Luke 13:7; John 15:1-6; Romans 7:4; Galatians 5:22; Philippians 4:17; Colossians 1:10; James 3:17

Life Lessons

Keys to answered prayer (Matthew 7:7-8). All our prayers are subject to God's sovereign will (1 John 5:14). Sin can put up a big roadblock to answered prayer (Psalm 66:18). Living righteously smooths the way for answered prayer (Proverbs 15:29).

Bearing fruit (Matthew 7:15-20). Spiritual fruit in your life is like a barometer by which you can measure your true relationship to Jesus. Ask yourself, *Is my life characterized by such things as peace, patience, gentleness, and self-control* (Galatians 5:22-23)? *Or is my life characterized more by turmoil, impatience, harshness, and lack of control?* If necessary, outline steps to make a midcourse correction in your life.

Verses to Remember

- "Ask, and it will be given to you; seek, and you will find; knock, and it will be opened to you" (Matthew 7:7).

- "Enter by the narrow gate. For the gate is wide and the way is easy that leads to destruction, and those who enter by it are many" (Matthew 7:13).

- "Not everyone who says to me, 'Lord, Lord,' will enter the kingdom of heaven, but the one who does the will of my Father who is in heaven" (Matthew 7:21).

Questions for Reflection and Discussion

1. What kind of fruit are you bearing in your life? What does your fruit reveal about your character?

2. How well built is your "house" according to Jesus's statement in Matthew 7:24-27?

3. What do you learn about faith in the account of the centurion (Matthew 8:5-13)?

My Father, I seem to have a simple but foundational choice to make every morning I awake. Will I build my life today on Jesus's words, or will I not? Please give me the strength of resolve to choose rightly. In Jesus's name, amen.

Day 12

Blasphemy Against the Holy Spirit

In yesterday's lesson we explored building our lives on Christ's teachings (Matthew 7:7-29; 8:5-13; 11:1-19; Luke 6:43–7:35). Now we give consideration to more teachings to live by.

Begin by reading Matthew 11:20-30; 12:22-45; Mark 3:20-30; and Luke 7:36–8:3; 11:14-32. As you read, remember that God's Word is the true source of hope (Psalm 119:81).

Chronological marker. The events of our study today happened in AD 28.

Overview of Today's Scripture Reading

Matthew 11:20-30. Jesus pronounced woes against unrepentant cities, indicating that degrees of punishment will be meted out at the future judgment.

Jesus gives a special commendation to "little children" (common folks) who were receptive to His teachings. This is in stark contrast to "the wise and understanding" (the legalistic Jewish leaders), who constantly stood against His ministry.

Jesus invites all who are burdened by religious legalism to come to Him for rest.

Luke 7:36-50. A sinful woman—perhaps a prostitute—anointed Jesus's head with an expensive perfume while He was a dinner guest in the home of Simon the Pharisee. Her weeping pointed to her repentance before the Lord. Simon said Jesus would have sent her away had He known her true character. Jesus defended her and pointed to her salvation.

Luke 8:1-3. Jesus greatly elevated women in a Jewish culture that held women in low regard. Three women whom Jesus helped continued to travel with His entourage.

Matthew 12:22-37; Mark 3:20-30; Luke 11:14-23. Jesus then healed a demon-oppressed man who was unable to speak. Instead of acknowledging that Jesus did the miracle in the power of the Holy Spirit, the Jewish leaders claimed He did the miracle in the power of Satan. Jesus said this was blasphemy against the Holy Spirit. (See Insights on Difficult Verses.)

Matthew 12:38-45; Luke 11:24-32. The scribes and Pharisees asked Jesus for a sign to prove He was who He claimed to be—the divine Messiah. Jesus knew that their hearts were hardened and that no sign would suffice. The only sign they'd get was the sign of Jonah—Jesus's resurrection from the dead after they killed Him.

Jesus then taught that the Jewish attempt to clean up one's life apart from the indwelling presence of the Holy Spirit leaves room for Satan to enter and wreak havoc. People's lives are changed only when they are filled with God's Word and God's Spirit.

Today's Big Ideas

- A lack of repentance brings judgment (Matthew 11:20-24).
- Come to Jesus, and He will give you rest (Matthew 11:25-30).
- Jesus warned against blasphemy of the Holy Spirit (Matthew 12:22-32; Mark 3:22-30).
- A person's true nature is revealed by the fruit he bears (Matthew 12:33-37).
- The person with many sins forgiven by God loves God greatly (Luke 7:47-48).

Insights on Difficult Verses

Matthew 12:32. Jesus did a miracle in the power of the Holy Spirit. The Jewish leaders said He did it in the power of the devil, the unholy spirit. This was an unforgivable sin against the Holy Spirit. After all, there is no other provision for human sin than the work of the one true Messiah as attested by the Holy Spirit.

Matthew 12:36-37. The Pharisees used careless (blasphemous) words by charging that Christ's miracles were performed not in the power of the Holy Spirit, but by the power of Satan (Matthew 12:22-24).

Matthew 12:40. Jesus was in the tomb for part of Friday, the entire Sabbath (Saturday), and part of Sunday. In Jewish reckoning, this constituted "three days and three nights" because any part of a day was reckoned as a complete day.

Major Themes

Degrees of punishment (Matthew 11:24). When the wicked face God in judgment, there will be degrees of punishment (Matthew 10:15; 16:27; Luke 12:47-48; Revelation 20:12-13; 22:12). God's judgment is just. Some people's judgment will be more tolerable than others' (Matthew 11:24).

Satan is called Beelzebub (Matthew 12:24). The term "Beelzebub" means "lord of the flies" and implies "lord of filth." The devil corrupts everything he touches. He is behind every form of moral filth in the universe.

Digging Deeper with Cross-References

Holy kiss (Luke 7:45)—Romans 16:16; 1 Corinthians 16:20; 2 Corinthians 13:12; 1 Thessalonians 5:26; 1 Peter 5:14

Father-Son unity (Matthew 11:27)—John 10:14-15; 14:6-7; 15:23-24; 16:15; 17:25-26

Life Lessons

Come to Jesus (Matthew 11:27-30). Are you burdened? Are you weighed down by the concerns of life? Jesus invites you to come to Him for spiritual rest. Jesus Himself is the source of your rest. Make it a daily habit to "come to Jesus."

You are either for or against Jesus (Matthew 12:30). There is no middle ground when it comes to Jesus. Every day of your life, you are either for Him or against Him. You have a choice to make. What will it be? Jesus calls for radical commitment.

Verses to Remember

- "Come to me, all who labor and are heavy laden, and I will give you rest. Take my yoke upon you, and learn from me, for I am gentle and lowly in heart, and you will find rest for your souls. For my yoke is easy, and my burden is light" (Matthew 11:28-30).

- "Whoever is not with me is against me, and whoever does not gather with me scatters" (Matthew 12:30).

Questions for Reflection and Discussion

1. How do the man who owed 500 denarii and the prostitute illustrate the principle that the person who is forgiven much loves much (Luke 7:36-48)?

2. What do you think it means that our rest is found in the person of Jesus and not merely in doing fewer things (Matthew 11:28-30)?

3. Do Jesus's words about the future judgment of careless words (Matthew 12:36-37) motivate you to clean up your speech?

My Father, again there are such rich truths in today's Scripture reading. I'm especially thankful that in a world that is in bondage to the tyranny of the urgent, I can experience spiritual rest in Jesus. I am also thankful that though I am a great sinner, I have a great Savior. In Jesus's name, amen.

DAY 13

Parables of the Kingdom, Part 1

Yesterday we considered more of Jesus's teachings to live by (Matthew 11:20-30; 12:22-45; Mark 3:20-30; Luke 7:36–8:3; 11:14-32). Today we will focus on some parables of the kingdom.

Begin by reading Matthew 12:46–13:30; Mark 3:31–4:29; and Luke 8:4-21. As you read, remember that great spiritual wisdom comes from studying God's Word (Psalm 119:98-104).

Chronological marker. Today's lesson features events that occurred in AD 28.

Overview of Today's Scripture Reading

Matthew 12:46-50; Mark 3:31-35; Luke 8:19-21. Jesus's true family members are those who do the will of the Father.

Matthew 13:1-23; Mark 4:1-20; Luke 8:4-15. Jesus taught a parable in which a sower threw seed on four different types of soil: wayside soil, rocky soil, thorn-ridden soil, and good soil. The parable portrays various responses to the preaching of God's Word. In some cases, God's Word takes root and bears fruit. In other cases, it doesn't.

Jesus's parables were designed to reveal secrets about the kingdom of God. A secret in the biblical sense is a truth that cannot be discerned simply by human investigation, but requires special revelation from God. In Matthew 13 (and parallel passages), Jesus provided information to believers (but not unbelievers) about the kingdom of heaven that had never been revealed before. Jesus's disciples were thus privileged to see and understand what the Old Testament prophets and other righteous people longed to see and understand.

Mark 4:21-25; Luke 8:16-18. Jesus taught that Christians need to let their light shine. Though it may be politically incorrect, Christians must openly and proactively stand for Christ and Christian values in a secularized society.

Mark 4:26-29. Jesus then told a parable (similar to the parable of the sower) to show that when God's Word is planted in the human heart, it will always produce fruit, albeit sometimes slowly (see 1 Peter 1:23-25).

Matthew 13:24-30. Jesus then told the parable of the wheat and the tares. The parable reveals that good and evil—true believers and false believers—will coexist in the world until the final judgment. Then they will be separated.

Today's Big Ideas

- Those who do the Father's will maintain the closest relationship with Jesus (Matthew 12:48-50; Mark 3:31-35).

- People have various responses to the preaching of God's Word (Matthew 13:3-9; Mark 4:1-9; Luke 8:4-8).

- True believers will be mingled with false believers until they are separated at the future harvest (Matthew 13:24-30).

Insights on Difficult Verses

Matthew 13:10-11. In Matthew 13, Jesus is in front of a multitude that includes believers and unbelievers. He did not attempt to separate the believers from the unbelievers and then instruct only the believers. Rather, He constructed His teaching so that believers would understand what He said but unbelievers would not, and He did this by using parables.

Mark 4:24-25. Those who respond positively to the truth they hear will be given more. Those who do not respond positively to the truth they hear will lose what they had.

Major Themes

Jesus was not being rude to His family (Matthew 12:46-50). Everyone knew how much Jesus loved His family. But when His mother and brothers were mentioned as being outside, Jesus used this teaching moment to emphasize that one's eternal allegiance to God is far more important than earthly loyalties.

Varied responses to the gospel (Matthew 13:3-23). As we've seen, Jesus told a parable showing that people have various responses to the gospel. People can be negatively influenced by such things as sin, peer pressure, money, materialism, fame, and various kinds of earthly attractions. But when the Word takes root in a life, the fruit is abundant.

Digging Deeper with Cross-References

Understanding secrets and mysteries (Matthew 13:11)—Matthew 11:25; 16:17; 1 Corinthians 2:10,14; Colossians 1:27; 1 John 2:20,27

The prophets yearned to see (Matthew 13:17)—John 8:56; Hebrews 11:13; 1 Peter 1:10-12

Choked by concern for worldly things (Luke 8:14)—Matthew 19:23; 1 Timothy 6:9-10

Life Lessons

"He who has ears, let him hear" (Matthew 13:9). Jesus often made similar statements after making important spiritual points (see, for example, verse 16 and Revelation 2–3). The idea here involves not just hearing what Jesus said, but applying His words to our lives. Many people hear and then choose to ignore. Jesus calls us to hear and obey.

The cares of the world (Matthew 13:22). Sin blinds us into thinking that the things of this world bring us meaning and security. Sin distracts us from the true source of meaning and security (Jesus Christ) so that we focus on the temporal rather than the eternal. People can be so busy trying to get ahead and trying to achieve that the tyranny of the urgent crowds out the important.

Verses to Remember

- "My mother and my brothers are those who hear the word of God and do it" (Luke 8:21).
- "They are those who hear the word, but the cares of the world

and the deceitfulness of riches and the desires for other things enter in and choke the word, and it proves unfruitful" (Mark 4:18-19).

- "Is a lamp brought in to be put under a basket, or under a bed, and not on a stand?" (Mark 4:21).

Questions for Reflection and Discussion

1. Why did Jesus's family conclude that Jesus was "out of his mind" (Mark 3:21)?

2. Why do you suppose Jesus constructed His parables so that believers would understand them but unbelievers would not (Matthew 13:10-11)? Some scholars believe Matthew 7:6 may relate. Do you agree?

3. Are you ever distracted by the cares of this world (Matthew 13:22)? Are there any thorns choking your commitment to Christ that you want to excise?

My Father, how easy it is to be distracted by the things of this world! You know me better than I know myself. Please help me to recognize and dig up any thorns choking my spiritual life. Help me to keep my life rooted in Your Word. I thank You. In Jesus's name, amen.

Parables of the Kingdom, Part 2

Yesterday we gave attention to some parables of the kingdom (Matthew 12:46–13:30; Mark 3:31–4:29; Luke 8:4-21). Today we turn our attention to more parables of the kingdom that pertain to its growth and incredible value to human beings.

Begin by reading Matthew 8:23-34; 13:31-52; Mark 4:30–5:20; and Luke 8:22-39; 13:18-21. As you read, remember that reading Scripture can strengthen your faith in God (Romans 10:17).

Chronological marker. Our study today focuses on events that took place in AD 28.

Overview of Today's Scripture Reading

Matthew 13:31-33; Mark 4:30-32; Luke 13:18-21. The kingdom of God will start small through the preaching of the disciples but will grow to be very large. Just as leaven spreads through a batch of dough, so the kingdom of God will spread and grow in influence.

Matthew 13:34-35; Mark 4:33-34. Jesus spoke in parables—word pictures that illustrate spiritual truths.

Matthew 13:36-43. Believers and unbelievers will coexist in the world until the eschatological end, when God's angels will gather unbelievers for eternal punishment.

Matthew 13:44-53. These verses communicate three ideas:

1. A person ought to be willing to pay any price for the blessings of the kingdom.

2. Good and evil will intermingle in the kingdom until the final judgment.

3. The new spiritual insights the disciples have gleaned from Jesus's parables should be understood in light of the old truths.

Matthew 8:23-27; Mark 4:35-41; Luke 8:22-25. Jesus is not only the sovereign Lord over humanity. He is also the sovereign Lord over the created universe—including the stormy sea. This means Jesus can calm the storms in our lives as easily as He calmed the storm on the lake with His disciples.

Matthew 8:28-34; Mark 5:1-20; Luke 8:26-39. Jesus is also the sovereign Lord over the demonic realm. The demons recognized this, for they addressed Jesus as "Son of the Most High God." Jesus cast countless demons out of a man and into pigs, who then ran into a lake and drowned.

Today's Big Ideas

- Jesus told various parables about the growth of the kingdom and its incredible value to people (Matthew 13:31-52; Mark 4:26-34; Luke 13:18-21).

- Jesus, Creator of the universe (John 1:3), exercised power over the natural realm (Matthew 8:23-27).

- Jesus, Creator of the angelic realm (Matthew 8:28-34; Colossians 1:16), exercised authority over fallen angels (demons).

Insights on Difficult Verses

Matthew 13:42. Weeping and gnashing teeth are expressions of grief and anger. These will be responses to the environment, the company, the remorse and guilt, and the shame that are part and parcel of hell.

Matthew 13:44-46. Jesus points to the incredible value of the kingdom of heaven. Those who truly see its importance will do anything in their power to possess it. Put in modern vernacular, the kingdom is a must-have.

Major Themes

Jesus has the power to calm storms (Matthew 8:26). Jesus created the entire universe. "All things were made through him, and without him was not any thing made that was made" (John 1:3). As the Creator (Colossians 1:16), He exercises providential control over that which He created (Colossians 1:17; see also Hebrews 1:3). Jesus reigns!

The kingdom of God starts small but becomes very big (Matthew 13:31-33). A tiny mustard seed can produce a large plant—more than 15 feet high. Likewise, the kingdom of heaven starts small but will grow to be incredibly large.

Digging Deeper with Cross-References

Jesus rebuked doubt (Matthew 8:26)—Matthew 6:30; 14:31; 16:8; 17:17; Mark 4:40; 9:19; Luke 8:25; 24:25; John 20:27; James 1:6

Jesus calmed the storm (Matthew 8:26)—Psalms 65:7; 89:9; 93:4; 107:29; Jonah 1:15; Matthew 14:32

The harvest at the end of the age (Matthew 13:39)—Joel 3:13; Revelation 14:15

Life Lessons

Be sensitive to your hearers (Mark 4:33). Jesus spoke the Word to His followers "as they were able to hear it." This reminds us of John 16:12, where Jesus said, "I still have many things to say to you, but you cannot bear them now." There are two applications for us: (1) Always seek to be ready to comprehend whatever the Lord wants to teach you, and (2) be sensitive to the receptivity of those with whom you share spiritual truth.

Go tell your friends (Mark 5:19). After Jesus delivered a man from demons, He told the man, "Go home to your friends and tell them how much the Lord has done for you, and how he has had mercy on you." In other words, Jesus told the man to go share his testimony. Giving our testimony is an effective way to evangelize our friends.

Verses to Remember

- "The kingdom of heaven is like a grain of mustard seed that a man took and sowed in his field. It is the smallest of all seeds, but when it has grown it is larger than all the garden plants and becomes a tree, so that the birds of the air come and make nests in its branches" (Matthew 13:31-32).

- "Who then is this, that he commands even winds and water, and they obey him?" (Luke 8:25).

Questions for Reflection and Discussion

1. Does today's lesson motivate you to get more involved in personal evangelism so you can participate firsthand in the growth of the kingdom?

2. Are you presently facing any storms in your life that you need the Lord to calm? Why not turn to Him in prayer now?

3. Do you think you ever give Jesus a reason to ask you, "Why are you afraid, O you of little faith?" (Matthew 8:26).

My Father, I thank You for the forgiveness I have in Jesus. I am grateful that Jesus is a Savior full of compassion. I am at peace knowing that Jesus has the power to calm the storms of my life. What a wonder is Jesus! I pray in His name, amen.

Day 15

Healing a Woman and Raising a Dead Girl

In the previous lesson we discussed more parables of the kingdom that pertain to its growth and incredible value to human beings (Matthew 8:23-34; 13:31-52; Mark 4:30–5:20; Luke 8:22-39; 13:18-21). Today we explore a number of healings Jesus performed in accordance with people's faith.

Begin by reading Matthew 9:18-34; 13:53-58; Mark 5:21–6:6; and Luke 4:16-30; 8:40-56. As you read, keep in mind that God desires you not only to hear His Word but also to do it (James 1:22).

Chronological marker. The events in this lesson took place in late AD 28 or early AD 29.

Overview of Today's Scripture Reading

Matthew 9:18-26; Mark 5:21-43; Luke 8:40-56. Jesus engaged in two rapid-fire miracles, which were signs of His identity as the divine Messiah—His divine ID card. He healed a woman with a hemorrhage and raised the daughter of a synagogue ruler from the dead. One must not forget the biblical teaching that Jesus Himself is the Creator of the universe (John 1:3; Colossians 1:16). Healing people and bringing the dead back to life are therefore in perfect keeping with His role as Creator. He who is the Creator exercises authority over that which He created.

Matthew 9:27-34. The Old Testament prophets prophesied that when the divine Messiah came, "the eyes of the blind shall be opened, and the ears of the deaf unstopped; then shall the lame man leap like a deer, and the tongue of the mute sing for joy" (Isaiah 35:5-6). Jesus's healing of the blind men was one of many signs that pointed to Jesus's identity as the divine Messiah.

Matthew 13:53-58; Mark 6:1-6; Luke 4:16-30. When Jesus came to Nazareth (where He grew up), some of the locals spoke of Him with a contempt born of familiarity. To them, Jesus was nothing special.

Today's Big Ideas

- Jesus compassionately healed many people (Matthew 9:18-26; Mark 5:21-43; Luke 8:40-56).
- Jesus emphasized the role of personal faith in healings (Matthew 9:22,28-29; Mark 5:34; Luke 8:48).
- Jesus was rejected in Nazareth, His hometown (Matthew 13:53-58; Mark 6:1-6; Luke 4:16-30).

Insights on Difficult Verses

Mark 6:4-5. It is not that Jesus was unable or incapacitated in performing a miracle in Nazareth. Rather, Jesus *could not* do miracles there in the sense that He *would not* do so in view of the pervasive unbelief in that city.

Luke 8:51-52. Jesus used the term "sleep" to indicate that the girl's condition was not permanent. He may have been saying that when He is included in the situation, death is like sleep, for it is temporary. As effortlessly as a parent awakens a child from sleep, so Jesus miraculously awakened the young girl from her temporary state of death (compare with John 11:11-14). Jesus will just as effortlessly resurrect you and me from the dead (1 Corinthians 15:50-51; 1 Thessalonians 4:13-17).

Major Themes

Jesus's healing power (Luke 8:46). Jesus was always in complete control of His divine miraculous power (see John 2:1-11; 4:50-52; 5:8-9; 11:40-44). The reason the woman was healed when she touched Jesus's garment was that He willed her to be healed as a result of her faith. The woman's touching of Jesus's cloak was an expression of her faith.

The devil does not cause all illness (Matthew 9:33). The devil and demons can cause such illnesses as dumbness, blindness (12:22), and epilepsy (17:15-18). But Scripture distinguishes natural illnesses from demon-caused illnesses (Matthew 4:24; Mark 1:32; Luke 7:21; 9:1; Acts 5:16). Demons do not cause all illnesses.

Digging Deeper with Cross-References

Laying on hands for healing (Mark 5:23)—Matthew 8:3; Mark 6:5; 7:32; 8:23,25; Luke 4:40; 13:13; Acts 9:12,17; 28:8

Elijah and rain (Luke 4:25)—1 Kings 17:1-9; 18:1; James 5:17

Son of David, the Messiah (Matthew 9:27)— 2 Samuel 7:12-16; Matthew 1:1; 12:23; 15:22; 20:30-31

Life Lessons

Those closest to you may not accept you and your spiritual beliefs (Luke 4:24). Jesus was not accepted as a prophet in His hometown. His neighbors were not impressed. In fact, they were offended at Him. It is possible that people in your neighborhood, your office, or even your home may not accept you once you become a Christian. No worries. Just stay close to Jesus, pray, stay in God's Word, and be a good witness. Keep in mind that you now have a huge family of God that stands with you (see Mark 10:29-31).

Have faith (Mark 5:34). In our lesson, those who experienced miracles at Jesus's hand had faith in Him. By contrast, those who did not experience miracles (like the residents of Nazareth) did not have faith in Him. This brings to mind Hebrews 11:6: "Without faith it is impossible to please him, for whoever would draw near to God must believe that he exists and that he rewards those who seek him." Keep your faith in God strong.

Verses to Remember

- "The Spirit of the Lord is upon me, because he has anointed me to proclaim good news to the poor. He has sent me to proclaim liberty to the captives and recovering of sight to the blind, to set at liberty those who are oppressed, to proclaim the year of the Lord's favor" (Luke 4:18-19).

- "A prophet is not without honor, except in his hometown and among his relatives and in his own household" (Mark 6:4).

Questions for Reflection and Discussion

1. Do you think Jesus still does supernatural things in our lives today as He did in New Testament times? Can you think of an example?

2. What have you learned in this lesson about receiving hostile reactions when you stand for the truth?

3. Would you say you have a strong faith or a weak faith in God? How might Romans 10:17 help you in this regard?

My Father, You have proclaimed good news to me and set me free. You have removed my spiritual blindness and relieved my oppression. You have brought me favor. I am so thankful to You. In Jesus's name, amen.

Jesus Sends Out 12 Apostles

Yesterday we focused on a number of healings Jesus performed in accordance with peoples' faith (Matthew 9:18-34; 13:53-58; Mark 5:21–6:6; Luke 4:16-30; 8:40-56). Today we zero in on Jesus's commission of 12 apostles to proclaim the kingdom of God.

Begin by reading Matthew 9:35–10:42; 14:3-12; Mark 6:6-13,17-29; and Luke 9:1-6. As you read, stop and meditate on any verses that speak to your heart (Joshua 1:8; Psalm 1:1-3).

Chronological marker. This lesson considers events that occurred in early AD 29.

Overview of Today's Scripture Reading

Matthew 9:35-38. Jesus's compassion motivated Him to heal people of diseases and afflictions. Jesus lamented the pastoral negligence of the Jewish leaders. He encouraged prayer for raising up laborers to participate in the evangelistic harvest.

Matthew 10:1-15; Mark 6:6-13; Luke 9:1-6. Jesus commissioned His 12 apostles to spread His message about the kingdom of God.

Matthew 10:16-42. Jesus informed His apostles that they'd experience persecution as they spread the news about the kingdom. Indeed, we can say that all those who serve Christ will experience some level of persecution. There is no need to fear, however, because God sovereignly watches over and guides all believers.

Interestingly, Jesus then said, "I have not come to bring peace, but a sword." In other words, as evangelism takes place, some will accept Christ and others will reject Him—even within the same family. The work of evangelism is like a spiritual sword that divides people. Jesus urged unqualified allegiance to Him regardless of people's response.

Matthew 14:3-12; Mark 6:17-29. Herod imprisoned John the Baptist because John condemned Herod's adulterous marriage to his brother Philip's wife, Herodias. At an opportune moment, she imposed on Herod to have John executed by beheading.

Today's Big Ideas

- The harvest is plentiful, but the workers are few (Matthew 9:35-38).

- Jesus sent out 12 apostles to proclaim, "The kingdom of God is at hand" (Matthew 10:1-15; Mark 6:7-13; Luke 9:1-6).

- Jesus warned the apostles of persecution, but He told them not to fear (Matthew 10:16-33).

- Jesus did not come to bring peace, but a sword (Matthew 10:34-39).

- John the Baptist was executed (Matthew 14:3-12; Mark 6:6-13,17-29).

Insights on Difficult Verses

Matthew 10:5-6. The good news of the kingdom was to be preached first to the Jews—God's covenant people (2 Samuel 7:12-14). But the Abrahamic covenant said Gentiles would also be blessed through Messiah (Genesis 12:3). Gentile inclusion becomes predominant in the book of Acts (see Acts 10).

Matthew 10:32-33. We might paraphrase Jesus this way: "Whoever acknowledges me before others [the way you disciples have been doing], I will also acknowledge before my Father in heaven. But whoever disowns me before others [the way these Pharisees do on every occasion they get], I will disown before my Father in heaven" (NIV).

Major Themes

Peter was one among a number of leaders (Matthew 10:2-4; Mark 3:16-19; Luke 6:14-16). Peter played a dominant role in the early church, but he did not become the first pope. He viewed himself not as preeminent, but as a "fellow elder" (1 Peter 5:1). James, not Peter, exercised primacy at the Council of Jerusalem (Acts 15:1-21). Peter wrote two New Testament books—the apostle Paul wrote thirteen.

Jesus and family breakups (Matthew 10:21-22). Jesus taught that commitment to following Him would be tested by all the significant relationships in life—civil, religious, and family. Discord and contention often erupt in families when one family member becomes a Christian.

Digging Deeper with Cross-References

Sheep without a shepherd (Matthew 9:36)—Numbers 27:17; 1 Kings 22:17; 2 Chronicles 18:16; Ezekiel 34:5; Zechariah 10:2; Mark 6:34

Prediction of Judas's betrayal (Matthew 10:4)—Matthew 26:25; 27:3; Mark 14:44; John 6:64; 12:4; 13:2,26-27

Sodom and Gomorrah (Matthew 10:15)—Genesis 18:20–19:29; Matthew 11:23-24; 2 Peter 2:6; Jude 7

Life Lessons

Wise as serpents and innocent as doves (Matthew 10:16). The apostles were to be wise as serpents in the sense of being circumspect, discreet, judicious, and sensible in the way they handled themselves before others. They were also to be innocent as doves. The Greek word translated "innocent" carries the idea, "without any mixture of deceit," "without falsity," "unadulterated," "harmless," "pure." Bottom line: The disciples were to be wise and honest in their interactions with others.

Be like Jesus (Matthew 10:25). In New Testament times, a disciple would seek to be like his teacher. The goal of every believer is to be like Jesus. As we walk in the Spirit, the fruit of the Spirit grows in our lives (Galatians 5:16,22). This fruit involves the very character of Jesus—things like love, joy, peace, patience, kindness, goodness, faithfulness, gentleness, and self-control. Do you want to be like Jesus? Then walk in the Spirit.

Verses to Remember

- "The harvest is plentiful, but the laborers are few; therefore pray earnestly to the Lord of the harvest to send out laborers into his harvest" (Matthew 9:37-38).

- "Everyone who acknowledges me before men, I also will acknowledge before my Father who is in heaven, but whoever denies me before men, I also will deny before my Father who is in heaven" (Matthew 10:32-33).

- "Whoever loves father or mother more than me is not worthy of me, and whoever loves son or daughter more than me is not worthy of me. And whoever does not take his cross and follow me is not worthy of me" (Matthew 10:37-38).

Questions for Reflection and Discussion

1. Why do you think the judgment is so harsh for people who reject the words of the apostles (Matthew 10:14-15)?

2. What do you think was Jesus's meaning in citing the four creatures in Matthew 10:16?

3. What do you think it means to take up your cross and follow Jesus (Matthew 10:38)?

My Father, I perceive from today's study that You are calling me to supreme commitment. You are calling me to take up my cross and follow Jesus. Please help me to understand all the implications of what that means, and give me the strength of will to make it happen. In Jesus's name, amen.

Day 17

Feeding 5000 and Walking on Water

In yesterday's lesson we explored Jesus's sending out of 12 apostles to proclaim the kingdom of God (Matthew 9:35–10:42; 14:3-12; Mark 6:6-13,17-29; Luke 9:1-6). Now we give consideration to Jesus miraculously feeding 5000 and then walking on water.

Begin by reading Matthew 14:1-2,13-33; Mark 6:14-16,30-52; Luke 9:7-17; and John 6:1-21. As you read, notice how the Word of God is purifying your life (John 17:17-18).

Chronological marker. The events of our study today happened in early AD 29.

Overview of Today's Scripture Reading

Matthew 14:1-2; Mark 6:14-16; Luke 9:7-9. Herod concluded that Jesus, with all His miracles, must be John the Baptist risen from the dead.

Matthew 14:13-21; Mark 6:30-44; Luke 9:10-17; John 6:1-15. Jesus repeatedly displayed a power over natural forces that could belong only to God, the Author of these forces. This should not surprise us, for Christ Himself is the Creator (John 1:3; Colossians 1:16; Hebrews 1:2). We should fully expect Christ to exercise control over that which He Himself brought into being.

In today's Scripture reading, we witness Jesus multiplying five small loaves of bread and two small fish into enough food to satisfy a huge crowd—5000 men plus women and children (Matthew 14:21). The total number of people eating could well be over 10,000. Using a small boy's lunch, which one of the disciples located, Jesus multiplied the meager serving of five loaves and two fish until everyone in the vast crowd was more than satisfied. There were 12 baskets of leftovers (John 6:12-13).

Matthew 14:22-33; Mark 6:45-52; John 6:16-21. Later that evening, Jesus dismissed the disciples and sent them back to Capernaum by boat across the northwest corner of the Sea of Galilee. As they rowed, they suddenly noticed a human figure walking toward them on the water. As the figure gained on them, they became terrified and cried out in fear, thinking they were being pursued by a ghost. When Jesus approached them, He said, "It is I; do not be afraid" (John 6:20). After witnessing this miracle—and seeing Jesus empower Peter to walk on water momentarily—the disciples worshipped Jesus in the boat, saying, "Truly you are the Son of God" (Matthew 14:33).

Today's Big Ideas

- Jesus miraculously fed more than 5000 people (Matthew 14:13-21; Mark 6:30-44; Luke 9:10-17; John 6:1-15).
- Jesus walked on the water (Matthew 14:22-33; Mark 6:45-52; John 6:16-21).

Insights on Difficult Verses

Matthew 14:25. The Romans divided the night into four military watches. These watches ended at nine p.m., twelve a.m., three a.m., and six a.m, so Jesus was seen walking on water sometime between three and six in the morning.

Mark 6:46. Jesus had no need to pray from the perspective of His divine nature, but only from the perspective of His humanity. As our High Priest and Mediator (1 Timothy 2:5), it was proper that Jesus prayed to the Father.

Mark 6:51-52. The disciples' hearts were hardened in that they had missed the main point of the miracle of multiplying food. That miracle was a sign of His identity as the divine Messiah. They were doubting because they still didn't have a firm grip on His true identity.

Major Themes

The miracle of bread (John 6:1-15). Jesus's multiplying of bread to feed more than 5000 recalls God's provision of food for the Israelites in the wilderness: "The LORD said to Moses, 'Behold, I am about to rain bread from heaven for you, and the people shall go out and gather a day's portion every day'" (Exodus 16:4).

Jesus and His singular focus (John 6:15). Jesus was incredibly popular. The people were ready to make Him king. Of course, that would have interfered with Jesus's main goal—to establish the kingdom of God and secure humanity's salvation. He would allow nothing to distract Him from that goal.

Digging Deeper with Cross-References

The Prophet (John 6:14)—Deuteronomy 18:15,18; Acts 3:22; 7:37

Walking on water (Matthew 14:25)—Job 9:8; Psalm 77:19; Isaiah 43:16

Jesus as the Son of God (Matthew 14:33)—Psalm 2:7; Matthew 16:16; 26:63; 27:54; Mark 1:1; Luke 22:70; John 1:49; 6:69; Romans 1:4

Life Lessons

Contagious blessings (Matthew 14:19). Notice that Jesus gave the loaves of bread to the disciples, and then the disciples gave the loaves to the people. This illustrates how God often works through people. As Paul put it in 1 Corinthians 11:23, "I received from the Lord what I also delivered to you." Paul also speaks of the "God of all comfort, who comforts us in all our affliction, so that we may be able to comfort those who are in any affliction, with the comfort with which we ourselves are comforted by God" (2 Corinthians 1:3-4).

God can turn something small into something great (John 6:8-9). The boy gave what little food he had, and God (Jesus) multiplied it into something great. You and I may sometimes feel that we are insignificant, that we don't have much to offer God. But offer to God what little you have—your talents, your spiritual gifts, your time, and the like. God can turn these into something great.

Verses to Remember

- "He saw a great crowd, and he had compassion on them and healed their sick" (Matthew 14:14).
- "O you of little faith, why did you doubt?" (Matthew 14:31).

Questions for Reflection and Discussion

1. What lesson did the disciples learn about Jesus in His feeding of the 5000? Why was this important for them to learn?
2. What do you think Jesus's purpose was in walking on water instead of walking around the lake to meet the disciples? What lesson was Jesus intending to teach?
3. What can you give to God that He could multiply into something great?

My Father, Jesus's miracles are staggering to my mind. Like You, He has the ability to alter and control things in the realm of nature. When life is hard, knowing that I am in a personal relationship with a God of miracles brings me comfort. In Jesus's name, amen.

Day 18

The Bread of Life

Yesterday we considered Jesus miraculously feeding 5000 and then walking on water (Matthew 14:1-2,13-33; Mark 6:14-16,30-52; Luke 9:7-17; John 6:1-21). Today we will focus on the supremacy of God's Word and Jesus as the bread of life.

Begin by reading Matthew 14:34–15:20; Mark 6:53–7:23; and John 6:22-71. As you read, keep in mind that the Word of God brings spiritual maturity (1 Corinthians 3:1-2; Hebrews 5:12-14).

Chronological marker. Today's lesson features events that occurred in mid–AD 29.

Overview of Today's Scripture Reading

Matthew 14:34-36; Mark 6:53-56. Jesus continued His ministry of miracles by healing many sick and diseased people in the land of Gennesaret. Such miracles continued to attest to His identity as the divine Messiah.

John 6:22-59. Jesus had just performed a tremendous miracle in feeding 5000 people with five barley loaves and two fishes. The crowd had eaten a meal that satisfied their physical hunger. Christ now wanted to satisfy their spiritual hunger and give them eternal life. This happens by partaking of the bread of life, Jesus Himself. Our passage informs us that just as one must consume physical food to sustain physical life, so one must spiritually appropriate Christ to have spiritual life. Just as Israel depended on manna (bread) in the wilderness to sustain physical life, so we depend on Jesus (the bread of life) for our spiritual life.

John 6:60-71. The word "disciple" comes from the Greek word *mathetes*, which literally means "a learner." A disciple is therefore a learner. He is one who learns about and learns from Jesus Christ. Some of Jesus's "learners" reacted negatively to His words about eating of Him and drinking of Him for eternal life. They "turned back and no longer walked with him" (verse 66).

Matthew 15:1-20; Mark 7:1-23. The scribes and Pharisees were critical of Jesus's disciples because they didn't follow Jewish cleansing rituals. These individuals focused on external issues while ignoring the inner person. Jesus responded that it is not the external eating of food but rather the internal impure thoughts and ideas that emerge from the fallen human heart that defile a person.

Today's Big Ideas

- Jesus elevated the Word of God over Jewish tradition (Matthew 15:1-9; Mark 7:1-13).
- Out of the human heart comes various forms of evil (Matthew 15:10-20; Mark 7:14-23).
- Jesus is the bread of life (John 6:22-59).
- Jesus speaks words of eternal life (John 6:60-71).

Insights on Difficult Verses

John 6:27. Jesus Himself is the food that endures to eternal life. By simply believing in Him, a person "partakes of this food" and receives the gift of eternal life.

John 6:53. When Jesus said "this is my body" in reference to bread in His hand (Matthew 26:26), He was present in His physical body, the hands of which were holding the very bread that He said was His body. He was obviously speaking figuratively. Otherwise, we must believe that Christ was holding His own body in His hands.

Major Themes

The Father draws people to Christ (John 6:44). Jesus indicated that people can't come to Him strictly on their own initiative. The Father sovereignly draws them to Jesus. People are so deeply engulfed in sin, they would never come to Christ unless the Father drew them.

Vain worship (Matthew 15:9). Jesus cited the words of Isaiah: "In vain do they worship me, teaching as doctrines the commandments of men." Worship becomes vain whenever there is more focus on external requirements and rituals than heartfelt commitment to and honor of God. The Pharisees were often guilty of vain worship.

Digging Deeper with Cross-References

"I am" (John 6:35)—John 4:26; 8:12; 9:5; 10:7-9,11-14; 11:25; 14:6; 15:1-5

Heart change versus legalism (Matthew 15:8-9)—1 Samuel 15:22; Psalm 51:17; Isaiah 1:13-17; 29:13; Hosea 6:6; Matthew 23:23; Mark 12:29-31; Acts 15:5-11; 2 Corinthians 3:6; Galatians 2:16; 3:2-5; 6:2

Life Lessons

Beware of religious traditions (Matthew 15:1-9). Jesus criticized the Jewish leaders for placing a higher priority on their traditions than on the Word of God. Traditions have a habit of making religion a routine matter of going through the motions. Such religious externalism is one reason so many people today have exited the Christian church. How much better it is to focus on the Word of God—the Bible, which is a "Jesus book."

Stay committed (John 6:66-69). Some disciples misunderstood what Jesus meant when He spoke about eating His flesh and drinking His blood. "After this many of his disciples turned back and no longer walked with him" (verse 66). Peter and the others remained, trusting in Jesus no matter what. Will you trust Jesus even if you don't fully understand everything? Even when things get tough? That is what the Lord desires of you.

Verses to Remember

- "What comes out of the mouth proceeds from the heart, and this defiles a person. For out of the heart come evil thoughts, murder, adultery, sexual immorality, theft, false witness, slander. These are what defile a person" (Matthew 15:8-9).

- "I am the bread of life; whoever comes to me shall not hunger, and whoever believes in me shall never thirst" (John 6:35).

Questions for Reflection and Discussion

1. What do we learn about Jesus from the "bread of life" metaphor (John 6:22-59)?

2. Are you having any heart problems (see Mark 7:21-23)?

3. For what reasons does Jesus call the Pharisees hypocrites (Matthew 15:7-9)? Do you ever see hypocrisy in yourself?

My Father, it is much easier to give the outer appearance of being pure than to be pure in my heart. It is much easier to wear a pious mask—to be a hypocrite—than to let others see me as I really am, a fallen and wounded sinner with many hang-ups. Please help me grow into an authentic Christian. In Jesus's name, amen.

DAY 19

Miraculous Proofs of Christ's Identity

Yesterday we gave attention to the supremacy of God's Word and Jesus as the bread of life (Matthew 14:34–15:20; Mark 6:53–7:23; John 6:22-71). Today we turn our attention to further miraculous proofs of Christ's identity as the divine Messiah.

Begin by reading Matthew 15:21–16:20; Mark 7:24–8:30; and Luke 9:18-21. As you read, remember that the Word of God can help you be spiritually fruitful (Psalm 1:1-3).

Chronological marker. Our study today focuses on events that took place in mid–AD 29.

Overview of Today's Scripture Reading

Matthew 15:21-28; Mark 7:24-30. Jesus was amazed that the Gentile woman had such great faith, especially because Jesus had spoken to many Jews who had no faith. At first glance, Jesus may have seemed a bit indifferent to the woman. But His conversation with her was engineered to increase her faith even further.

Matthew 15:29-31; Mark 7:31-37. Jesus continued to heal the lame, the blind, the crippled, the mute, and many others. All these miracles attested to His identity as the divine Messiah.

Matthew 15:32-39; Mark 8:1-10. Jesus again multiplied food to feed the masses. Jesus had previously fed more than 5000 Jews in a Jewish territory. Now He fed more than 4000 non-Jews in a Gentile territory. This shows that Jesus has compassion for all people, both Jew and Gentile.

Matthew 16:1-4; Mark 8:11-13. The Pharisees and Sadducees asked Jesus for a sign to prove He was who He claimed to be—the divine

Messiah. Jesus knew that their hearts were hardened and that no sign would suffice. They'd only receive the sign of Jonah—Jesus's resurrection from the dead after they arranged to have Him killed.

Matthew 16:5-12; Mark 8:14-21. Jesus warned His disciples that the false teachings of the Jewish leaders were penetrating and corrupting the entire nation.

Mark 8:22-26. Unlike other miracles of Jesus, this miracle took place in two stages. First the man was given partial sight, and then he was healed completely. Some believe that because sight can be a metaphor for understanding, perhaps this two-stage miracle represents how the man's spiritual sight was gradually increasing in response to Jesus.

Matthew 16:13-20; Mark 8:27-30; Luke 9:18-21. Jesus asked the disciples who people said He was. Many flattering answers were given, but none were right. When Jesus asked the disciples about their opinion, Peter said, "You are the Christ, the Son of the living God." The term "Christ" is equivalent to "Messiah." Jesus is the One to whom all the Old Testament messianic prophecies point.

Today's Big Ideas

- Receiving a miracle from the Lord hinges on faith (Matthew 15:28; Mark 7:29).

- Jesus again multiplied food to feed the masses (Matthew 15:32-39; Mark 8:1-10).

- Only the sign of Jonah would be given to the Pharisees and Sadducees (Matthew 16:1-4; Mark 8:11-13).

- Beware of the pervasive unbelief and hypocrisy demonstrated by the Pharisees and Sadducees (Matthew 16:5-12; Mark 8:14-21).

Insights on Difficult Verses

Matthew 15:22-28. Jesus had come specifically to offer the nation of Israel the kingdom that had been promised in the Davidic covenant (2 Samuel 7:12-14). It would not be appropriate for Him to pour out blessings on a Gentile woman before such blessings were bestowed on Israel. The woman, with great faith, continued her plea. Jesus therefore granted her request. How ironic that the Gentile woman's faith was in great contrast to the hypocritical Jewish leaders' lack of faith.

Matthew 15:24. The lost sheep of Israel were the Israelites to whom Jesus was preaching in Judah and in Galilee who were in a "lost" condition in God's eyes.

Major Themes

Beware of the growth of unbelief and hypocrisy (Mark 8:15). Pharisaic unbelief and hypocrisy—once it was introduced and admitted into the heart of Jewish society—spread so pervasively that it rendered true spirituality impossible. The spiritual state of the nation had become abysmal.

The rock upon which the church is built (Matthew 16:18). The foundation upon which the church would be built is apparently Jesus's rock-solid identity as the Christ, which Peter just acknowledged (1 Corinthians 3:11; Ephesians 2:20; Colossians 1:17-18; 1 Peter 2:7).

Digging Deeper with Cross-References

Little faith (Matthew 16:8)—Matthew 6:30; 8:26; 14:31; Mark 9:22; Luke 12:28; 24:21; John 11:37

Great faith (Matthew 15:28)—Matthew 8:10; 9:21-22; Mark 10:51; Luke 7:9; Romans 4:19; Hebrews 11:19

Life Lessons

Be persistent (Matthew 15:21-28). Jesus commended the Gentile woman for her faithful persistence. This recalls Jesus's words in Matthew 7:7-8, where "ask," "seek," and "knock" are in the present tense, indicating continuous activity. We are to keep on asking, keep on seeking, and keep on knocking.

It's the inside that counts (Matthew 15:16-20). We all spend a lot of time trying to look our best with nice clothes, nice haircuts, and the like. But what's in the heart is more important to God. God is in the business of heart transformation (see Psalm 51:10; Romans 12:2; 2 Corinthians 3:18; Galatians 5:22; Philippians 1:6; 2 Timothy 3:15-17).

Verses to Remember

- "Great crowds came to him, bringing with them the lame, the blind, the crippled, the mute, and many others, and they put them at his feet, and he healed them" (Matthew 15:30).
- "'Who do you say that I am?' Simon Peter replied, 'You are the Christ, the Son of the living God'" (Matthew 16:15-16).

Questions for Reflection and Discussion

1. Has hypocrisy ever been like leaven in your own life, starting small but then becoming pervasive?

2. The disciples wanted to send the miracle-seeking woman away (Matthew 15:23). Do you think people could be so concerned about the business of ministry that they become blind to the needs of people nearby?

3. Do you think Jesus could have been showing a sense of humor, with a wink in His eye, when He spoke the words in Matthew 15:26?

My Father, I fear that unbelief and hypocrisy sometimes creep into my spiritual life. Please continue transforming me and root out any inkling of these from my life. I'm appreciative. In Jesus's name, amen.

The Transfiguration

In the previous lesson we discussed further miraculous proofs of Christ's identity as the divine Messiah (Matthew 15:21–16:20; Mark 7:24–8:30; Luke 9:18-21). Today we explore Jesus's prediction of His death and resurrection, and His requirement of radical commitment from His followers.

Begin by reading Matthew 16:21–17:20; Mark 8:31–9:29; and Luke 9:22-43. Read with the anticipation that the Holy Spirit has something important to teach you today (see Psalm 119:105).

Chronological marker. The events in this lesson took place in mid–AD 29.

Overview of Today's Scripture Reading

Matthew 16:21-28; Mark 8:31–9:1; Luke 9:22-27. Jesus revealed to the disciples that He would go to Jerusalem to suffer and die but then be raised on the third day. Peter, not understanding the plan of salvation, rebuked Jesus and tried to talk Him out of it. Jesus saw Satan's work in Peter's words.

The Lord then revealed that discipleship involves a cost. The path of discipleship means turning from self and ambition to a life of sacrifice and total submission to Christ.

Matthew 17:1-13; Mark 9:2-13; Luke 9:28-36. In the transfiguration, Jesus allowed His intrinsic glory to shine forth in all its splendor. "His face shone like the sun, and his clothes became white as light" (Matthew 17:2).

A question then came up. If Jesus was truly the Messiah, as the transfiguration just proved Him to be, why had Elijah not yet appeared, as prophesied? Jesus indicated that Elijah *had* appeared in the sense that John the Baptist's ministry was carried out in the spirit and power of Elijah.

Matthew 17:14-20; Mark 9:14-29; Luke 9:37-43. Jesus had given the disciples the power to cast out demons. In the present case, however, they were unable to do so because of unbelief. Jesus cast out the demon, and the boy was healed.

Today's Big Ideas

- Jesus foretold His death and resurrection (Matthew 16:21-23; Mark 8:31-33; Luke 9:22).

- Jesus requires radical commitment from His followers (Matthew 16:24-28; Mark 8:34-38; Luke 9:23-27).

- Jesus allowed His divine glory to shine forth (Matthew 17:1-13; Mark 9:1-13; Luke 9:28-36).

Insights on Difficult Verses

Luke 9:31. The Greek word translated "departure" literally means "exodus." In the exodus from Egypt, God's people were liberated from bondage and brought into liberty and freedom. Christ viewed His death as an act that would liberate Him from this period of bondage (on earth) to which He had subjected Himself by the Incarnation (Philippians 2:5-11). Using similar language, the apostle Paul in 2 Timothy 4:6 spoke of his approaching death: "The time of my departure has come" (see also 2 Peter 1:15).

A bright cloud (Matthew 17:5). We often witness a bright cloud in manifestations of God's glory (Exodus 13:21-22; 34:5-7; 1 Kings 8:10-13). The cloud typically indicates God's presence. Recall the scene with Moses and the Israelites at Mount Sinai: "On the morning of the third day there were thunders and lightnings and a thick cloud on the mountain and a very loud trumpet blast, so that all the people in the camp trembled" (Exodus 19:16).

Major Themes

Jesus was transfigured (Mark 9:2-13). In the transfiguration, Christ pulled back the veil so that His intrinsic divine glory shone forth in all its splendor. He was "transfigured" (Matthew 17:2), and "the appearance of his face changed" (Luke 9:29 NIV) so that it "shone like the sun" and His clothing "became as white as light" (Matthew 17:2).

Evil spirits and physical symptoms (Luke 9:39). In our passage, a demon caused convulsions in a person. However, not all convulsions—not all physical symptoms—are caused by demons. Plenty of verses speak of peoples' physical symptoms without mentioning a demon (such as John 9:1-7).

Digging Deeper with Cross-References

Jesus is glorified (Matthew 17:1-13)—Mark 9:2-8; 16:19; Luke 9:28-36; John 1:14; 17:5,24; Ephesians 1:21-22; Philippians 2:9-10; Colossians 1:15-18; 1 Peter 3:22; Revelation 5:7-14; 19:11-16

"My beloved Son" (Matthew 17:5)—Psalm 2:7; Matthew 3:17; 12:18; Mark 1:11; Luke 3:22; 2 Peter 1:17

Life Lessons

Take up your cross (Mark 8:34). Jesus was communicating this: "If you really want to follow Me, do not do so in word only, but put your life on the line and follow Me on the path of the cross—a path that will involve sacrifice, self-denial, and possibly even suffering and death for My sake" (see Romans 14:7-9; 15:2-3).

Be cautious following a mountaintop experience (Matthew 17:14-18). As soon as the disciples came down the mountain, they immediately encountered a man bound by a demon that they could not cast out. Jesus Himself had to deal with the demon. Some Bible expositors suggest that after mountaintop experiences (such as that experienced by the disciples when they witnessed Jesus's glory on the mountain), the devil is often waiting and ready to attack. Christian beware (Ephesians 6:11)!

Verses to Remember

- "If anyone would come after me, let him deny himself and take up his cross and follow me. For whoever would save his life will lose it, but whoever loses his life for my sake will find it" (Matthew 16:24-25).

- "If you have faith like a grain of mustard seed, you will say to this mountain, 'Move from here to there,' and it will move, and nothing will be impossible for you" (Matthew 17:20).

Questions for Reflection and Discussion

1. What do you think is the significance of Jesus's face shining like the sun and His clothes becoming as white as the light?

2. How do you think that losing one's life actually enables one to find it?

3. Practically speaking, how does one take up his cross to follow Jesus? What does that look like in real life?

My Father, I see so much selfishness in my life. I sometimes wonder if I could ever be the kind of Christian that could engage in self-denial and sacrifice in order to take up the cross and follow Jesus. Please work in my life and transform me into a cross-bearing Christian. In Jesus's name, amen.

Day 21

Restoration and Forgiveness

Yesterday we focused on Jesus's prediction of His death and resurrection and His requirement of radical commitment from His followers (Matthew 16:21–17:20; Mark 8:31–9:29; Luke 9:22-43). Today we zero in on Jesus's teachings on a variety of subjects, including humility, taking steps to overcome sin, and forgiving others.

Begin by reading Matthew 17:22–18:35; Mark 9:30-50; Luke 9:43-50; and John 7:1-9. As you read, remember that the Word of God is alive and working in you (Hebrews 4:12).

Chronological marker. This lesson considers events that occurred in mid–AD 29.

Overview of Today's Scripture Reading

Matthew 17:22-23; Mark 9:30-32; Luke 9:43-45. Jesus again predicted His death and resurrection. The disciples were distressed.

Matthew 17:24-27. Jesus sovereignly controlled a fish with a coin in its mouth so that the coin could be used to pay the yearly temple tax for Himself and Peter.

Matthew 18:1-5; Mark 9:33-37; Luke 9:46-48. Jesus went against traditional wisdom in saying that the path to greatness in the kingdom of God is becoming like a little child. The way up is down. One must be humble, dependent, and trusting.

Mark 9:38-41; Luke 9:49-50. Meanwhile, the disciples sought to stop an anonymous exorcist from driving out demons in Jesus's name. They apparently thought he was making unauthorized use of Jesus's name. Jesus corrected their narrow exclusivism.

Matthew 18:6-10; Mark 9:42-50. Jesus urged against causing any kind of offense that could bring temptation to others—especially the "little ones." Radical steps should be taken to thwart sin.

Matthew 18:12-14. Using an illustration of a shepherd, Jesus emphasized how much the Father cares for each of His little ones.

Matthew 18:15-20. Jesus outlined progressive steps to take if another Christian sins against you. First speak privately with the person. If he does not listen, take two or three witnesses (Deuteronomy 19:15). If he still does not listen, take the matter before the church. It he still does not listen, he is to be treated as an outsider. Sin is too serious to ignore.

Matthew 18:21-35. Every Christian has been forgiven an incalculably large debt of sin by God. That being so, every Christian ought to forgive all the sins of others, which pale in comparison.

John 7:1-9. Jesus's brothers did not believe He was the promised Messiah. They mockingly urged Him to go to Jerusalem and attend the Feast of Booths, where He could openly declare to the crowds that He was the Messiah. Jesus told them His time had not yet come.

Today's Big Ideas

- The one who humbles himself like a child is the greatest in the kingdom of heaven (Matthew 18:1-5; Mark 9:33-37; Luke 9:46-48).

- One must take radical steps to thwart sin (Matthew 18:7-9; Mark 9:43-48).

- Sinning Christians must be confronted (Matthew 18:15-20).

- One must forgive others without limit (Matthew 18:21-35).

Insights on Difficult Verses

Matthew 18:10. Scripture reveals that many multitudes of angels are always available to render help and protection to Christians whenever there is a need (2 Kings 6:17; Psalm 91:9-11).

Mark 9:39-40. Though there are many who follow Jesus, not all follow Him in the same way. The man in our passage did not follow Jesus the way the disciples did, but he had nevertheless crossed the line to be on Jesus's side.

Major Themes

The Feast of Booths (John 7:2). The backdrop of the Feast of Booths was that the Israelites lived in temporary shelters (or booths) after God brought them out of Egypt (Deuteronomy 16:13-15; 31:10). The feast, which lasted eight days, commemorated the desert wanderings following the exodus from Egypt, during which the people made for themselves shelters made of branches.

Woe to the one (Matthew 18:7). It is to be expected that unbelievers in the world will seek to cause Christians to sin and stumble. They will be judged for that in the future. But believers should never cause their fellow Christians to sin or stumble.

Digging Deeper with Cross-References

Become like a child (Matthew 18:3)—Matthew 19:14; Mark 10:15; Luke 18:17; 1 Peter 2:2

If your brother sins (Matthew 18:15)—Leviticus 19:17; Luke 17:3; Galatians 6:1; James 5:19-20; 1 John 5:16

Life Lessons

Become like a child (Matthew 18:1-5). Jesus is not saying that adults should behave childishly. Rather, He is pointing to the need to have the same type of faith that little children exhibit. The most trusting people in the world are children. They have not acquired the obstructions to faith that often come with experience in a fallen world.

We ought to forgive others without limit (Matthew 18:21-22). The Pharisees taught that righteousness demanded that a person be forgiven twice. The Jewish rabbis taught that one could be magnanimous by forgiving up to three times. When Peter asked Jesus about forgiving someone seven times, he no doubt thought he was being quite generous. Jesus went far beyond that, saying we should forgive seventy-seven times—that is, without limit.

Verses to Remember

- "I say to you, unless you turn and become like children, you will never enter the kingdom of heaven. Whoever humbles himself like this child is the greatest in the kingdom of heaven" (Matthew 18:3-4).

- "If your eye causes you to sin, tear it out and throw it away. It is better for you to enter life with one eye than with two eyes to be thrown into the hell of fire" (Matthew 18:9).

Questions for Reflection and Discussion

1. What do you think Jesus meant when He said, "Whoever receives one such child in my name receives me" (Mark 9:37)?

2. Have you ever encountered territorial or exclusive Christians? What did you learn from the encounter?

3. Do you have a childlike trust in God? If not, how can you make that a reality?

My Father, my faith sometimes wavers. I desire to have the same type of faith that little children naturally exhibit. Please work in my life to make this a reality. I love You. In Jesus's name, amen.

Counting the Cost

In yesterday's lesson we explored Jesus's teachings on a variety of subjects, including humility, taking steps to overcome sin, and forgiving others (Matthew 17:22–18:35; Mark 9:30-50; Luke 9:43-50; John 7:1-9). Now we give consideration to the cost and benefits of following Jesus.

Begin by reading Matthew 8:18-22; 19:1-2; Mark 10:1; Luke 9:51-62; and John 7:10–8:20. As you read, remember that those who obey the Word of God are truly blessed (Psalm 119:2; Luke 11:28).

Chronological marker. The events of our study today happened in mid to late AD 29.

Overview of Today's Scripture Reading

Matthew 19:1-2; Mark 10:1; Luke 9:51. Jesus left Galilee and entered Judea.

Luke 9:52-56. Jesus and the disciples passed through a Samaritan village that rejected Jesus. The disciples responded harshly, for which Jesus rebuked them.

Matthew 8:18-22; Luke 9:57-62. Sharing the good news of the gospel is the single most important task a person could do. And yet the human tendency is to offer excuses to get out of it. Jesus indicated that such excuses are invalid.

John 7:10-31. We've seen that Jesus's unbelieving brothers mockingly urged Him to go to Jerusalem and attend the Feast of Booths, where He could openly declare to the crowds that He was the Messiah. Jesus told them His time had not yet come and instructed them to go to the feast.

Jesus later went to the feast privately. He soon began teaching at the temple and acknowledged that His teachings came from the Father. Some wondered, "Is this the Christ?" The Jewish leaders wanted to arrest Him.

John 7:32-53. The Pharisees sent officers to arrest Jesus. Jesus told the Pharisees He would be with them a little longer, but then He would go to a place where they could not come. His meaning was that they would die in their sins (John 8:24) and not go to heaven, as He would.

Jesus taught that living waters would soon flow from the hearts of His followers. This would involve the ministry of the Holy Spirit, whom they could not yet receive, for Jesus had not yet gone to heaven.

John 8:1-11. The religious leaders brought to Jesus a woman caught in the act of adultery. They persisted in asking Jesus whether they should carry out the Law of Moses and stone her to death. Jesus answered that the man who had no sin should cast the first stone at her. Finding no one to accuse her, Jesus sent the woman away with the admonition to sin no further.

John 8:12-20. Jesus affirmed He is the light of the world who will deliver people from darkness (see 1 John 1:7). This caused the Pharisees to become even angrier.

Today's Big Ideas

- Following Jesus can entail a substantial personal sacrifice (Matthew 8:18-22; Luke 9:57-62).

- Believers will experience living water flowing within their hearts through the ministry of the Holy Spirit (John 7:37-39).

- Jesus is the light of the world (John 8:12-20).

Insights on Difficult Verses

Matthew 18:18. Members of the church who sin but then repent are to be "loosed"—that is, they are to be restored to fellowship. Those who are unrepentant are to be "bound"—that is, they are to be removed from fellowship.

Luke 9:60. Jesus's meaning might be paraphrased this way: "Let the spiritually dead bury the physically dead. You, however, have a higher priority, for I have now called you to the greater work of proclaiming the kingdom of God to other people."

Major Themes

Jesus, the Son of Man (Matthew 8:20). The term "Son of Man" is an important messianic title (Daniel 7:13). Notice how the title is often used in contexts of Christ's deity. It is as the Son of Man that Jesus forgives sins (Mark 2:10; see also Isaiah 43:25). Christ will come in glory at the second coming as the Son of Man (Matthew 26:63-64).

The Messiah and light (John 8:12). The Lord and light are often connected in Old Testament revelation. Psalm 27:1 affirms, "The Lord is my light and my salvation." Speaking prophetically of the coming of the Messiah, Isaiah 60:19 promises, "The Lord will be your everlasting light."

Digging Deeper with Cross-References

Anyone who is thirsty (John 7:37)—Isaiah 55:1; John 4:10,14; 6:35; Revelation 22:17

Jesus, the light of the world (John 8:12)—Isaiah 9:1-2; John 1:4-5,9; 3:19; 9:5; 12:35-36,46; 2 Corinthians 4:6

Life Lessons

Rivers of living water (John 7:37-39). This living water is identified as the Holy Spirit within the believer. The Holy Spirit is a continual and blessed source of joy, comfort, and satisfaction. He brings a sense of the very presence of God. Drink richly of the Holy Spirit.

Jesus doesn't condemn (John 8:3-11). Jesus exhorted the woman caught in adultery: "Go, and from now on sin no more" (verse 11). This brings to mind John 3:17: "God did not send his Son into the world to condemn the world, but in order that the world might be saved through him."

Verses to Remember

- "If anyone thirsts, let him come to me and drink. Whoever

believes in me, as the Scripture has said, 'Out of his heart will flow rivers of living water'" (John 7:37-38).

- "I am the light of the world. Whoever follows me will not walk in darkness, but will have the light of life" (John 8:12).

Questions for Reflection and Discussion

1. What comfort do you find in Jesus's response to the woman caught in adultery (John 8:3-11)?
2. What does Jesus's identity as "the light of the world" tell you about Him (John 8:12)?
3. Are you satisfied with your relationship with the Holy Spirit?

My Father, how appreciative I am that Jesus is the light of the world and that by following Him, I am no longer in darkness. I ask that You enable me to walk in the light as He is in the light. I am truly grateful. In Jesus's name, amen.

The Good Samaritan

Yesterday we considered the cost and benefits of following Jesus (Matthew 8:18-22; 19:1-2; Mark 10:1; Luke 9:51-62; John 7:10–8:20). Today we will focus on Jesus's parable of the good Samaritan and other key teachings.

Begin by reading Luke 10 and John 8:21-59. As you read, keep in mind that just as we eat food for physical nourishment, so we need the Word of God for spiritual nourishment (1 Corinthians 3:2; Hebrews 5:12; 1 Peter 2:2).

Chronological marker. Today's lesson features events that occurred in late AD 29.

Overview of Today's Scripture Reading

John 8:21-30. Jesus again indicated that He would go to a place where the Jewish leaders could not come. His meaning was that they would die in their sins (verse 24) and not go to heaven, as He would. He indicated that rejecting Him bars them from salvation.

John 8:31-59. Jesus said that though the Jews were Abraham's physical descendants, their rejection of Jesus proved that they were not Abraham's spiritual descendants. Their rank unbelief proved that God was not their Father. Rather the devil was their father (see Ephesians 2:2-3; 1 John 3:8-10).

Luke 10:1-16. Jesus sent out 72 of His followers after empowering them to teach and heal. Jesus indicated that at the judgment, cities would be held accountable for their response. He pronounced woes against unrepentant cities, indicating that degrees of punishment will be handed out at the future judgment.

Luke 10:17-24. Jesus's 72 followers returned and rejoiced at their great success. Jesus told them they should rejoice that their names are written in heaven.

Jesus then thanked God for hiding these things from the "wise and understanding" (the self-assured Jewish leaders) and revealing them to "little children" (followers of Christ). It is to these followers of Christ that the Messiah and His gospel message have been revealed. The prophets of old yearned to hear this message.

Luke 10:25-37. A lawyer asked Jesus about how to inherit eternal life. Jesus affirmed the lawyer's summary of the law: Love God supremely (Deuteronomy 6:4-5) and love your neighbor (Leviticus 19:18). But the lawyer asked, "Who is my neighbor?"

Jesus told the parable of the good Samaritan to demonstrate the meaning of showing compassion to a neighbor. Ironically, the people in the parable that one would naturally expect to show compassion (the priest and the Levite) showed no compassion. The one not expected to show compassion (the Samaritan) showed compassion.

Luke 10:38-42. Jesus visited Mary and Martha, who learned not to let the tyranny of the urgent take a higher priority than the Word of God and spiritual growth and commitment.

Today's Big Ideas

- The truth will set you free (John 8:31-38).
- Satan is a liar and a murderer who stands against Christ (John 8:44).
- Jesus identified Himself as "I am" (John 8:48-59).
- Be a good Samaritan (Luke 10:25-37).
- Don't be anxious and troubled about many things (Luke 10:38-42).

Insights on Difficult Verses

John 8:28. Jesus and the Father have the same divine nature. This being so, Jesus as the Son of God could never do anything contrary to the Father because they are of the same nature and never act separately from one another.

John 8:56. Abraham rejoiced that he would see Jesus's day. This may be related to Abraham's encounter with the Angel of the Lord, which was apparently an appearance of the preincarnate Christ (Genesis 22:17-18; Exodus 3:6).

Major Themes

Satan is the father of lies (John 8:44). The word "father" is used in this verse metaphorically of the originator of a family or company of persons animated by a deceitful character. Satan was the first and greatest liar. He motivates others to lie.

Jesus is the eternal "I am" (John 8:58). "I am" echoes God's name in Exodus 3:14 ("I AM WHO I AM"), so Jesus was here revealing His identity as eternal God. Jesus's eternal nature as God is in contrast to Abraham, who had a beginning.

Digging Deeper with Cross-References

"I am he" (John 8:24)—Exodus 3:14-15; John 4:26; 8:28; 13:19

Jesus's oneness with the Father (John 8:29)—Mark 9:37; John 1:18; 5:19,30; 6:57; 8:16; 10:30,38; 12:45; 14:7,10,20; 15:23; 16:15; 17:10-11,21-22; Acts 10:38; 1 Corinthians 3:23; 2 Corinthians 5:19; Philippians 2:6; 2 John 9

Being set free (John 8:32)—Romans 8:2; 2 Corinthians 3:17; Galatians 5:1,13

Life Lessons

Pray for evangelism (Luke 10:2). Jesus said, "The harvest is plentiful, but the laborers are few. Therefore pray earnestly to the Lord of the harvest to send out laborers into his harvest." Do you ever wonder what to pray about? Here's one prayer need! Pray that God would raise up evangelists and missionaries, and ask what God would have you do in reaching others for Christ.

Jesus sets us free (John 8:32). The truth that Jesus reveals to us sets us free from doctrinal error, from self-deception, from Satan's trickery, and from slavery to sin. Jesus set us free not so we can do whatever we want but rather so we can follow God.

Verses to Remember

- "If you abide in my word, you are truly my disciples, and you will know the truth, and the truth will set you free" (John 8:31-32).
- "Rejoice that your names are written in heaven" (Luke 10:20).

Questions for Reflection and Discussion

1. In your day-to-day life, do you feel that you have been set free (John 8:32)? If not, what have you learned in this lesson that might help you?

2. Can you think of anyone to whom you might be a good Samaritan this week?

3. Are you ever anxious and troubled about many things, like Martha? What can you do to change?

My Father, I must confess that all too often I feel anxious and troubled about many things. This is an anxious and troubled world. Please help me escape the tyranny of the urgent. In Jesus's name, amen.

Day 24

Prayer, Anxiety, and Watchfulness

Yesterday we gave attention to Jesus's parable of the good Samaritan and other key teachings (John 8:21-59; Luke 10:1-42). Today we turn our attention to Jesus's teachings on prayer, covetousness, anxiety, and watchfulness.

Begin by reading Luke 11:1-13,33-54; 12:1-48. As you read, remember that storing God's Word in your heart can help you to avoid sinning (Psalm 119:9,11).

Chronological marker. Our study today focuses on events that took place in late AD 29.

Overview of Today's Scripture Reading

Luke 11:1-13. Jesus modeled prayer in the Lord's Prayer. In this one prayer we find praise (verse 2), a personal petition (verse 3), a request for forgiveness (verse 4), and a request for deliverance from temptation (verse 5). Jesus indicated we must be persistent in prayer.

Luke 11:33-36. A clear or healthy eye represents one's ability to comprehend truth as it is—that is, to "see" clearly. By contrast, a bad eye represents the inability to comprehend truth as it is—that is, to not "see" clearly.

Luke 11:37-54. Jesus pronounced woes on the Pharisees and scribes because of their hypocrisy, their preoccupation with external matters in religion, and their dishonesty, pride, and spiritual blindness. They're all show with no substance. They preach but do not practice. They load heavy spiritual burdens on the common people. And they were Jesus's most forceful critics. Jesus's most condemning words were directed to the Pharisees, Sadducees, and scribes.

Luke 12:1-12. Jesus instructed His disciples to beware of the pervasive hypocrisy of the Pharisees. He also warned against the blasphemy of the Holy Spirit—an unforgivable sin.

Luke 12:13-21. We ought to have a top-down perspective, seeking eternal, heavenly rewards instead of temporal, earthly rewards. We must live with eternity's values in mind. Life on earth is short.

Luke 12:22-34. Focusing only on earthly values naturally results in anxiety. Focusing on eternity's values prevents anxiety, for the Lord oversees everything. The sovereignty of God relieves us of worry.

Luke 12:35-48. Those who profess to serve Christ must make a pivotal choice: Be faithful servants, doing the Lord's will at all times, or be unfaithful servants, neglecting God's will and living self-indulgently. The faithful will be rewarded at the Lord's return, but the unfaithful will be punished.

Today's Big Ideas

- Jesus demonstrated how Christians ought to pray (Luke 11:1-13).

- Jesus pronounced woes on the scribes and Pharisees (Luke 11:37-54).

- Jesus warned against blasphemy of the Holy Spirit (Luke 12:10-12).

- Be on guard against covetousness (Luke 12:13-21).

- Trust in God instead of being anxious (Luke 12:22-34).

- Be in watchful readiness at all times (Luke 12:35-48).

Insights on Difficult Verses

Luke 11:7-9. God is not resistant to answering our prayers. Christ's parable is intended to motivate Christians to persist in prayer. After all, God longs to give good gifts to them.

Luke 12:6. Sparrows are inexpensive, but God values each one.

Luke 12:9. This does not refer to something like Peter's temporary threefold denial, after which he repented. This refers to a definitive and final denial of Christ, refusing to confess Him as Lord and Savior.

Major Themes

Personal possessions (Luke 12:33). Do not base your fundamental security in life on the things you own. This verse should not be twisted out of context to teach that it is sinful to possess things or even be wealthy. God blessed both Abraham and Job with great wealth.

Degrees of punishment (Luke 12:47-48). People's punishment in hell will be commensurate with the light they have received. This is the primary teaching of Luke 12:47-48. Other Scripture verses on this issue include Matthew 10:15; 16:27; Revelation 20:12-13; 22:12.

Digging Deeper with Cross-References

An hour you do not expect (Luke 12:40)—Matthew 24:36-44; 1 Thessalonians 5:2-4; 2 Peter 3:10; Revelation 3:3; 16:15

Don't be anxious (Luke 12:11)—Psalm 127:2; Matthew 6:25,34; 10:19; 13:22; Mark 4:19; Luke 8:7,14; 10:40-41; 12:11,22,29; 14:18; 21:34; 1 Corinthians 7:32; 1 Peter 5:7

Life Lessons

Beware of hypocrisy (Luke 12:1-2). Hypocrisy was pervasive among the Pharisees, and it's pervasive in the modern church as well. People often present an outer appearance of respectability when in reality their hearts are far from God. If you're struggling with this, it's never too late to get on the right track.

Don't give in to peer pressure (Luke 12:4-5). Sometimes our fear of other people can prevent us from being effective witnesses for Christ. Our passage tells us not to fear people but rather to fear (or reverence) God. Here's a suggestion: Imitate the early believers by praying for boldness (Acts 4:29).

Verses to Remember

- "Everyone who speaks a word against the Son of Man will be forgiven, but the one who blasphemes against the Holy Spirit will not be forgiven" (Luke 12:10).

- "Take care, and be on your guard against all covetousness, for one's life does not consist in the abundance of his possessions" (Luke 12:15).

- "You also must be ready, for the Son of Man is coming at an hour you do not expect" (Luke 12:40).

Questions for Reflection and Discussion

1. Do you think Christians can commit the "unforgivable sin" today? Why or why not?

2. Do you have a problem with covetousness? What have you learned in this lesson that might help you with this?

3. Do you ever struggle with anxiety? What can you surrender to the Lord's keeping to relieve this anxiety?

My Father, in our materialistic society, it often seems hard to be free of covetousness. As ugly a sin as I think it is, I'm as guilty as anyone in this department. Please help me develop a Christlike perspective on issues related to possessions and ownership. In Jesus's name, amen.

DAY 25

The Good Shepherd

In the previous lesson we discussed Jesus's teachings on prayer, covetousness, anxiety, and watchfulness (Luke 11:1-13,33-54; 12:1-48). Today we explore more of Jesus's teachings, His healing of a blind man, and His role as the Good Shepherd.

Begin by reading Luke 12:49–13:17 and John 9:1–10:21. As you read, remember that the Word of God teaches us, trains us, and corrects us (2 Timothy 3:15-17).

Chronological marker. The events in this lesson took place in late AD 29.

Overview of Today's Scripture Reading

Luke 12:49-53. As evangelism takes place, some will accept Christ and others will reject Him, even within the same family. Christ is much like a spiritual sword that divides people.

Luke 12:54-59. People seem able to read the signs of nature, understanding that dark clouds indicate the approaching rain. But they seem blind to the spiritual signs indicating that Jesus is the divine Messiah.

People also seem blind to common sense. They ought to make peace with their accusers before they go to trial in court and end up in prison.

Luke 13:1-9. Some Galileans were slain by Pilate's soldiers while offering sacrifices at the temple, so their blood was mixed with that of the sacrifices. Christ indicated that this horrible thing did not happen to them because they were worse sinners than others. All people need to repent. "Unless you repent, you will all likewise perish."

Jesus then told a parable of a fruitless fig tree, symbolizing the Jewish people who feigned religion but bore no spiritual fruit.

Luke 13:10-17. More criticism comes against Jesus for healing a woman with a crooked back on the Sabbath. Jesus rebutted the criticism by observing that even animals can be fed water on the Sabbath. Why not take care of this woman, who is of far greater worth than an animal?

John 9:1-41. Isaiah prophesied that when the Messiah arrives on the scene, "the eyes of the blind shall be opened" (Isaiah 35:5). Jesus's healing of the blind man should have caused the Pharisees to recognize Jesus as the promised Messiah. The real blind people were the Pharisees.

John 10:1-21. Jesus is the Good Shepherd. He has an intimate relationship with His sheep, calling them by name. They listen to His voice and follow and obey Him. He liberates His sheep so they are truly free and unfettered. The Good Shepherd loves His sheep so much that He lays down His life for them.

Today's Big Ideas

- Jesus came not to give peace on earth, but division (Luke 12:49-53).

- Seek reconciliation with your accuser before legal action is necessary (Luke 12:57-59).

- Repent or perish (Luke 13:1-5).

- God will judge those who appear fruitful but are not (Luke 13:6-9).

- Jesus is the Good Shepherd who gives His life for the sheep (John 10:1-21).

Insights on Difficult Verses

Luke 12:49. The fire may relate to bringing judgment to the earth (John 9:39). Or it may refer to the Holy Spirit (Luke 3:16; Acts 2:1-4).

John 9:1-7. The Jews believed there were two reasons for birth defects: prenatal sin and parental sin. They claimed that when a pregnant woman worshipped in a heathen temple, the fetus committed idolatry as well. They also believed that the sins of the parents were visited on the children (Exodus 20:5; Psalm 109:14; Isaiah 65:6-7). Jesus corrected such misguided thinking.

Major Themes

"The sheep follow him" (John 10:4). In the West, shepherds typically drive the sheep from behind. Near Eastern shepherds lead the sheep from the front, using their voices to call them. Jesus, the Good Shepherd, leads us and calls us to follow Him.

Jesus has "other sheep" (John 10:16). The Jews were "the lost sheep of the house of Israel" (Matthew 10:6; 15:24). Jews who followed Christ were His sheep. Jesus's "other sheep" are Gentile believers. Jewish and Gentile believers are to be one flock with one shepherd (see also Galatians 3:28).

Digging Deeper with Cross-References

"God does not listen to sinners" (John 9:31)—Job 27:8-9; Psalms 34:15-16; 66:18; 145:19; Proverbs 15:29; Isaiah 1:15; Jeremiah 11:11; 14:12; Micah 3:4; Zechariah 7:13

Repentance (Luke 13:1-5)—2 Chronicles 7:14; Psalm 51:17; Proverbs 28:13; Ezekiel 18:30–32; Matthew 3:2; Acts 3:19; 2 Corinthians 7:10; 1 John 1:9

Life Lessons

The importance of testimony (John 9:25). The Jewish leaders gave the healed blind man a tough time because his healing took place on the Sabbath. The man had no intention of getting into a theological debate. He simply responded, "One thing I do know, that though I was blind, now I see." He gave a testimony they could not refute. You and I can also make good use of our testimonies when sharing the gospel with others.

The abundant life (John 10:10). Jesus came to give us a life that is better than anything we could possibly imagine. He offers us a rich, full, vibrant, dynamic, joyful life—one overflowing with divine blessing. The divine Shepherd cares the utmost for His sheep, seeking for them green pastures and quiet waters (Psalm 23).

Verses to Remember

- "I came that they may have life and have it abundantly" (John 10:10).

- "I am the good shepherd. The good shepherd lays down his life for the sheep" (John 10:11).

Questions for Reflection and Discussion

1. How is the blind man's response to the Jewish leaders a good model to use for our encounters with those antagonistic to the gospel (John 9:25)?

2. Are you experiencing the abundant life Jesus promised His followers (John 10:10)? If not, what do you think may be the reason?

3. Do you find comfort in Jesus's role as the Good Shepherd?

My Father, I'm like a sheep—weak, prone to get lost, insufficient in myself, and often in need of rescue. I'm so thankful that Jesus is the Good Shepherd, who loved me so much that He gave up His life for me. What a rescue! I pray in His name, amen.

The Narrow Door

Yesterday we focused on more of Jesus's teachings, His healing of a blind man, and His role as the Good Shepherd (Luke 12:49–13:17; John 9:1–10:21). Today we zero in on different ways that people respond to Jesus.

Begin by reading Matthew 23:37-39; Luke 13:22–15:10; and John 10:22-42. As you read, never forget that you can trust everything that is recorded in the Word of God (Matthew 5:18; John 10:35).

Chronological marker. This lesson considers events that occurred in late AD 29 and early AD 30.

Overview of Today's Scripture Reading

John 10:22-42. Jesus affirmed yet again that He is the Christ, the Son of God, and is one with the Father. The Jews promptly tried to stone Him for blasphemy, but He escaped.

Luke 13:22-30. The way to eternal life is narrow and difficult. One should be wary of deceptive claims regarding Christianity which make it seem as if it includes everyone and is easy.

Matthew 23:37-39; Luke 13:31-35. Jesus lamented over Jerusalem's rejection of Him as the divine Messiah. Jesus sought them, but they were not willing. The consequence? The city and its temple would be destroyed.

Luke 14:1-6. Jesus healed a man of dropsy. Receiving criticism from the Jewish leaders for healing on the Sabbath, He noted that the Law allowed for rescuing an animal. Why, then, criticize the healing of a man?

Luke 14:7-14. Jesus told two parables that emphasized one of His most common themes—that the way of humility leads to real advancement. In the Beatitudes, Jesus had taught that the meek will inherit the earth (Matthew 5:5). God shows grace to humble sinners instead of the proud Pharisees (Luke 18:9-14).

Luke 14:15-24. Jesus's next parable portrayed how Jesus repeatedly offered the kingdom to Israel but the Jews consistently rejected it. Israel refused to repent and turn to Him. The Jewish people are thus turned away from the messianic feast while Gentiles from around the world are brought in to take their place at the table (Romans 15:16).

Luke 14:25-35. In Jesus's ethic, we do not actually have the prerogative of hating anyone. We are to love even our enemies (Luke 6:27). The fifth commandment instructs us to honor our parents (Exodus 20:12), a commandment repeated in the New Testament (Ephesians 6:1-3). When Jesus says we must hate our family, His intended meaning is that we are to love our parents less than we love Jesus. (In the Hebrew mindset, to hate can mean to "love less.")

Luke 15:1-7. Using an illustration of a shepherd with a single lost sheep, Jesus emphasized how much heaven rejoices when a single sinner repents.

Luke 15:8-10. In the parable of the lost coin, Jesus illustrated how much joy there is in heaven over each sinner who repents.

Today's Big Ideas

- Jesus and the Father are one (John 10:22-42).
- Some who claim to be Christians will one day hear Christ say, "I do not know where you come from" (Luke 13:27).
- Jesus lamented Jerusalem's unwillingness to come to Him (Matthew 23:37-39; Luke 13:31-35).
- Everyone who exalts himself will be humbled, and he who humbles himself will be exalted (Luke 14:7-11).
- Because the Jews rejected Jesus, Gentiles are invited to the messianic feast (Luke 14:12-24).
- Jesus calls for radical commitment (Luke 14:25-33).

- There is great joy in heaven when a single sinner repents (Luke 15:1-7).

Insights on Difficult Verses

John 10:34. We might paraphrase Jesus, "If even human judges are called 'gods' with a small 'g,' based on their work of making life-and-death decisions over people, then how much more can I call myself the Son of God in view of my many miraculous works."

Luke 14:26. Our supreme love must be for Christ alone.

Matthew 23:39. The Jewish people would not see Jesus teaching or ministering publicly any further. However, just prior to the second coming of Christ, the Jews will finally recognize Him as the divine Messiah.

Major Themes

Jesus and the Father are one (John 10:30). Jesus and the Father are one in nature, each being divine. The Jewish leaders understood Jesus to be claiming to be God. That is why they sought to stone Him (verse 33). They thought He committed blasphemy (Leviticus 24).

Scripture cannot be broken (John 10:35). Scripture is inspired, inerrant, and authoritative, and nothing can undo that.

Digging Deeper with Cross-References

True disciples (Luke 14:25-33)—Deuteronomy 6:5; Matthew 6:33; Mark 10:28; John 15:8; Galatians 5:24; Colossians 3:1-3; 2 Timothy 2:15; Revelation 3:19

Radical commitment (Luke 14:26)—Deuteronomy 33:9; Matthew 16:24; Mark 8:34; Luke 9:23; 18:29; John 12:25

Life Lessons

Jesus wants to help (Luke 13:34). Considering Jesus's words to the Jews in Luke 13:34, I sometimes wonder if Jesus has ever lamented from heaven, "How often I wanted to bless you, dear Christian, but you were unwilling to turn away from sin and toward Me." Something to think about.

Heavenly rewards (Luke 14:13-14). When you bless people who cannot possibly repay you, you can look forward to the Lord Himself repaying you in the afterlife. Heaven rewards generous givers on earth.

Verses to Remember

- "If anyone comes to me and does not hate his own father and mother and wife and children and brothers and sisters, yes, and even his own life, he cannot be my disciple. Whoever does not bear his own cross and come after me cannot be my disciple" (Luke 14:26-27).

- "There will be more joy in heaven over one sinner who repents than over ninety-nine righteous persons who need no repentance" (Luke 15:7).

Questions for Reflection and Discussion

1. What have you learned in this lesson about the cost of discipleship (Luke 14:7-33)?

2. What kinds of excuses have you heard people offer for not wanting to get involved in Christianity (Luke 14:18)?

3. What aspect of today's lesson impacted you most?

My Father, I don't want to be a Christian in name only. I want to be a Christian disciple who lives according to Jesus's kingdom ethics. Please continue transforming me into that kind of Christian. In Jesus's name, amen.

The Prodigal Son

In yesterday's lesson we explored different ways that people respond to Jesus (Matthew 23:37-39; Luke 13:22–15:10; and John 10:22-42). Now we give consideration to more of Christ's teachings, including how God welcomes repentant sinners into His arms.

Begin by reading Luke 15:11–17:10. As you read, trust God to open your eyes so you can discover wondrous things from His Word (Psalm 119:18).

Chronological marker. The events of our study today happened in early AD 30.

Overview of Today's Scripture Reading

Luke 15:11-32. The parable of the prodigal son reveals God's boundless love toward those who are lost and turn to Him for forgiveness. This parable gives hope to every sinner.

Luke 16:1-18. Jesus tells a parable depicting a business manager who was commended for ingeniously using present opportunities and relationships to prepare for the future. Likewise, we ought to use ingenuity in this life to serve the interests of the kingdom.

The Pharisees—lovers of money—ridiculed Jesus, probably because He was a poor man teaching poor men about money. Jesus taught that God looks beyond external wealth to see what is in the heart. This is where the Pharisees fell so terribly short.

Luke 16:19-31. Jesus told a parable about a rich man who had everything in earthly life but gave no thought to God or eternal matters. Lazarus, by contrast, was a poor man who had very little in earthly life but depended on God. Once they died, the rich man's money was no help in averting his eternal suffering. Lazarus, by contrast, enjoyed paradise.

Luke 17:1-10. Jesus urged against causing any kind of offense that could bring temptation to others—especially the "little ones," of whom He had just spoken. Radical steps should be taken to thwart sin (17:1-2). Jesus then spoke about the extent to which we should forgive others. If your brother sins against you seven times, forgive him seven times.

Jesus closed with a parable indicating that a servant should expect no special reward for doing what was expected of him in the first place. When Christ's disciples obey His instructions, they are simply fulfilling their duty to Him.

Today's Big Ideas

• God welcomes repentant sinners into His arms (Luke 15:11-32).

• One is wise to plan for the future (Luke 16:1-13).

• A life devoted solely to earthly pleasures comes to sudden ruin in the afterlife (Luke 16:19-31).

Insights on Difficult Verses

Luke 16:1-8. Jesus commended the manager not for his dishonesty but for taking shrewd, resolute action in the midst of a crisis. It is important not to read more into this parable than is intended. It would be a violation of the text to conclude that Jesus was teaching His disciples to handle themselves dishonestly. His only point from the parable was that they should use present opportunities and relationships to prepare for the future, just as the shrewd manager did.

Luke 16:22-26. Some have claimed that Jesus's description of Lazarus and the rich man in Abraham's bosom is just a story and is not based on reality. However, whenever Jesus taught people using parables, He always cited real-life situations. For example, Jesus spoke of a prodigal son who returned home after squandering his money (Luke 15:11-32), a man who found a buried treasure in a field (Matthew 13:44), and a king who put on a wedding feast for his son (Matthew 22:1-14). Jesus never illustrated His teaching with a fairy tale.

Major Themes

Everyone will be conscious in the afterlife (Luke 16:19-31). Believers (like Lazarus and Abraham) will be conscious in the afterlife (contrary to the doctrine of soul sleep). Christian martyrs in heaven are fully conscious (Revelation 6:9-11). For the Christian, to be apart from the body is to be at home with the Lord (2 Corinthians 5:8; Philippians 1:21).

Unbelievers will also be conscious in the afterlife. The rich man was in conscious woe. Second Peter 2:9 affirms that "the Lord knows how to...keep the unrighteous under punishment until the day of judgment."

Digging Deeper with Cross-References

> *Repentance (Luke 15:17)*—Psalms 38:18; 51:4; Matthew 21:29; Luke 18:13; 22:62
>
> *Reclothed to reflect a change in status (Luke 15:22)*—Genesis 41:42; Zechariah 3:4; Revelation 6:11
>
> *Confession of sin (Luke 15:18)*—Psalms 25:11; 32:5; 38:18; 41:4; 51:3; 69:5; 119:176; Luke 18:13; Acts 19:18

Life Lessons

Material wealth (Luke 16:13). Jesus said, "You cannot serve God and money." Jesus wasn't forbidding making a living. He wasn't even forbidding wealth. He was warning against letting money become a god. Keep in mind that no one can take money into the afterlife.

Confession (15:21). Like the prodigal son (and the tax collector in Luke 18:13), you and I should confess our sins—preferably as soon as we become aware of them. When we Christians sin, we break fellowship with God. We restore that fellowship through confession (see Proverbs 28:13; John 1:9).

Verses to Remember

- "No servant can serve two masters, for either he will hate the one and love the other, or he will be devoted to the one and despise the other. You cannot serve God and money" (Luke 16:13).

- "If you had faith like a grain of mustard seed, you could say to this mulberry tree, 'Be uprooted and planted in the sea,' and it would obey you" (Luke 17:6).

Questions for Reflection and Discussion

1. Have you ever been a prodigal son as a Christian? What did you learn in the experience?

2. What steps can you take to avoid falling into the trap of trying to serve two masters (Luke 16:13)?

3. Do you need to confess anything to God?

My Father, I am so thankful for this teaching about the prodigal son. It blesses me beyond words to see that Your arms are wide open to receive those who repent and turn to You. You are awesome. In Jesus's name, amen.

The Resurrection and the Life

Yesterday we considered more of Christ's teachings, including the way God welcomes repentant sinners into His arms (Luke 15:11–17:10). Today we will focus on Jesus as the resurrection and the life, and the response of the Jewish leaders.

Begin by reading Luke 17:11-37 and John 11. As you read, allow the Word of God to bring revival to your soul (Psalm 119:25,93,107).

Chronological marker. Today's lesson features events that occurred in early AD 30.

Overview of Today's Scripture Reading

John 11:1-44. Jesus learned that Lazarus, whom He loved deeply, was ill. He affirmed that Lazarus's situation would ultimately bring much glory to God. Notice He didn't say Lazarus would not die, but only that the final outcome would not be death. Jesus would raise Lazarus from the dead, thereby validating His claim to be the resurrection and the life.

It is particularly relevant that Jesus didn't head toward Lazarus's home as soon as He heard of the illness. By the time Jesus arrived, Lazarus had been dead four days. This made Christ's miracle of raising him from the dead all the more impressive. Christ issued the command, and life emerged out of death. Lazarus was now alive again.

John 11:45-57. Many of the Jews who witnessed the miracle believed in Jesus. Others ran off to tell the Pharisees. The Jewish Sanhedrin met and decided that Jesus had to go. They made plans on how to kill Him.

Luke 17:11-19. Jesus then healed ten lepers, again pointing to His identity as the divine Messiah. Amazingly, only one of them gave thanks to Jesus.

Luke 17:20-37. The Pharisees asked when the kingdom of God would come, and Jesus replied, "The kingdom of God is in the midst of you." His meaning was that the kingdom of God was already present because Christ the King was present. Jesus then shifted His thoughts to the future, when He would come again in glory and judgment.

Today's Big Ideas

- Jesus is the resurrection and the life (John 11:1-27).

- Jesus raised Lazarus back to life to prove He is the resurrection and the life (John 11:38-44).

- The Jewish leaders plotted how to kill Jesus (John 11:45-57).

- As it was in the days of Noah, so it will be in the days prior to the second coming (Luke 17:20-37).

Insights on Difficult Verses

John 11:11-14. The term "sleep," when used in contexts of death in Scripture, always refers to the body, not the soul. Sleep is an appropriate figure of speech for the death of the body, which takes on the appearance of sleep (Acts 7:60; 1 Corinthians 15:20; 1 Thessalonians 4:13-18).

Luke 17:34-37. Jesus's affirmation that one will be taken and the other left has been interpreted by some as a reference to the rapture. Such a view is unlikely, however. The disciples asked Jesus *where* these individuals would be taken. Jesus replied, "Where the corpse is, there the vultures will gather." Jesus's answer points to judgment. This judgment takes place at the second coming. Those who are left are invited into Christ's millennial kingdom.

Major Themes

God cares for our hurts (John 11:33-36). A common theme in Scripture is that God cares immensely for our hurts. In the present case, Lazarus's death caused Jesus to be "deeply moved in his spirit and greatly troubled." He wept, and the people commented, "See how he loved him!" Jesus likewise cares for our hurts.

Walking by faith (John 11:38-39). Martha's conflict was between walking by sight and walking by faith. By sight, Martha recognized that Lazarus's body had been in the tomb four days. Walking by faith looks beyond circumstances to the Lord of miracles. When Jesus raised Lazarus from the dead, Martha learned a lot about walking by faith.

Digging Deeper with Cross-References

Sleeping in death (John 11:11)—Daniel 12:2; Matthew 9:24; 27:52; Mark 5:39; Luke 8:52; Acts 7:60; 1 Corinthians 11:20

Resurrection promised (John 11:23-24)—Daniel 12:2; John 5:28-29; Acts 24:15; Philippians 3:21; 1 Thessalonians 4:14

Life Lessons

God is always aware of our suffering (John 11:7,11). Notice that Jesus omnisciently pronounced to His disciples that Lazarus had died. No one informed Him. Sometimes we might feel as if God is not aware of what we're going through. Be assured—He knows everything that is going on in your life. So trust Him even if He seems to be silent. He is weaving the tapestry of your life behind the scenes.

God allows suffering (John 11:3-4,6). As is evident in the case of Lazarus, Mary, and Martha, God sometimes allows His children to go through tough times even though He loves them greatly. He does this because He knows that in the end, He will be glorified in the outcome He brings about. Perhaps you are now going through a time of suffering that will ultimately bring glory to God.

Verses to Remember

- "I am the resurrection and the life. Whoever believes in me, though he die, yet shall he live, and everyone who lives and believes in me shall never die" (John 11:25-26).

- "Just as it was in the days of Noah, so will it be in the days of the Son of Man. They were eating and drinking and marrying and being given in marriage, until the day when Noah entered the ark, and the flood came and destroyed them all" (Luke 17:26).

Questions for Reflection and Discussion

1. Do you consider your relationship with Jesus as a friendship, as did Mary, Martha, and Lazarus?

2. What have you learned in this lesson that changes the way you view difficulties in your life?

3. How does Caiaphas, the high priest, inadvertently preach the gospel in John 11:49-50?

My Father, my years seem to pass faster and faster. I am becoming increasingly aware that my time on this earth is limited. But I rejoice in the reality that You will resurrect me from the dead. Even though I die, I shall yet live. For that, I praise You. I am grateful. In Jesus's name, amen.

Prayer, Humility, Wealth, and Marriage

Yesterday we gave attention to Jesus as the resurrection and the life, and the response of the Jewish leaders (John 11; Luke 17:11-37). Today we turn our attention to Jesus's teachings on prayer, humility, the blinding effects of wealth, and marriage.

Begin by reading Matthew 19:3-30; Mark 10:2-31; and Luke 18:1-30. As you read, never forget that God urges you to quickly obey His Word in all things (Psalm 119:60).

Chronological marker. Our study today focuses on events that took place in early AD 30.

Overview of Today's Scripture Reading

Luke 18:1-8. Jesus's parable emphasizes the need for persistence in prayer. This is in keeping with Jesus's teaching in Matthew 7:7: "Ask, and it will be given to you." Literally, the Greek reads, "Keep on asking, and it will be given you." Be persistent!

Luke 18:9-14. The Pharisee was full of pride in his prayer. He considered himself worthy. He elevated himself and looked down on others. Because of his sense of self-righteousness, he did not appeal to God's mercy. The tax collector, by contrast, was humble in his prayer. He considered himself a sinner and unworthy. He appealed to God's mercy. The Pharisee's prayer was not accepted by God, but the tax collector's was.

Matthew 19:3-12; Mark 10:2-12. God Himself created the institution of marriage, and He intended it to be permanent (Genesis 2:18-25). Divorce was never a part of God's original plan, and Scripture says God hates divorce (Malachi 2:16). The marriage relationship was originally to be dissolved only when one of the marriage partners died (Romans 7:1-4; 1 Corinthians 7:8-9; 1 Timothy 5:14). Here, however, Jesus allowed for divorce in the event that one's spouse engages in sexual immorality.

Matthew 19:13-15; Mark 10:13-16; Luke 18:15-17. People brought their children to Jesus so He could pray for them. The disciples—perhaps a bit overprotective and maybe a bit territorial—rebuked the people for doing this. Here's a paraphrase of Jesus's response to them: "Guys, relax. Take a deep breath. Let the children come to Me. They're My kind of people—kingdom people."

Matthew 19:16-30; Mark 10:17-31; Luke 18:18-30. A rich young ruler asked Jesus how to inherit eternal life. Jesus told him to follow the commandments of God. The ruler responded he had kept the commandments. Jesus said he must do one thing more—sell all that he had and give it to the poor. The man became sad, for he had great wealth.

Jesus wasn't teaching salvation by works. He was helping the man see that his unwillingness to give money to the poor indicated he had not kept even the first great commandment to love God more than anything else, such as money (see Matthew 22:36-37).

Today's Big Ideas

- We should be persistent in our prayer requests to God (Luke 18:1-8).

- Everyone who exalts himself will be humbled, but the one who humbles himself will be exalted (Luke 18:9-14).

- It is difficult for rich people to enter the kingdom of heaven (Matthew 19:16-30; Mark 10:17-31; Luke 18:18-30).

- Jesus set forth strict rules for marriage (Matthew 19:3-12; Mark 10:1-12).

Insights on Difficult Verses

Luke 18:8. The primary characteristic of people on earth at the time of Christ's second coming will be unbelief (2 Thessalonians 2:3-4).

Jesus apparently asked the question about finding faith on earth to spur His own disciples on to faithfulness.

Luke 18:24-25. Jesus used a hyperbole to emphasize that it is hard for a rich person to turn to God in the midst of his wealth, for he has little sense of need for God. Of course, many rich persons have become Christians throughout church history and have used their wealth for great good.

Major Themes

Jesus is good (Mark 10:17-18). Jesus asked a young man to examine the implications of his calling Jesus "Good Teacher." In effect, Jesus said to him, "Do you realize what you are saying when you say I am good? Only God is good. Are you saying I am God?" Jesus was helping the young man understand Christ's deity.

Inheriting eternal life (Luke 18:18). A person cannot do anything to receive an inheritance of any kind—including eternal life. An inheritance by its very nature is a gift. Eternal life is presented throughout Scripture as a gift (John 3:36; 5:24; 20:31; Romans 6:23; 1 John 5:13), so one cannot do anything to earn it (Romans 4:4-5).

Digging Deeper with Cross-References

Humility (Matthew 19:14)—Luke 14:7-11; Romans 12:3; Ephesians 4:2; Philippians 2:3-4

Wealth and money (Matthew 19:16-30; Mark 10:17-31; Luke 18:18-30)—Ecclesiastes 5:10; Jeremiah 49:4; Matthew 6:24; 1 Timothy 3:2-3; 6:9-10; Hebrews 13:5; 1 Peter 5:2

Life Lessons

The hundredfold return (Mark 10:30). This verse is speaking specifically of those who forsake home and loved ones for the sake of Jesus and the gospel. These individuals will receive a hundredfold return in the sense that they become a part of a large community of believers.

Two attitudes in praying (Luke 18:9-14). The wrong attitude is to pray pridefully, arrogantly, and self-righteously—like the Pharisees in New Testament times. The right attitude is to pray humbly, recognizing that one is a fallen and wounded sinner. God looks mercifully on repentant sinners (Proverbs 28:13).

Verses to Remember

- "When the Son of Man comes, will he find faith on earth?" (Luke 18:8).

- "Truly, I say to you, whoever does not receive the kingdom of God like a child shall not enter it" (Mark 10:15).

- "How difficult it will be for those who have wealth to enter the kingdom of God" (Mark 10:23).

Questions for Reflection and Discussion

1. What do we learn about rightly relating to God in Luke 18:9-14?

2. Have you ever found money or wealth to be a distraction regarding your commitment to God?

3. Are you enjoying your hundredfold return (Mark 10:30)?

My Father, there is much to ponder in this lesson—persistence in prayer, pursuing humility, keeping wealth in proper perspective... These are life-changing insights. Please enable me to flesh them out in my life. In Jesus's name, amen.

Bartimaeus and Zacchaeus

In the previous lesson we discussed Jesus's teachings on prayer, humility, the blinding effects of wealth, and marriage (Matthew 19:3-30; Mark 10:2-31; Luke 18:1-30). Today we explore Jesus's foretelling of His death and resurrection along with more key teachings and miracles.

Begin by reading Matthew 20; Mark 10:32-52; and Luke 18:31–19:10. As you read, ask God to help you understand His Word (Psalm 119:73).

Chronological marker. The events in this lesson took place in early AD 30.

Overview of Today's Scripture Reading

Matthew 20:1-16. Jesus told a parable in which the workers labored for different lengths of time—some long, some short—and yet all were paid the same at the end of the day. Jesus's point was not to teach economics. His main point was that every believer ought to be willing to continually serve the Lord, knowing that the Lord will abundantly care for each of His workers. Our main goal is to serve, not to see how much reward we can get out of it, and not to insist on our personal rights.

Matthew 20:17-19; Mark 10:32-34; Luke 18:31-34. Jesus again reveals to His disciples that He will be executed in Jerusalem. The good news is that He will be resurrected on the third day after His death.

Matthew 20:20-28; Mark 10:35-45. The mother of James and John—two of Jesus's disciples—wanted Jesus to give her sons prominent places in His kingdom. Jesus responded that such matters are in the Father's hands. Besides, the one who wants to be great in the kingdom must become a humble servant. The way up is down.

Matthew 20:29-34; Mark 10:46-52; Luke 18:35-43. As noted previously, the Old Testament prophets predicted that when the divine Messiah came, "the eyes of the blind [would] be opened" (Isaiah 35:5-6). Jesus's healing of the blind men was one of many signs that pointed to Jesus's identity as the divine Messiah.

Luke 19:1-10. Jesus personally sought out Zacchaeus to save him and fellowship with him. The lesson we learn here is that Jesus is not just interested in teaching the multitudes. He is interested in the individual sinner as well.

Today's Big Ideas

- The believer must be willing to freely serve Christ without seeking exaltation or sticking up for personal rights (Matthew 20:1-16; Mark 10:35-45).

- Jesus foretold His death and resurrection (Matthew 20:17-19; Mark 10:32-34; Luke 18:31-34).

- Whoever wants to be great in the kingdom of heaven must become a servant (Matthew 20:20-28).

Insights on Difficult Verses

Matthew 20:29-34. This passage should not be seen as a contradiction of Mark 10:46-52 and Luke 18:35-43. The healing addressed in these passages took place as Jesus was leaving *old* Jericho and was nearing *new* Jericho (there were two Jerichos in those days). If Jesus were at a place between the two Jerichos, then depending on one's perspective, He could be viewed as leaving one Jericho or entering the other Jericho. There is no contradiction.

Mark 10:38. The disciples had no idea what they were asking. For them to share in Christ's glory, they would also have to share in His suffering. They would have to drink the cup Christ drank (suffering and death).

Major Themes

A lack of understanding (Luke 18:34). Jesus explained to His disciples that in Jerusalem He would be mocked, flocked, killed, and resurrected. "They understood none of these things." Perhaps they were more focused on His sensational miracles and the reality of the coming kingdom. They did not perceive how Christ's death could possibly be a part of God's plan for the Messiah. Things got clearer after the resurrection.

Jesus, Son of David (Luke 18:38-39). The blind man understood that Jesus was the Messiah, prophesied to be a descendant of David (2 Samuel 7:12-13). How interesting that he understood this while people with good sight missed it entirely!

Digging Deeper with Cross-References

Selfishness and ambition (Mark 10:35-37)—Proverbs 28:25; Matthew 19:21-22; Mark 8:34-37; Luke 12:15-21; 16:19-31; Philippians 2:3

Ransom for many (Mark 10:45)—Isaiah 53:5-6; Romans 5:6-8, 15-19; 1 Corinthians 15:3; 2 Corinthians 5:21; Hebrews 9:15

Citizens of the kingdom (Matthew 20:1-16)—Matthew 7:13-23; 21:28-32; 1 Corinthians 4:20; James 2:5; 2 Peter 1:5-11

Life Lessons

Don't turn a deaf ear to prophecy (Matthew 20:17-19). Jesus prophetically foretold to the disciples that He would go to Jerusalem and be betrayed, condemned to death, scourged, crucified, and resurrected. When these events actually took place, the disciples scattered like cowards and seem to have been befuddled at what had happened. Don't allow prophecy to go in one ear and out the other. Pay close attention to prophecy and allow it to strengthen your faith. (More than one-fourth of the Bible is prophecy.)

Salvation manifests itself (Luke 19:8-10). After Zacchaeus became a Christian, he affirmed to the Lord, "The half of my goods I give to the poor. And if I have defrauded anyone of anything, I restore it fourfold." If you are a believer in fellowship with the Lord, your life will change. You will progressively take on the family likeness, becoming more like Jesus.

Verses to Remember

- "The last will be first, and the first last" (Matthew 20:16).

- "Whoever would be great among you must be your servant, and whoever would be first among you must be slave of all" (Mark 10:43-44).

Questions for Reflection and Discussion

1. Do you know any Scripture verses that reveal how prophecy is life changing? (If not, here's a good one: Titus 2:13-14.)

2. How are some of Jesus's ideas counterintuitive (Matthew 20:1-16)?

3. What does it mean to you personally that Jesus gave His life as your ransom (Matthew 20:28)?

My Father, every time I think about Jesus's death for me, I am awed all over again. At the cross He took what was mine (my sin) so that He could give me what is His (eternal life). He provided me a great exchange. And He did it by ransoming me by His death. Thank You for sending Him into the world. In Jesus's name, amen.

CHAPTER 3

Passion Week

DAY 31

The Triumphal Entry

Yesterday we focused on Jesus's foretelling of His death and resurrection, along with more key teachings and miracles (Matthew 20; Mark 10:32-52; Luke 18:31–19:10). Today we zero in on Jesus's brief teaching on faithful service, His anointing in anticipation of His death, and His riding into Jerusalem on a colt.

Begin by reading Matthew 21:1-11; 26:6-13; Mark 11:1-11; 14:3-9; Luke 19:11-40; and John 12:1-19. As you read, remember that God's Word is the true source of hope (Psalm 119:81).

Chronological marker. This lesson considers events that occurred in early AD 30.

Overview of Today's Scripture Reading

Luke 19:11-27. This parable teaches that believers will be held accountable for how they managed God's resources and their time during earthly life. Jesus illustrated this with ten servants who were each given the same amount of money to manage while He was away. Some servants invested it and made more money, for which they were commended by the nobleman. The servant who played it safe—storing the money without earning any return—was criticized. Application: You and I ought to use our time and resources wisely for God's glory.

Matthew 26:6-13; Mark 14:3-9; John 12:1-11. A woman anointed Jesus's head with an expensive perfume. Jesus interpreted this gesture as a special anointing in preparation for His soon death and burial. Therefore the woman should not be criticized (as the disciples attempted to do). (See Life Lessons.)

Matthew 21:1-11; Mark 11:1-11; Luke 19:28-40; John 12:12-19. Jesus had taught multitudes and healed countless people over three years, and now He was riding into Jerusalem on a colt, as prophesied of the divine Messiah (Zechariah 9:9). We are now in the spring of AD 30, the Sunday before crucifixion day. The people were jubilant, shouting out hallelujahs and hosannas, apparently because they thought their moment of deliverance from Roman oppression had finally come. They seemed blind to the reality that His real mission was to bring spiritual salvation. (See Major Themes.)

Today's Big Ideas

- We are held accountable for our management of God's resources (Luke 19:11-27).

- Blessed is he who comes in the name of the Lord! Hosanna in the highest! (Matthew 21:1-11; Mark 11:1-11; Luke 19:28-40; John 12:12-19).

Insights on Difficult Verses

Luke 19:11. Christ had to correct the impression that the kingdom of God would begin right away. How does this relate to the disciples? The disciples occasionally held false notions as human beings. However, there is no indication in Luke 19:11 or any other text of Scripture that the disciples or prophets ever taught such false notions as part of God's "Thus saith the Lord" revelation to humankind. Whenever the prophets or apostles were speaking as God's mouthpieces to humanity, they never communicated any false notions (see 2 Samuel 23:2; 1 Corinthians 2:13).

John 12:16. After Jesus entered into glory, the disciples "remembered that these things had been written about him." What things? Among other things, His riding into Jerusalem on a colt (Zechariah 9:9), His death on a cross (Isaiah 53:7; Zechariah 12:10), and His resurrection from the dead (Psalm 16:10).

Major Themes

Jesus on a donkey (Matthew 21:7). The Messiah was prophesied to come into Jerusalem on a donkey: "Behold, your king is coming to you...humble and mounted on a donkey" (Zechariah 9:9). In the Old Testament, donkeys are associated with leaders (see Judges 10:4; 1 Kings 1:33).

Hosanna (Matthew 21:9). "Hosanna" literally means "save us, we pray." This is highly significant. From the perspective of the people, the phrase "save us, we pray" carries the idea, "save us now from Roman dominion." The people were praising Jesus but for the wrong reason.

Digging Deeper with Cross-References

The kingship of Jesus (Matthew 21:5)—Psalm 118; Zechariah 9:9; Luke 19:28-44; Ephesians 1:19-23; Philippians 2:5-11; Colossians 1:17-18; 2:10; Revelation 4:9–5:14

He is humble (Matthew 21:5)—Zechariah 9:9; Matthew 11:29; 20:28; Luke 22:27; John 8:50; 12:15; 13:5; 2 Corinthians 8:9; Philippians 2:8; Hebrews 5:5

Life Lessons

Use what the Lord has given you (Luke 19:13). The lesson of the parable is that the Lord has given each of us gifts and talents and time, and He wants us to "engage in business" until that future day when there will be an accounting at the future judgment seat of Christ (Romans 14:10; 2 Corinthians 5:10). Every day we arise, our attitude should be, "Today I will serve the Lord with enthusiasm and gladness."

Never a waste (Mark 14:4). When the woman poured an expensive ointment on Jesus, the disciples commented on what a waste it was. Jesus corrected them. He said she did a wonderful thing on His behalf. The important thing is not the value of the ointment itself, but the woman's high valuation of Jesus. We learn from this that anything we do as an expression of our high valuation of Jesus is a worthy endeavor.

Verses to Remember

• "Hosanna! Blessed is he who comes in the name of the Lord!

Blessed is the coming kingdom of our father David! Hosanna in the highest" (Mark 11:9-10).

- "Behold, your king is coming to you, humble, and mounted on a donkey, on a colt, the foal of a beast of burden" (Matthew 21:5).

Questions for Reflection and Discussion

1. Does the fact that you will have to give a future accounting at the judgment seat of Christ motivate you to use your God-provided gifts and talents in service to Him?

2. Contrary to the misconception of the people in Jerusalem, what do you think the term "hosanna" really communicates about Jesus's identity?

3. What aspect of this lesson impacted you most?

My Father, truly, blessed is he who comes in the name of the Lord! Hosanna in the highest! I am so thankful that Jesus is my blessed Savior. He saves me not only in terms of my eternal salvation, but He's also right there with me when life throws me a punch. I am thankful, Father. Truly thankful. In Jesus's name, amen.

Day 32

Cleansing the Temple

In yesterday's lesson we explored Jesus's brief teaching on faithful service, His anointing in anticipation of His death, and His riding into Jerusalem on a colt (Matthew 21:1-11; 26:6-13; Mark 11:1-11; 14:3-9; Luke 19:11-40; John 12:1-19). Now we give consideration to the Jewish rejection of Jesus and its consequences, Jesus's cleansing of the temple, His cursing of the fig tree, and several key teachings.

Begin by reading Matthew 21:12-27; Mark 11:12-33; Luke 19:41–20:8; and John 12:20-50. As you read, remember that great spiritual wisdom comes from studying God's Word (Psalm 119:98-104).

Chronological marker. The events of our study today happened at the beginning of the second quarter of AD 30.

Overview of Today's Scripture Reading

Luke 19:41-44. Jesus again lamented over Jerusalem's rejection of Him as the divine Messiah. The consequence? Jerusalem and its temple would be destroyed.

Matthew 21:12-17; Mark 11:15-19; Luke 19:45-48. Jesus had earlier cleansed the temple at the beginning of His ministry (John 2:13-16). He is now cleansing the temple again on the Monday prior to crucifixion day. The scribes and Pharisees were just like the temple—appearing good on the outside but utterly corrupt on the inside.

John 12:20-50. Now, on the Tuesday before crucifixion day, a group of Gentiles who had heard about Jesus's miracles and teachings came to see Him. Jesus used the opportunity to reveal that the time of His salvific death was drawing near. He indicated He is the light of the world that provides salvation for both Jews and Gentiles—that is, the entire world. But He requires radical commitment.

Matthew 21:18-22; Mark 11:12-14,20-25. The fig tree had leaves on it, giving the appearance of being fruitful. Upon closer examination, there was no fruit at all. Jesus's cursing of the fig tree was an acted-out parable. It taught that God will judge those who give an outer appearance of fruitfulness but in fact are not fruitful at all (like the Pharisees).

Matthew 21:23-27; Mark 11:27-33; Luke 20:1-8. The Jewish leaders asked Jesus where He got His authority. He answered their question with a question: "The baptism of John, from where did it come?" If they affirmed John's ministry came from God, that would put them in a bad light because they did not follow John. If, however, they said John taught merely man-made ideas, they might trigger an uprising because John was so popular. They copped out by saying, "We do not know." Jesus replied, "Neither will I tell you by what authority I do these things."

Today's Big Ideas

- The Jews rejected Jesus, so Jerusalem and its temple would be destroyed (Luke 19:41-44).

- Jesus cleansed the temple of money-changers (Matthew 21:12-17; Mark 11:15-19; Luke 19:45-48).

- God judges those who appear fruitful on the outside but are not truly fruitful (Matthew 21:18-22; Mark 11:12-14).

- Whoever loves his life loses it, and whoever hates his life in this world will keep it for eternal life (John 12:20-26).

- When Jesus is lifted up at the cross, His saving grace will be available to all people (John 12:27-36).

Insights on Difficult Verses

Matthew 21:12. Pigeons and other animals were sold within the temple complex. The only coins allowed for buying and selling in the temple were ancient Hebrew shekels. Other coins had to be exchanged for shekels. The money-changers made a profit with each exchange. *Mark 11:23-24.* God answers prayer, but there are conditions. He answers prayer when people abide in Him and His Word abides in them (John 15:7). Christians cannot "ask wrongly" out of selfishness (James 4:3). All requests must be submitted to God's sovereign will (1 John 5:14-15). We must avoid sin (Psalm 66:18) and pursue righteousness (Proverbs 15:29).

Major Themes

Righteous indignation (Matthew 21:12). Jesus responded to the money-changers in the temple with righteous indication. The temple was supposed to be a holy environment, but the Jewish leaders defiled it with their profit-driven activities.

Moving mountains (Mark 11:23). A common metaphor in biblical times was "rooter up of mountains." The phrase was typically used of great rabbis who accomplished mighty feats. Jesus adapted the metaphor to illustrate the great power of faith in God.

Digging Deeper with Cross-References

Unbelief (John 12:36-43)—Numbers 14:11-12; 2 Kings 17:14, 18-20; Luke 12:8-9; John 3:18,36; Romans 9:30-33; Hebrews 4:2-3,6,11

If you have faith (Matthew 21:22)—Matthew 17:20; 21:21; Luke 17:6; 1 Corinthians 13:2; Hebrews 11:1-6; James 1:6; 5:13-18; 1 John 5:14

Life Lessons

Beware of religious scammers (Matthew 21:12-13). The money-changers in the temple were nothing but religious scammers. They preyed on innocent worshippers for financial gain. We have religious scammers today too. Christian beware!

Prayer and forgiveness (Mark 11:25-26). Jesus said that if you are praying and remember that you have something against someone, your top priority is to forgive that person. A lack of forgiveness in your heart shows that your heart is not right before God. So forgive the person and then bring your petitions to God with a peaceful heart.

Verses to Remember

- "Whatever you ask in prayer, believe that you have received it, and it will be yours. And whenever you stand praying, forgive, if you have anything against anyone, so that your Father also who is in heaven may forgive you your trespasses" (Mark 11:24-25).

- "Whoever loves his life loses it, and whoever hates his life in this world will keep it for eternal life" (John 12:25).

Questions for Reflection and Discussion

1. What sort of death do you think Christians need to experience before becoming fruitful (John 12:24)?

2. In what sense are Christ's followers to hate their lives (John 12:25)?

3. What do you think it means to be a son of light (John 12:36)?

My Father, some of the words in John's Gospel seem particularly hard to take, such as death before bearing fruit and hating this life to keep eternal life. Please help me to have a right understanding of all this. I want to be a truly biblical Christian. In Jesus's name, amen.

DAY 33

The Parable of the Tenants

Yesterday we considered the Jewish rejection of Jesus and its consequences, Jesus's cleansing of the temple, His cursing of the fig tree, and several key teachings (Matthew 21:12-27; Mark 11:12-33; Luke 19:41–20:8; John 12:20-50). Today we will focus on how Jewish leaders will one day be punished for their religious hypocrisy and their rejection of the divine Messiah.

Begin by reading Matthew 21:28–22:22; Mark 12:1-17; and Luke 20:9-26. As you read, remember that reading Scripture can strengthen your faith in God (Romans 10:17).

Chronological marker. Today's lesson features events that occurred at the beginning of the second quarter in AD 30.

Overview of Today's Scripture Reading

Matthew 21:28-32. In this parable, Jesus contrasted the Pharisees and repentant sinners. The Pharisees are pictured as the son who promised to work in the vineyard but did not. They were supposed to be doing God's work but instead were fixated on their own traditions and rituals. Sinners are pictured as the son who initially refused but then went to work anyway. These repentant sinners—and not the hypocritical Pharisees—become citizens of the kingdom.

Matthew 21:33-46; Mark 12:1-12; Luke 20:9-19. The master of the house in this parable is God. The tenants represent the religious leaders of Israel. The master's servants represent God's prophets. The parable indicates that down through the centuries, the Jewish leaders resisted and even killed God's prophets (see 1 Kings 22:24; 2 Chronicles 24:20-21; 36:15-16; Nehemiah 9:26; Jeremiah 2:30). They eventually killed the master's son—that is, Jesus Christ. In judgment, the master invites other tenants in—referring to Gentiles who will become a part of the church.

Matthew 22:1-14. In this parable Jesus showed how He repeatedly offered the kingdom to Israel, but it was consistently rejected. Israel refused to repent and turn to Him, the divine Messiah. As a result, the Jewish people will be turned away from the messianic feast, while Gentiles from around the world will be brought in to take their place at the table (see Romans 15:16).

Matthew 22:15-22; Mark 12:13-17; Luke 20:20-26. God gave the land of Israel to the Jewish people. The Romans, who charged a tribute, did not truly own the land even though they were in military control over it. Knowing this, the Pharisees sought to entrap Jesus with a dilemma. If Christ agreed that a tribute should be paid to Rome, that would amount to disloyalty to Israel. If Jesus said a tribute should not be paid to Rome, the Pharisees could report Him to the Romans. Jesus defeated their logic with the image on a simple coin.

Today's Big Ideas

- Religious hypocrites will not enter God's kingdom, but repentant sinners will (Matthew 21:28-32).

- The Jewish leaders will one day be punished for having rejected the prophets and now rejecting the divine Messiah (Matthew 21:33-46; Mark 12:1-12; Luke 20:9-19).

- Because the Jewish people rejected the Messiah, they will be turned away from the messianic feast, and Gentiles will take their place (Matthew 22:1-14).

Insights on Difficult Verses

Matthew 21:42. "The stone that the builders rejected" refers to Christ in His crucifixion. The statement that He "has become the cornerstone" refers to Christ in His resurrection.

Matthew 22:14. While God issues a general call to sinners inviting them to receive His salvation, there is also a specific call—or election—of some. At the same time, it is clear from the parable that human beings are responsible for their decision to receive or reject Christ, whether it is the result of indifference (verse 5), rebellion (verse 6), or self-righteousness (verse 12).

Major Themes

The Herodians (Matthew 22:16). The Herodians were Jewish political sympathizers of Herodian rulers (Mark 3:6; Luke 20:20). The Herodian party was made up mostly of Sadducees. The fact that the Herodians and Pharisees joined together against Jesus shows how much they viewed Him as a threat.

Roman coinage (denarius) (Matthew 22:19). A Roman denarius was worth about 15 cents, which was the daily wage of laborers in biblical times. (In those days, 15 cents had a lot more buying power than it does today.)

Digging Deeper with Cross-References

Prophets killed (Mark 12:5)—2 Chronicles 24:21; 36:15-16; Nehemiah 9:26; Matthew 23:34-37; Acts 7:52; 1 Thessalonians 2:15

Hatred of Christ (Luke 20:14)—Matthew 26:4,59; 27:1,23; Mark 11:18; 12:12; 14:55; 15:13; Luke 22:2; 23:21; John 11:57; 15:18,23,25; 19:6,15

Life Lessons

Give to Caesar what belongs to Caesar, and give to God what belongs to God (Luke 20:25). Believers have a dual citizenship and responsibility. We are citizens of a nation on earth. But more importantly, we are citizens of heaven. Our behavior on earth ought to be governed by our heavenly citizenship. We live *now* in view of *then* (see Philippians 1:27; 3:20).

The cornerstone (Mark 12:10). The cornerstone in a building was used as a kind of baseline measurement to ensure that all the other stones of the building were straight and level. Jesus is metaphorically called a cornerstone because His life and teachings constitute the foundation of the church. He is likewise the foundation of each of our lives.

Verses to Remember

- "The stone that the builders rejected has become the cornerstone; this was the Lord's doing, and it is marvelous in our eyes" (Matthew 21:42).

- "Give back to Caesar what is Caesar's, and to God what is God's" (Matthew 22:21 NIV).

Questions for Reflection and Discussion

1. Do you ever act like either of the two sons in Matthew 21:28-30? Why do you think it is easy for us to act in those ways?

2. Is Jesus your rock-solid foundation—that is, is He the heart and center of your life as a Christian (Mark 12:10)?

3. How does your awareness that you are a citizen of heaven impact the way you live?

My Father, I am so thankful that Jesus is my rock-solid foundation. He is the heart and center of my life as a Christian. He is the cornerstone of my life. I'm so appreciative to You for sending Him. In Jesus's name, amen.

Day 34

The Greatest Commandment

Yesterday we gave attention to how Jewish leaders will one day be punished for their religious hypocrisy and their rejection of the divine Messiah (Matthew 21:28–22:22; Mark 12:1-17; Luke 20:9-26). Today we turn our attention to several important issues, such as no marriage in the afterlife, the greatest commandments, and Jesus's pronouncement of woes on the scribes and Pharisees.

Begin by reading Matthew 22:23–23:36; Mark 12:18-44; and Luke 20:27–21:4. As you read, keep in mind that God desires you not only to hear His Word but also to do it (James 1:22).

Chronological marker. Our study today focuses on events that took place during Passion Week at the beginning of the second quarter in AD 30. The crucifixion is drawing near, and Christ is giving some of His final teachings.

Overview of Today's Scripture Reading

Matthew 22:23-33; Mark 12:18-27; Luke 20:27-40. The Sadducees—who denied the doctrine of the resurrection—tried to trap Jesus. They asked whom a woman would be married to in the afterlife if she had been married to several different men on earth. Jesus's answer is simple and to the point. There is no marriage in the afterlife.

Matthew 22:34-40; Mark 12:28-34. A Pharisee asked Jesus about the greatest commandment. Jesus said the first is to love God supremely with our whole being (Deuteronomy 6:4-5). The second is to love our neighbor (Leviticus 19:18). These two commands constitute a summary of God's law.

Matthew 22:41-46; Mark 12:35-37; Luke 20:41-44. Christ now cornered the Pharisees by asking them a question relating to the person of the Messiah. He said that if the Messiah was the son (or descendent) of David, "how is it then that David, in the Spirit, calls him Lord?" (Matthew 22:43). That the Messiah was David's son testified to the humanity of the Messiah. But David's reference to "my Lord" also points to the undiminished deity of the Messiah, since "Lord" (*Adonai*) was a title for deity. The Messiah would be David's son, but He would also be David's God. The Messiah would be both God and man.

Matthew 23:1-36; Mark 12:38-40; Luke 20:45-47. Jesus pronounced woes on the scribes and Pharisees because of their hypocrisy, their preoccupation with external matters in religion, and their dishonesty, pride, and spiritual blindness. They were all show with no substance. They preached but did not practice. They consistently inflicted heavy spiritual burdens on the common people.

Mark 12:41-44; Luke 21:1-4. Jesus praised a poor woman whose offering was more sacrificial than a much larger gift from a richer person. She donated so much that she would not be able to eat again until she earned more. This widow obviously loved God with all her heart, soul, mind, and strength.

Today's Big Ideas

- There is no human marriage in the afterlife (Matthew 22:23-33; Mark 12:18-27; Luke 20:27-40).

- You shall love the Lord your God with all your heart and with all your soul and with all your mind, and you shall love your neighbor as yourself (Matthew 22:34-40; Mark 12:28-34).

- Jesus pronounced woes on the scribes and Pharisees (Matthew 23:1-36).

Insights on Difficult Verses

Matthew 22:30. Once believers receive their glorified resurrection bodies, the need for procreation—one of the fundamental purposes for marriage (Genesis 1:28)—will no longer exist. We will share this one characteristic with the angels—we will not be married.

Matthew 23:2-3. "Moses' seat" was the place in the synagogue where the teacher of the law would sit during the Scripture reading. Generally the most distinguished Jewish elder would sit in this chair, which was placed next to the Torah in the synagogue.

Major Themes

Brothers marrying widows (Matthew 22:24). The Levirate marriage law affirmed that if a man died, his brother had to marry his wife. This was done for two reasons—to take care of the widow and to ensure that the dead brother's family line was kept intact (Deuteronomy 25:5-10).

The God of the living (Luke 20:38). The Sadducees taught that the soul dies with the body. Jesus directly contradicted them. In effect, Jesus said, "Abraham, Isaac, and Jacob, though they died many years ago, are actually living today. For God, who calls Himself the God of Abraham, Isaac, and Jacob, is not the God of the dead but of the living."

Digging Deeper with Cross-References

Love your neighbor (Matthew 22:39)—Leviticus 19:18; Matthew 5:43; 19:19; Mark 12:31; Luke 10:27; Romans 13:9; Galatians 5:14; James 2:8

Hypocrisy (Matthew 23:1-36)—Isaiah 29:13; Ezekiel 33:30-32; Malachi 1:6-14; Matthew 16:5-12; Romans 2:17-24; Titus 1:16

Life Lessons

The greatest commandment (Matthew 22:35-40). The greatest commandment involves supreme love for God. The second involves loving one's neighbor. Interestingly, they're related. Loving our neighbor is an outgrowth of our supreme love for God.

Shun legalism (Matthew 23:13). Nobody could ever successfully follow all of the scribes and Pharisees' legalistic rules and regulations. As it was in Bible times, so it is today. A spirituality based on legalism is doomed to failure. Never forget, "Grace and truth came through Jesus Christ" (John 1:17).

Verses to Remember

- "You shall love the Lord your God with all your heart and with all your soul and with all your mind. This is the great and first commandment. And a second is like it: You shall love your neighbor as yourself" (Matthew 22:37-39).

- "The greatest among you shall be your servant. Whoever exalts himself will be humbled, and whoever humbles himself will be exalted" (Matthew 23:11-12).

Questions for Reflection and Discussion

1. How would you rate yourself in loving God and loving your neighbor?

2. Do you ever find yourself slipping into legalism? How does legalism affect your sense of closeness to the Lord?

3. Are Jesus's words about the Pharisees—not practicing what they preach, working hard to appear pious, being enamored with popularity—ever true of you? (*Ouch!*)

My Father, I have learned that I am called to love You and my neighbor, and also that loving my neighbor is actually a reflection of my love for You. Please help me to be consistent in loving. In Jesus's name, amen.

The Olivet Discourse, Part 1

In the previous lesson we discussed several important issues, such as no marriage in the afterlife, the greatest commandments, and Jesus's pronouncement of woes on the scribes and Pharisees (Matthew 22:23–23:36; Mark 12:18-44; Luke 20:27–21:4). Today we explore Jesus's comments on the signs of the end of the age.

Begin by reading Matthew 24; Mark 13; and Luke 21:5-38. As you read, stop and meditate on any verses that speak to your heart (Joshua 1:8; Psalm 1:1-3).

Chronological marker. The events in this lesson took place during Passion Week at the beginning of the second quarter in AD 30.

Overview of Today's Scripture Reading

Matthew 24:1-28; Mark 13:1-23; Luke 21:5-24. The Olivet Discourse is so named because Jesus delivered this message "as he sat on the Mount of Olives" (Matthew 24:3). The disciples had asked, "What will be the sign of your coming and of the end of the age?" The Olivet Discourse is Jesus's response. Highlights include Jesus's prediction of the appearance of false Christs, wars, earthquakes, famines, and cosmic disturbances.

Matthew 24:29-31; Mark 13:24-27; Luke 21:25-28. There will be cosmic disturbances during the tribulation period. However, no such disturbances will be able to block the glory of the second coming of Christ. Once He arrives, His angels will gather the elect.

Matthew 24:32-35; Mark 13:28-31; Luke 21:29-33. Jesus indicated that God has revealed certain things in prophecy that ought to cause people who know the Bible to understand that a fulfillment of prophecy is taking place. Jesus desired His followers to be accurate observers of the times.

Matthew 24:36-44; Mark 13:32-37; Luke 21:34-36. In the days of Noah, people were carousing and unprepared, just as people will be prior to the second coming of Christ. At the second coming, one will be taken and one will be left. This does not refer to the rapture, for the one that is taken is taken to judgment (Luke 17:34-36). Those who are left enter into Christ's millennial kingdom (Matthew 25:31-46).

Matthew 24:45-51; Luke 21:37-38. Those who profess to serve Christ must make a pivotal choice—to be faithful servants, doing the Lord's will at all times, or to be unfaithful servants, neglecting God's will and living self-indulgently. The faithful will be rewarded at the Lord's return, entering His kingdom; the unfaithful will be punished, being excluded from His kingdom.

Today's Big Ideas

- Jesus revealed the signs of the end of the age (Matthew 24:3-14; Mark 13:3-13).

- Jesus revealed events that will take place during the tribulation period (Matthew 24:15-28; Mark 13:14-23; Luke 21:10-24).

- Jesus spoke of His second coming (Matthew 24:29-31; Mark 13:24-27; Luke 21:25-28).

- No one knows the day or the hour of end-time events (Matthew 24:36-51).

Insights on Difficult Verses

Matthew 24:34. Those people who witness the signs stated just earlier in Matthew 24 (verses 15-31) will see the coming of Jesus Christ within that very generation.

Mark 13:32. Jesus in the Incarnation had two natures. In His human nature, Jesus knew hunger (Luke 4:2), weariness (John 4:6), and the need for sleep (Luke 8:23). In His divine nature, He was omniscient (John 2:24-25; 11:11; 16:30; 21:17), omnipresent (John 1:48), and omnipotent (John 11). In Mark 13:32, Jesus was speaking only from the vantage point of His humanity.

Major Themes

The Mount of Olives (Matthew 24:3). The Mount of Olives was a high hill to the east of Jerusalem that derived its name from the dense olive groves that covered it. Zechariah 14:4 tells us that at the second coming Christ's feet will touch the Mount of Olives—the same mountain from which He ascended from earth (Acts 1:10-11).

Lesson from the fig tree (Matthew 24:32). We are never to predict the dates of end-time events (Matthew 24:36). We do not know the specific day or hour of Jesus's coming (Acts 1:7), but we can know the general season of the Lord's return by virtue of the signs of the times (Matthew 24:33).

Digging Deeper with Cross-References

Cosmic disturbances (Matthew 24:29)—Isaiah 13:10; 34:4; Ezekiel 32:7; Joel 2:10,31; 3:15; Revelation 6:12-13

Jesus's return (Matthew 24:29-31)—Mark 13:1-23; Luke 21:5-24; Acts 1:10-12; 1 Corinthians 15:50-57; 2 Thessalonians 2:1-10; 2 Timothy 3:1-5; Revelation 19

Life Lessons

Beware of false teachers (Matthew 24:4). When Jesus was speaking about the end times, He warned the disciples, "See that no one leads you astray." The only way to avoid deception is to consistently use Scripture as a barometer of truth (Acts 17:11; 1 Thessalonians 5:21).

No one knows the day or hour (Matthew 24:36). Here are four reasons why people shouldn't predict the dates of end-time events:

1. Over the past 2000 years, the guesses have been 100 percent wrong.

2. Those who make these predictions may make harmful decisions for their lives.

3. These predictions can damage one's faith.

4. The timing of end-time events is in God's hands, and we haven't been given the details (Acts 1:7).

Verses to Remember

- "See that no one leads you astray. For many will come in my name, saying, 'I am the Christ,' and they will lead many astray" (Matthew 24:4-5).

- "Look at the fig tree, and all the trees. As soon as they come out in leaf, you see for yourselves and know that the summer is already near. So also, when you see these things taking place, you know that the kingdom of God is near" (Luke 21:29-31).

Questions for Reflection and Discussion

1. Do any of the prophecies Jesus speaks about seem to be coming to pass in our own day (Matthew 24:4-14)?

2. Can you think of any false prophets in the world today (Matthew 24:24)?

3. How might our days be similar to the days of Noah (Matthew 24:37-39)?

My Father, prophecy gives me comfort because it assures me that You are in control of our world. Prophecy is also a strong motivation for me to live righteously. Thank You for these teachings on the end times. In Jesus's name, amen.

The Olivet Discourse, Part 2

Yesterday we focused on Jesus's comments on the signs of the end of the age (Matthew 24; Mark 13; Luke 21:5-38). Today we zero in on Jesus's words on being in a state of watchful readiness at all times and His summary of the judgment of the nations that follows the second coming.

Begin by reading Matthew 25. As you read, notice how the Word of God is purifying your life (John 17:17-18).

Chronological marker. This lesson considers events that occurred during Passion Week at the beginning of the second quarter in AD 30.

Overview of Today's Scripture Reading

Matthew 25:1-13. This parable refers to the future seven-year tribulation period. In context, it speaks of people who are unprepared for the second coming of Christ, which follows the tribulation period.

Matthew 25:14-30. In this parable, Jesus urges believers to be good stewards of the gifts and abilities the Lord gives them. Those who are faithful will be fruitful. By contrast, those who are unfaithful will be unfruitful.

Matthew 25:31-46. Following the second coming, Jesus will judge the nations. The nations are comprised of sheep and goats (the saved and the lost among the Gentiles). They are intermingled and require separation by a special judgment. The basis of the judgment is how they treated Christ's brothers—apparently the 144,000 Jewish evangelists of Revelation 7 and 14. (Only believers would dare feed them and make provisions for them during the tribulation period, for the antichrist is against them.) The result of the judgment is twofold: The righteous (sheep) enter into Christ's millennial kingdom, and the unrighteous (goats) are cast into the lake of fire.

Today's Big Ideas

- Jesus urged His followers who live during the tribulation period to be in a state of watchful readiness at all times (Matthew 25:1-13; Mark 13:32-37; Luke 12:35-48).

- Believers are to be good stewards of the gifts and abilities granted to them by the Lord (Matthew 25:14-30).

- The judgment of the nations will follow Christ's second coming (Matthew 25:31-46).

Insights on Difficult Verses

Matthew 25:1-13. Believers during the tribulation period will anticipate Jesus's coming and seek to be prepared for it, living their lives accordingly. Jesus's return will terminate the opportunity for people to prepare themselves (trust in Jesus) to enter His kingdom. Only those who are previously prepared (saved by trusting in Christ) will be permitted to enter.

Matthew 25:41. Some expositors believe the fire of hell is literal. Others believe it is a metaphorical way of expressing the great wrath of God. Scripture tells us, "The Lord your God is a consuming fire" (Deuteronomy 4:24; Jeremiah 4:4; Hebrews 12:29). Perhaps both views are correct.

Major Themes

Descriptions of hell (Matthew 25:41). The eternal fire of our passage is one of many descriptions of hell in the Bible. Others include the lake of burning sulfur (Revelation 19:20; 20:14-15), a fiery furnace (Matthew 13:42), destruction (2 Thessalonians 1:8-9), and eternal punishment (Matthew 25:46). One thing is certain. Hell will be worse than human words can describe.

The second coming (Matthew 25:31). The second coming is that event when Jesus Christ will return to the earth in glory following the seven-year tribulation period. The very same Jesus who ascended into heaven will come again at the second coming (Acts 1:9-11). Christ will come as the King of kings and Lord of lords (Revelation 19:11-16). Every eye will see Him (Revelation 1:7).

Digging Deeper with Cross-References

Faithfulness to the end (Matthew 25:21)—Luke 12:35-40; 1 Timothy 6:12-14; Titus 2:11-13; James 5:7-9; 1 Peter 1:13-15

Inheriting God's kingdom (Matthew 25:34)—Luke 22:30; 1 Corinthians 15:50; Galatians 5:21

Helping those in need (Matthew 25:35-36)—Job 31:32; Isaiah 58:7; Hebrews 13:3; James 2:15-16

Life Lessons

Meeting others' needs (Matthew 25:35-40). Those who are commended in this passage are told that by feeding Christ's brothers, giving them drink, giving them clothing, and visiting them in prison, they were in fact doing these very things to Christ Himself. Doing such things is an outward manifestation of one's inward faith. This reminds us of the teaching in James that "faith by itself, if it does not have works, is dead" (James 2:17).

Faithful service (Matthew 25:21). As we look forward to Christ's coming, we are called to be faithful servants. This means we are to use our time, talents, and treasures in our service to Him. This doesn't mean we have to go into full-time ministry. It means that regardless of our professions, we are to consistently serve the Lord.

Verses to Remember

- "Well done, good and faithful servant. You have been faithful over a little; I will set you over much. Enter into the joy of your master" (Matthew 25:21).

- "I was hungry and you gave me food, I was thirsty and you gave me drink, I was a stranger and you welcomed me, I was naked and you clothed me, I was sick and you visited me, I was in prison and you came to me...Truly, I say to you, as you

did it to one of the least of these my brothers, you did it to me"
(Matthew 25:35-40).

Questions for Reflection and Discussion

1. What do you learn in Matthew 25:31-46 about the active
   nature of our faith in the Lord?

2. Doing something for a Christian brother is ultimately doing
   that same thing to the Lord. Does that reality motivate you to
   change the way you treat others?

3. Are there perhaps any prison ministries you might want to
   participate in? Food banks? Ministries to the poor?

*My Father, one thing that comes through loud and clear in this lesson is that
my faith in You shows itself in the way I treat other people. I fear I often
fail in that regard. Please enable me to keep a mindset of action-oriented
faith—a faith that is alive in my actions. In Jesus's name, amen.*

Washing the Disciples' Feet

In yesterday's lesson we explored a prophecy of the judgment of the nations (Matthew 25). Now we give consideration to Jesus's celebration of the Passover with the disciples and His prediction of Judas's betrayal.

Begin by reading Matthew 26:1-5,14-25; Mark 14:1-2,10-21; Luke 22:1-13; and John 13:1-30. As you read, keep in mind that the Word of God brings spiritual maturity (1 Corinthians 3:1-2; Hebrews 5:12-14).

Chronological marker. It is Thursday, April 2, AD 30, the night before the crucifixion.

Overview of Today's Scripture Reading

Matthew 26:1-5; Mark 14:1-2; Luke 22:1-2. The events here described take place on the Wednesday of Passion Week. Jesus was soon to be betrayed. The Jewish Sanhedrin plotted to arrest and kill Jesus. They knew they needed to be careful about this because Jesus was extremely popular.

Matthew 26:14-16; Mark 14:10-11; Luke 22:3-6. Judas's betrayal of Jesus was largely money driven. He betrayed Jesus for 30 pieces of silver—equivalent to a little more than a month's wages for a common laborer.

Matthew 26:17-19; Mark 14:12-16; Luke 22:7-13. Jesus instructs His disciples to make preparations for their celebration of the Jewish Passover. This Passover would have been especially meaningful to Jesus since the time of His death was imminent ("My time is at hand").

John 13:1-20. Normally a guest's feet were washed by a household servant, not the master of the household. By washing the disciples' feet,

Jesus placed Himself in the role of a servant. This was a living parable of humility and self-denial—things the disciples would need in the days ahead after His death and resurrection.

Matthew 26:20-25; Mark 14:17-21; John 13:21-30. In ancient times, eating a meal with a person implied, "I am fellowshipping with you and therefore wish you well; I mean you no harm." However, as Jesus and His disciples were enjoying the Passover meal together, Jesus identified Judas as His betrayer. Judas asked, "Is it I?" Jesus did not hesitate: "You have said so."

Today's Big Ideas

- Jesus washes the disciples' feet to illustrate the need for humility and self-denial (John 13:1-20).

- Jesus predicts Judas's betrayal (Matthew 26:14-25; Mark 14:10-21; Luke 22:3-6,21-23; John 13:21-30).

Insights on Difficult Verses

Mark 14:10-11. Part of Judas's motive in betraying Jesus was the love of money (Matthew 26:15). However, we are also told that Satan entered his heart and motivated him (John 12:6; 13:2,27). Satan has a long history of seeking to hinder and even kill the Messiah (Matthew 16:22-23; John 8:44; Revelation 12:4-6).

Matthew 26:18. Jesus apparently made clandestine arrangements with a man not known to those in Jesus's inner circle of disciples to celebrate Passover at his house. This arrangement at the unknown man's house was necessary to prevent His premature betrayal by Judas.

Major Themes

Going back to God (John 13:3). Jesus derived strength by taking the long-term outlook. That is, He was able to face the betrayal, agony, and death on the cross because He knew He would soon be resurrected and exalted in heaven in the presence of the Father. This was the "joy that was set before him" that enabled Him to endure (see Hebrews 12:2).

A washing away of sin (John 13:6-10). There is a deeper spiritual significance of Jesus engaging in foot washing. This living parable indicates that unless Jesus, the Lamb of God, cleanses a person of sin, that person cannot have a personal relationship with God or a heavenly destiny. That is why Jesus told Peter, "If I do not wash you, you have no share with me."

Digging Deeper with Cross-References

Loyalty and obedience (Matthew 26:23-25)—Joshua 22:2-5; Psalm 119:33-37; John 21:15-17; Philippians 4:3; 1 Peter 1:14-16

Servanthood (John 13:5,15-16)—Matthew 20:25-28; John 12:24-26; Romans 14:16-19; 1 Corinthians 3:4-9; 2 Corinthians 3:4-6

Life Lessons

Taking the long look (John 13:3). Like Jesus, you and I ought to have a long-term outlook, especially when we are going through tough times. This helps us keep present circumstances in perspective. Every obstacle we face in this life is temporal, whereas our future life with God in heaven is eternal. These temporal obstacles can even serve a good purpose in refining our faith (1 Peter 1:6).

Authoritative but humble (John 13:3-4). Our text says of Christ, "The Father had given all things into his hands." Jesus is the highest authority in the universe, yet He engaged in the humble act of washing the disciples' feet. Great servants of God have often combined authority with humility. Examples include King David in the Old Testament (2 Samuel 7:18-21) and Paul in the New Testament (1 Timothy 1:15-16).

Verses to Remember

- "When Jesus knew that his hour had come to depart out of this world to the Father, having loved his own who were in the world, he loved them to the end" (John 13:1).

- "You call me Teacher and Lord, and you are right, for so I am. If I then, your Lord and Teacher, have washed your feet, you also ought to wash one another's feet" (John 13:13-14).

Questions for Reflection and Discussion

1. How is Jesus's death described in John 13:1,3? What is the relationship of these verses to Hebrews 12:2?

2. Do you think Judas was a Christian who severely backslid or an unbeliever who feigned being a Christian for a while?

3. Do you want to make any changes in your life after considering Jesus's living parable of washing the disciples' feet?

My Father, a big part of today's lesson is on humility. Jesus demonstrated this humility in washing the disciples' feet. This seems to be such a counter-cultural idea, for our culture emphasizes self and pride. Please help me not to be molded by the world, but instead let me be molded by Your Word through the Spirit. In Jesus's name, amen.

The Way, the Truth, and the Life

Yesterday we considered Jesus's celebration of the Passover with the disciples and His prediction of Judas's betrayal (Matthew 26:14-25; Mark 14:10-21; Luke 22:3-13; John 13:1-30). Today we will focus on Jesus's institution of the Lord's Supper, His prediction of Peter's denial, His promise of the coming of the Holy Spirit, and some key teachings.

Begin by reading Matthew 26:26-35; Mark 14:22-31; Luke 22:14-34; and John 13:31–14:31. As you read, remember that the Word of God can help you be spiritually fruitful (Psalm 1:1-3).

Chronological marker. It is Thursday, April 2, AD 30, the night before the crucifixion.

Overview of Today's Scripture Reading

John 13:31-35. Jesus was about to die. Knowing this, He gave the disciples the one crucial instruction that would keep them together in the days ahead: They were to love one another as Christ had loved them.

Matthew 26:26-29; Mark 14:22-25; Luke 22:14-23. Jesus instituted the Lord's Supper. The bread represented His body, and the cup represented His blood. The last Passover meal was thus transformed into the first celebration of the Lord's Supper.

Luke 22:24-30. Knowing that Jesus would soon die, the disciples' discussion deteriorated into an argument over which of them was greatest. Jesus said the humble servant is greatest in God's kingdom.

Matthew 26:30-35; Mark 14:26-31; Luke 22:31-34; John 13:36-38. Jesus then told the disciples what they surely did not want to hear: "You will all fall away because of me this night." Peter said no way. But the

Lord informed Peter that he would deny Him three times before the rooster crowed twice.

John 14:1-14. Jesus instructed the disciples that even though He was about to die, they shouldn't worry. The risen Christ would go to heaven and prepare a place for them. There would be a reconciliation in heaven. (And of course, there is only one way to get there—through faith in Christ.) Meanwhile, Christ's followers were to pray in His name and do great works.

John 14:15-31. Jesus promised believers some wonderful blessings:

- The Holy Spirit will be their Helper and Teacher.
- They will enjoy union with Christ.
- They will enjoy supernatural peace.

Today's Big Ideas

- Jesus instituted the Lord's Supper (Matthew 26:26-29; Mark 14:22-25; Luke 22:14-20).
- Jesus foretold Peter's denial of Him (Matthew 26:30-35; Mark 14:26-31; Luke 22:31-34; John 13:36-38).
- The path to greatness is to become a servant (Luke 22:24-30).
- Jesus is the way, and the truth, and the life (John 14:1-14).
- Jesus promised the coming of the Holy Spirit (John 14:15-31).

Insights on Difficult Verses

Matthew 26:28. Earlier in Matthew's Gospel, Jesus said that few find eternal life (7:14) and few are chosen (22:14). But Jesus said His blood was poured out not for a few but for many. By the word "many," Jesus apparently meant the whole human race. (The apostle Paul used this same type of terminology in Romans 5:15.)

Luke 22:31-32. Satan is on a leash. He cannot go beyond what our God will allow him. We see this not only here but also in the book of

Job, where Satan had to obtain permission from God before afflicting Job (Job 1:9-12).

Major Themes

I go to prepare a place (John 14:2-3). The same Jesus who created the entire stellar universe (John 1:3; Colossians 1:16) is preparing our eternal habitat in heaven. This is the New Jerusalem, the eternal city of the redeemed that will rest on the new earth (Revelation 21; 22:1-5).

I am the way (John 14:6). Jesus is the only way to a relationship with the Father. As Peter put it, "There is salvation in no one else, for there is no other name under heaven given among men by which we must be saved" (Acts 4:12; see also 1 Timothy 2:5).

Digging Deeper with Cross-References

The Holy Spirit, our Helper (John 14:16,26)—John 15:26; 16:7
Jesus is the way, the truth, and the life (John 14:6)—John 1:4,14,16; 8:32; 10:10; 11:25; Romans 5:2; Ephesians 2:18; Hebrews 10:20; 1 John 5:20

Life Lessons

Sing songs of worship (Mark 14:26). Immediately after Jesus instituted the Lord's Supper, He and the disciples sang a hymn. The Passover meal traditionally ended with the singing of Psalm 136, which has the repeated refrain, "His steadfast love endures forever." Colossians 3:16 admonishes us to sing "psalms and hymns and spiritual songs, with thankfulness in [our] hearts to God."

Don't be overconfident (Mark 14:29-31). After Jesus informed the disciples that they would all stumble, an overconfident Peter announced that he'd never stumble. Jesus gently informed him that he would deny Him three times before the rooster crowed twice. Though Peter denied he'd ever do that, he did as Jesus said and was devastated. Peter had too high a view of himself. This brings to mind 1 Corinthians 10:12: "Let anyone who thinks that he stands take heed lest he fall." Christian beware.

Verses to Remember

- "He took bread, and after blessing it broke it and gave it to them, and said, 'Take; this is my body.' And he took a cup, and when he had given thanks he gave it to them, and they all drank of it. And he said to them, 'This is my blood of the covenant, which is poured out for many'" (Mark 14:22-24).

- "Do this in remembrance of me" (Luke 22:19).

Questions for Reflection and Discussion

1. Jesus had taught the importance of love during His entire ministry. Why do you think He now calls His final instructions on love a "new commandment" (John 13:31-35)?

2. Do you believe Jesus is the only way to salvation (John 14:6)?

3. What is the purpose of celebrating the Lord's Supper? (See 1 Corinthians 11:23-30.)

My Father, we are living in a day when even some people in the church say there are many ways to salvation. Your Word is clear. There is only one way—through Jesus Christ. Help me to be a strong witness of this life-changing truth to others. In Jesus's name, amen.

The True Vine

Yesterday we gave attention to Jesus's institution of the Lord's Supper, His prediction of Peter's denial, His promise of the coming of the Holy Spirit, and several key teachings (Matthew 26:26-35; Mark 14:22-31; Luke 22:14-20,24-34; John 13:31–14:31). Today we turn our attention to Jesus's teaching about being the true vine, the Holy Spirit as the Helper, Christ's overcoming of the world, and His High Priestly prayer to the Father.

Begin by reading John 15–17. Read with the anticipation that the Holy Spirit has something important to teach you today (see Psalm 119:105).

Chronological marker. It is Thursday, April 2, AD 30, the night before the crucifixion. These are some of Jesus's last teachings.

Overview of Today's Scripture Reading

John 15:1-17. The Father wants every Christian to consistently bear fruit. God works in each believer's life to bring about maximum fruit. The Christian (branch) cannot bear fruit apart from union with and abiding in Christ (the vine). A key component of abiding is obedience to Christ.

John 15:18-27. Jesus warned that the world—that is, the anti-God world system characterized by evil and ruled by Satan—will hate and persecute Christians who abide in Christ and bear fruit (see John 12:31; 14:30; Ephesians 2:2; 1 John 2:15-17). Christians are targets of Satan and the world system.

John 16. Jesus taught that once He ascended into heaven, He would send the Holy Spirit to believers. The Holy Spirit is the Helper who guides believers into the truth. The Holy Spirit's purpose is to glorify Christ. Jesus then reiterated that He will soon die, but not to worry—He will be resurrected from the dead, and the disciples' sorrow will turn to joy.

John 17. Jesus prays His High Priestly prayer to the Father, in which He asks the Father to glorify Him so that He in turn can glorify the Father. He prays for the safety and sanctification of His followers and asks that they would maintain a spiritual oneness.

Today's Big Ideas

- Jesus is the true vine (John 15:1-17).
- The world will hate Christ's followers (John 15:18-27).
- The Holy Spirit is the Helper of believers (John 16:4-15).
- The disciples' sorrow will turn to joy at Christ's resurrection (John 16:16-24).
- Jesus has overcome the world (John 16:25-33).

Insights on Difficult Verses

John 15:2. Some interpreters believe this verse refers to the physical death of fruitless Christians. Others believe it refers to God's discipline in the lives of believers so they will be more fruitful. Still others believe Jesus was indicating that not all who claim to be followers of Jesus are true believers.

John 16:8-11. The Holy Spirit convicts and reproves people through apostles, evangelists, and preachers who set forth the Word of God in a clear light that all can understand. As the Word is proclaimed, the Holy Spirit enables people to understand what has been spoken (1 Corinthians 2:10-12).

Major Themes

Unless I go away (John 16:7). Jesus told His followers that unless He went to heaven, the Holy Spirit could not come to them. In John 7:39 we are told that "the Spirit had not been given, because Jesus was not

yet glorified." The implication is that the cross, resurrection, and glorification of Christ were necessary prior to the sending of the Spirit.
The only true God (John 17:3). In this verse Jesus affirms that the Father is the one true God (see 2 Chronicles 15:3; Isaiah 65:16; 1 Thessalonians 1:9; 1 John 5:20; Revelation 3:7).

Digging Deeper with Cross-References

> *Bearing fruit (John 15:1-17)*—Psalm 1:2-3; Micah 3:8; Zechariah 4:6; Matthew 13:23; 2 Corinthians 3:18; Galatians 5:22-23; Ephesians 3:16-17; Philippians 1:6; 2 Peter 1:5-8; 1 John 3:6
>
> *The vine (John 15:1)*—Psalm 80:8-19; Jeremiah 6:9; Ezekiel 15:1-6; 17:1-10; 19:10-14; Hosea 10:1; 14:7

Life Lessons

The joy of the Lord (John 15:11). Jesus affirmed, "These things I have spoken to you, that my joy may be in you, and that your joy may be full." The things Jesus had just spoken relate to Christians (branches) being connected to Him (the vine). Our joy comes from our close connection with Jesus.

Asking in Jesus's name doesn't guarantee blanket approval (John 16:24). This verse should not be isolated from other verses that qualify Jesus's meaning. In John 15:7, Jesus said, "If you abide in me, and my words abide in you, ask whatever you wish, and it will be done for you." Abiding is a condition for answered prayer. We are also told that "whatever we ask we receive from him, because we keep his commandments and do what pleases him" (1 John 3:22; see James 4:3; 1 John 5:14-15). In other words, obedience is tied to answered prayer.

Verses to Remember

- "Abide in me, and I in you. As the branch cannot bear fruit by itself, unless it abides in the vine, neither can you, unless you abide in me. I am the vine; you are the branches" (John 15:4-5).

- "Greater love has no one than this, that someone lay down his life for his friends" (John 15:13).

- "Truly, truly, I say to you, whatever you ask of the Father in my name, he will give it to you. Until now you have asked nothing in my name. Ask, and you will receive, that your joy may be full" (John 16:23-24).

Questions for Reflection and Discussion

1. Since we can do nothing apart from Jesus Christ (John 15:5), how important is it that Christians remain connected to the vine (Jesus Christ)?

2. Practically speaking, how can a Christian remain, or abide, in Jesus Christ? What does that look like?

3. How do you think the Holy Spirit convicts the world of sin, righteousness, and judgment (John 16:7-11)?

My Father, in John 15:5 I am told that I can do nothing apart from Jesus Christ. Yet I am told in Philippians 4:13 that I can do all things through Christ. Please remind me daily of the importance of staying connected to Jesus Christ. In Jesus's name, amen.

Betrayal and Arrest

In the previous lesson we discussed Jesus's teachings about His identity as the true vine, the Holy Spirit as the Helper, Christ's overcoming of the world, and His High Priestly prayer to the Father (John 15–17). Today we explore Jesus's praying in Gethsemane, His betrayal by Judas, and His arrest.

Begin by reading Matthew 26:36-56; Mark 14:32-52; Luke 22:35-53; and John 18:1-14. As you read, remember that the Word of God is alive and working in you (Hebrews 4:12).

Chronological marker. It is Thursday, April 2, AD 30, the night before the crucifixion.

Overview of Today's Scripture Reading

Luke 22:35-38. Jesus earlier told the disciples, "Take nothing for your journey, no staff, nor bag, nor bread, nor money; and do not have two tunics" (Luke 9:3). He likewise told the 72 witnesses that were sent out, "Carry no moneybag, no knapsack, no sandals" (10:4). In those early days, Christ's witnesses traveled light. But things had now changed. Tougher times were ahead. The disciples would have to not only provide for themselves but also bring swords for self-defense. There would be some threatening resistance to their work of evangelism.

Matthew 26:36-46; Mark 14:32-42; Luke 22:39-46. Jesus and His disciples entered Gethsemane to pray. On this occasion Jesus apparently experienced distress such as He had never experienced before in His short earthly life. In His hour of greatest need, the Lord wanted those dearest to Him to be there for Him in prayer.

Jesus preferred not to drink this cup. He was no doubt imagining the separation from the Father He would experience when the sins of all humanity would be poured out on Him (Matthew 27:46). Yet He willingly submitted His will to that of the Father (26:39).

Instead of offering up prayer support, the disciples fell asleep. In His hour of greatest need, Jesus ended up going it alone.

Matthew 26:47-56; Mark 14:43-52; Luke 22:47-53; John 18:1-14. Judas, in a monumental betrayal, led the temple guards sent by the Jewish Sanhedrin straight to the Garden of Gethsemane, where Jesus was praying. Judas identified Christ with a kiss. In this case, Judas turned a symbol of love and affection into an act of hypocritical betrayal.

Peter tried to defend Jesus by slicing the ear off of Malchus, a personal servant of Caiaphas. Jesus immediately instructed Peter, "Put your sword back into its place. For all who take the sword will perish by the sword" (Matthew 26:52).

Today's Big Ideas

- Jesus prayed in Gethsemane as He pondered what lay ahead at the cross (Matthew 26:36-46; Mark 14:32-42).

- Jesus was betrayed by Judas and arrested (Matthew 26:47-56; Mark 14:43-52; Luke 22:47-53; John 18:1-11).

Insights on Difficult Verses

Matthew 26:38-43. Jesus said, "My soul is very sorrowful, even to death." The Greek word translated "sorrowful" is *hlypeisthai,* meaning "to be grieved or sad to the point of distress." Jesus had never before experienced such distressing grief in His earthly life. The word "soul" is used here to refer to Jesus's entire being—His whole person. The sorrow was all-pervasive.

Luke 22:36-38. Jesus earlier instructed His disciples to turn the other cheek (Matthew 5:39). But now He revealed the future hostility they would face and encouraged them to buy a sword. The sword (Greek: *maxairan*) was a dagger typically used for self-defense against robbers, muggers, or even wild animals.

Major Themes

Jesus sweating blood (Luke 22:44). There are cases in medical history in which severe mental suffering produced the sweating of blood, resulting from the breakdown of blood vessels. In Jesus's case, His mental suffering was no doubt due to His awareness that even though He was completely holy, He would soon take the sins of all humanity upon Himself at the cross (2 Corinthians 5:21).

Sleeping as a result of great sorrow (Luke 22:45). The disciples were physically and emotionally exhausted. They couldn't bear with the strain. They apparently fell asleep in defeat instead of praying for strength, as Christ had commanded them (22:40).

Digging Deeper with Cross-References

Jesus taught in the temple (Matthew 26:55-56)—Mark 12:35; Luke 21:37; John 7:14,28; 18:20

My soul is troubled (Mark 14:34)—Psalms 42:6; 43:5; John 12:27

Jesus's companions scattered (Mark 14:50)—Psalm 88:8; John 16:32

Life Lessons

Obedience to death (Matthew 26:39). As Jesus faced death on the cross, He asked the Father if this cup might pass from Him. But then Jesus said to the Father, "Nevertheless, not as I will, but as you will." Jesus affirmed, "My food is to do the will of him who sent me" (John 4:34). He said, "I have come down from heaven, not to do my own will but the will of him who sent me" (John 6:38). How wonderful if all Christians could say, "Not as I will, but as You will."

Reverence for our glorious Jesus (John 18:5-6). When Jesus informed the Roman soldiers "I am he," they involuntarily fell to the ground. We recall that when the apostle John saw Christ in His glory, he "fell at his feet as though dead" (Revelation 1:17). Jesus is the God of glory. Let us always honor and revere Him.

Verses to Remember

- "Father, if it be possible, let this cup pass from me; nevertheless, not as I will, but as you will" (Matthew 26:39).

- "Watch and pray that you may not enter into temptation" (Matthew 26:41).

- "All who take the sword will perish by the sword" (Matthew 26:52).

Questions for Reflection and Discussion

1. What is the significance of Jesus saying "I am he" to the Roman soldiers? (See John 8:58.)

2. Do you need to pray about any temptations (see Luke 22:46)?

3. What do you learn about prayer in Mark 14:36?

My Father, this was a difficult lesson, for I learned much about the suffering of Jesus on my behalf. Please let me never forget the price Christ paid for me to have the free gift of salvation. In Jesus's name, amen.

Day 41

The Trial Before Caiaphas

Yesterday we focused on Jesus praying in Gethsemane, His betrayal by Judas, and His arrest (Matthew 26:36-56; Mark 14:32-52; Luke 22:35-53; John 18:1-14). Today we zero in on Jesus's trial before Caiaphas and Peter's denial of Him.

Begin by reading Matthew 26:57-75; Mark 14:53-72; Luke 22:54-71; and John 18:15-27. As you read, remember that those who obey the Word of God are truly blessed (Psalm 119:2; Luke 11:28; Revelation 1:3).

Chronological marker. It is now crucifixion Friday, April 3, AD 30.

Overview of Today's Scripture Reading

Matthew 26:57-68; Mark 14:53-65; Luke 22:66-71; John 18:19-24.
Even though Caiaphas the high priest was judging Jesus, Jesus perceived of Himself as a divine Judge. Caiaphas asked Jesus, "Are you the Christ, the Son of the Blessed?" Jesus responded, "I am, and you will see the Son of Man seated at the right hand of Power, and coming with the clouds of heaven."

In His answer to Caiaphas, Jesus was drawing on Old Testament imagery taken from Daniel 7. He informed Caiaphas that He—the Son of Man—will ultimately be the one to whom everlasting dominion is given. One should not miss the irony of Jesus's words. Although Jesus was standing before Caiaphas and the others as an indicted man, they will one day stand before Him at His tribunal, and He will be the sovereign Judge. In that day, it will be utterly horrific for all who have rejected Christ's gracious provision of salvation.

Matthew 26:69-75; Mark 14:66-72; Luke 22:54-65; John 18:15-18,

181

25-27. Even though Peter's love for Jesus was real, his love did not stand the test of fear. He denied Jesus three times. When a servant girl accused Peter of being with Jesus, Peter immediately responded, "I neither know nor understand what you mean." This is the exact phrase one would use in a Jewish court of law as a legal denial. He continued with a second and third denial. After the third denial, Peter swore, "I do not know this man of whom you speak." He swore, as if in a courtroom, to confirm the veracity of his denial. At the rooster's second crowing, Jesus looked directly into Peter's eyes from a distance. When they made eye contact, the reality of what had happened hit Peter like a ton of bricks, and he wept.

Today's Big Ideas

- Jesus was tried before Caiaphas and the council (Matthew 26:57-68; Mark 14:53-65; John 18:19-24).

- Peter denied Jesus three times (Matthew 26:69-75; Mark 14:66-72; John 18:15-18).

Insights on Difficult Verses

Matthew 26:60. Two witnesses at last came forward to testify against Jesus. Under Jewish law, at least two witnesses were always required to establish a formal charge against a person. Their testimony had to be in agreement.

Matthew 26:65. The high priest tore his clothes as an expression of horror at what he perceived to be Christ's blasphemy—claiming to be God.

Mark 14:72. Expositors have noted the progression of events that may have contributed to Peter's denial of Christ. First, he became overconfident (verses 29,31). Then he apparently failed to pray (verses 37,40-41). Then he was seen with secular guards instead of other believers (verse 54). Then came the denial.

Major Themes

The whole council (Matthew 26:59). This is the Jewish Sanhedrin, a supreme ruling and administrative council among the Jews in New Testament times composed of scribes, elders, chief priests, and the high priest (Matthew 5:22). This ruling body stood against Jesus, and later they would stand against Peter and John (Acts 4:1-23; 5:17-41), Stephen (Acts 6:12-15), and Paul (Acts 22:30; 23:1-10). *Another disciple (John 18:15-16)*. Some Bible expositors suggest that John may have been making an anonymous reference to himself.

Digging Deeper with Cross-References

Jesus abused (Matthew 26:67)—Matthew 16:21; 17:22-23; 20:18-19; 26:2

False witnesses (Mark 14:56)—Psalm 35:11; Proverbs 6:16-19; 19:5

The coming of the Son of Man (Mark 14:62)—Psalm 110:1; Daniel 7:13; Matthew 16:27; 24:30; Mark 8:38; 13:26; Acts 1:11; 1 Thessalonians 4:16; 2 Thessalonians 1:7; Revelation 1:7; 22:20

Life Lessons

Disciples in hiding (Mark 14:53-65). As soon as Jesus was arrested, the disciples "all left him and fled" (14:50). They were in hiding—with the exception of Peter, who watched from a distance. Some might find it easy to judge them. Perhaps we should all remember our own weaknesses before casting the first stone. Truthfully, we have all probably denied Christ sometime by our words and actions. Let's resolve to never do it again.

A look of compassion (Luke 22:61). Peter denied Jesus three times. Following the third denial, "the Lord turned and looked at Peter." Some believe Jesus looked at Peter to remind him of His prediction of the denial. I don't think so. Jesus loved Peter. And Jesus, as God, knows how weak we are. "He knows our frame; he remembers that we are dust" (Psalm 103:14). I think Jesus gave Peter a look of love and compassion.

Verses to Remember

- "I tell you, from now on you will see the Son of Man seated at

the right hand of Power and coming on the clouds of heaven"
(Matthew 26:64).

- "Peter remembered the saying of Jesus, 'Before the rooster
  crows, you will deny me three times.' And he went out and
  wept bitterly" (Matthew 26:75).

Questions for Reflection and Discussion

1. What thought process do you think Peter was going through
   in his denials?

2. If you put yourself in Peter's place, do you think it possible
   that you would have denied Jesus Christ (Luke 22:54-62)?
   Are you sure about your answer?

3. What do you learn from this lesson about how people can do
   wrong things with a religious motivation? Are there examples
   of that in today's world?

*My Father, I again find this lesson difficult to bear because it reveals how
much my Savior suffered on my behalf. It enhances my love for the Savior ever more. I again thank You for sending Him into the world. In Jesus's
name, amen.*

Judas's Death and the
Trial Before Pilate

In yesterday's lesson we explored Jesus's trial before Caiaphas and Peter's denial of Him (Matthew 26:57-75; Mark 14:53-72; Luke 22:54-71; John 18:15-27). Now we give consideration to Judas's hanging and Jesus's trial before Pilate.

Begin by reading Matthew 27:1-26; Mark 15:1-15; Luke 23:1-25; and John 18:28–19:16. As you read, keep in mind that just as we eat food for physical nourishment, so we need the Word of God for spiritual nourishment (1 Corinthians 3:2; Hebrews 5:12; 1 Peter 2:2).

Chronological marker. It is crucifixion Friday, April 3, AD 30.

Overview of Today's Scripture Reading

Matthew 27:3-10. Filled with remorse over betraying innocent blood, Judas went back to the Jewish officials and lamented that Jesus was not worthy of death. He wanted no part of the money he took earlier for his betrayal and threw it into the temple. Judas could no longer live with himself and committed suicide. Meanwhile, instead of using Judas's tainted money for the temple, the Jewish officials used it to buy a parcel of land to bury foreigners.

Matthew 27:1-2,11-14; Mark 15:1-5; Luke 23:1-17; John 18:28-40. The Jewish council took Jesus to Pilate, the governor of Judea, and brought false accusations against Him. They claimed Jesus opposed paying taxes to Caesar. Jesus actually said to give to Caesar what was his (Luke 20:25). They charged him with misleading the people, but Pilate thought Him innocent. Because the Jewish leaders would not let down, Pilate sent Jesus to Herod.

Herod interrogated Jesus, but Jesus kept silent. Herod mocked Jesus by dressing Him up as a false king. He then sent Jesus back to Pilate without rendering any kind of verdict.

Pilate again affirmed that he saw no crime in Jesus. Pilate thought Jesus should be released and said, "I will therefore punish and release him." But the crowds would not have it.

Matthew 27:15-26; Mark 15:6-15; Luke 23:18-25; John 19:1-16. The governor customarily released a prisoner each year at Passover in order to gain acceptance with the Jews. On this day, the Jewish people demanded that Pilate release Barabbas—a known insurrectionist—and not Jesus. The crowd shouted against Jesus, "Crucify, crucify him." Pilate finally consented.

Today's Big Ideas

- Judas hanged himself in remorse for his betrayal (Matthew 27:3-10).
- Jesus experienced several rigged trials (Matthew 27:11-14; Mark 15:1-5; Luke 23:1-16; John 18:28-32).
- Jesus affirmed His kingdom is not of this world (John 18:33-40).
- Pilate delivered Jesus to be crucified (Matthew 27:24-26; Mark 15:6-15; Luke 23:18-25; John 19:1-16).

Insights on Difficult Verses

Matthew 27:5. Taken together with Acts 1:18, we deduce that Judas first hanged himself. Then, at some point, the rope either broke or loosened so that his body slipped from it and fell to the rocks below and burst open. Neither account is complete. Taken together, we have a composite picture of what happened.

John 18:28. The Jewish authorities would not enter into the governor's headquarters, a dwelling place of Gentiles that would render them unclean. Notice, however, that they saw nothing defiling in falsely testifying against Jesus and seeking to arrange for His brutal execution.

Major Themes

Judas died unconverted (Matthew 27:4). Some have suggested that because Judas showed remorse over his action, he must have repented and turned to God for salvation. But Judas didn't die with the relief of forgiveness. He is an example of 2 Corinthians 7:10: "Godly grief produces a repentance that leads to salvation without regret, whereas worldly grief produces death."

Flogging (Matthew 27:26). This was an unusually cruel form of punishment utilizing a leather whip with pieces of sharpened bone and metal attached. It not only scarred the victim but sometimes left open wounds and even exposed organs.

Digging Deeper with Cross-References

Remaining silent (Matthew 27:12)—Isaiah 53:7; Matthew 26:63; John 19:9; 1 Peter 2:22

His blood be on us (Matthew 27:25)—2 Samuel 1:16; 14:9; Jeremiah 51:35; Acts 5:28; 18:6; 20:26

Jesus, the King (John 18:33)—Isaiah 9:6; 11:10; John 12:15; Acts 2:30; 1 Timothy 6:15; Revelation 17:14; 19:16

Life Lessons

Jesus's kingdom is not of this world (John 18:36-37). Jesus let Pilate know that He indeed was a King, but His kingdom was not of this world. His is a spiritual kingdom where people are redeemed and lives are forever changed. Entry is by simple faith in Christ (John 3:16-17). The good news is that following death, the Christian goes to be face-to-face with the King of light (2 Corinthians 5:8; Philippians 1:21-23).

Fearing men (Mark 15:8). The crowd described in this verse sided with the Jewish leaders. What happened to the earlier crowd that cheered when Jesus rode a donkey into Jerusalem? They had cried out, "Hosanna! Blessed is he who comes in the name of the Lord" (Mark 11:9), but then they apparently went into hiding. They should have remembered Psalm 118:6: "The LORD is on my side; I will not fear. What can man do to me?"

Verses to Remember

- "Pilate said to the chief priests and the crowds, 'I find no guilt in this man'" (Luke 23:4).

- "You brought me this man as one who was misleading the people. And after examining him before you, behold, I did not find this man guilty of any of your charges against him" (Luke 23:14).

- "Crucify, crucify him!" (Luke 23:21).

Questions for Reflection and Discussion

1. Judas's suicide was motivated by remorse. Why do you suppose he did not turn back to the Lord for forgiveness?

2. Can you think of a time when you were betrayed by someone close to you? What did it feel like? Have you thought of turning to Jesus in your pain, knowing that He, too, experienced betrayal?

3. What significance do you see in Pilate finding Jesus innocent (Luke 23:13-16,22)?

My Father, Your love is absolutely amazing. You so loved the world that You gave Your only Son, that whoever believes in Him should not perish, but have eternal life. You sent Him despite knowing the pain He would go through. What amazing love! In Jesus's name, amen.

Day 43

The Crucifixion

Yesterday we considered Judas's hanging and Jesus's trial before Pilate (Matthew 27:1-26; Mark 15:1-15; Luke 23:1-25; John 18:28–19:16). Today we will focus on the soldiers' mocking of Jesus and His subsequent crucifixion.

Begin by reading Matthew 27:27-44; Mark 15:16-32; Luke 23:26-43; and John 19:17-30. As you read, remember that storing God's Word in your heart can help you to avoid sinning (Psalm 119:9,11).

Chronological marker. It is crucifixion Friday, April 3, AD 30.

Overview of Today's Scripture Reading

Matthew 27:27-31; Mark 15:16-20. Jesus's kingship was treated with utter scorn by the Roman soldiers. They took Him into the Praetorium, or governor's headquarters, and ridiculed Him. They stripped Him, put a scarlet robe on Him, twisted together a crown of thorns and placed it on His head, and put a staff in His right hand. They then knelt before Him, acclaiming, "Hail, king of the Jews!" They spat on Him, took away the staff, and struck Him on the head. Following this, they took off the robe, put His clothes back on Him, and led Him away to be crucified.

Matthew 27:32; Mark 15:21; Luke 23:26-32. Jesus was forced to carry the crossbeam of His cross by Himself (John 19:17). Even for a healthy young man in good shape, this would have been difficult. Jesus, who had just been severely scourged, quickly became too weak and needed assistance. Simon was thus drafted into service. We know little of the man. He was probably in Jerusalem to celebrate the Passover and had no idea that he would play this role in aiding Jesus to the place of execution.

189

Matthew 27:33-44; Mark 15:22-32; Luke 23:33-43; John 19:17-30.
Once Jesus arrived at Golgotha, or the Place of a Skull, He was offered
wine mixed with gall, a first-century painkilling narcotic. Jesus refused
it. He then suffered Roman crucifixion, a slow and torturous form of
death generally reserved for criminals, slaves, and non-Romans. Such
crucifixion was not only painful but also caused the victim to slowly
suffocate.

In crucifixions, it was common to post a sign stating the crime of
the victim. In Jesus's case, the sign read, "This is Jesus, the King of the
Jews." Jesus was mocked and taunted by people who were passing by as
well as the Jewish leaders. Oh, the utter blindness of such individuals!

Today's Big Ideas

- Jesus was mocked and ridiculed (Matthew 27:27-31; Mark
  15:16-20).

- Jesus was crucified (Matthew 27:32-44; Mark 15:21-32; Luke
  23:26-43; John 19:17-28).

Insights on Difficult Verses

Luke 23:28-31. Jerusalem and its temple were utterly destroyed in
AD 70 at the hands of Titus and his Roman warriors. Barren women
living during that time would be considered blessed, for it would be
better for women not to have any children than for them to have children experience such suffering as would come in AD 70.

John 19:30. The phrase "it is finished" can also be translated "paid in
full." In ancient days, whenever someone was found guilty of a crime,
the offender was put in jail and a record of debt detailing the crime
was posted on the jail door (see Colossians 2:14). Upon release, the
offender was given the record of debt, and on it was stamped, "Paid in
full." Christ took the record of debt of all our lives and nailed it to the
cross. He paid our debt in full.

Major Themes

Wine mixed with gall (Matthew 27:34). This combination was an ancient painkiller. Gall was derived from plants or tree bark. Jesus refused the painkilling cocktail, choosing instead to suffer in full for the sins of humankind. Mark 15:23 adds that myrrh was part of the mix. Myrrh may be the same thing as gall, or it may be a different substance. *The Place of a Skull (John 19:17)*. This place derived its name either because this part of the hill looked like a human skull or because so many people were executed there. The exact location of this place is unknown.

Digging Deeper with Cross-References

Christ's sacrifice (Mark 15:21-32)—John 3:16; Romans 5:6-8; Philippians 2:5-8; Hebrews 12:1-3

It is finished (John 19:30)—John 1:29; Hebrews 9:11-15,24-28; 10:11-14

Say to the mountains, "Fall on us" (Luke 23:30)—Isaiah 2:19; Hosea 10:8; Revelation 6:16

Life Lessons

Jesus saves (Mark 15:31). Some onlookers mocked Jesus on the cross, saying, "He saved others; he cannot save himself." Think about it. Though the mockers didn't mean it this way, the truth is that Jesus loved us so much that He *dared not* save Himself, choosing instead to save us. This brings to mind John 15:13: "Greater love has no one than this, that someone lay down his life for his friends." Jesus is our greatest friend!

Forgiveness (Luke 23:34). Lessons on forgiveness often surface in the four Gospels. For example, Jesus instructs us to pray, "Forgive us our debts, as we also have forgiven our debtors." Jesus explained, "If you forgive others their trespasses, your heavenly Father will also forgive you, but if you do not forgive others their trespasses, neither will your Father forgive your trespasses" (Matthew 6:12,14).

Verses to Remember

- "They mocked him, saying, 'Hail, King of the Jews'" (Matthew 27:29).

- "They led him out to crucify him" (Mark 15:20).

- "When they came to the place that is called The Skull, there they crucified him" (Luke 23:33).

- "Jesus said, 'Father, forgive them, for they know not what they do'" (Luke 23:34).

Questions for Reflection and Discussion

1. How is the soldiers' mocking of Jesus similar to the way many today react to Him (Mark 15:16-20)?

2. Have you ever been mocked because of your commitment to Jesus? Read Matthew 5:11-12 for a blessing.

3. Are you able to pray Jesus's prayer in Luke 23:34 regarding those who have wronged you?

My Father, today's lesson brought to my mind Romans 5:8: "God shows his love for us in that while we were still sinners, Christ died for us." Thank You for showing this love to me, a sinner. In Jesus's name, amen.

Day 44

Jesus's Death and Burial

Yesterday we gave attention to the soldiers' mocking of Jesus and His crucifixion (Matthew 27:27-34; Mark 15:16-32; Luke 23:26-43; John 19:17-30). Today we turn our attention to Jesus's death and burial, and the Roman guards who were posted at the tomb.

Begin by reading Matthew 27:45-66; Mark 15:33-47; Luke 23:44-56; and John 19:31-42. As you read, remember that the Word of God teaches us, trains us, and corrects us (2 Timothy 3:15-17).

Chronological marker. It is crucifixion Friday, April 3, AD 30.

Overview of Today's Scripture Reading

Matthew 27:45-56; Mark 15:33-41; Luke 23:44-49; John 19:31-37. Jesus was crucified, and then at midday, darkness covered the land. During this time of darkness, Jesus became the sin offering for humanity and was forsaken by the Father. This was the greatest pain of the crucifixion for Jesus, far worse than physical pain. Jesus shouted out, "My God, my God, why have you forsaken me?" Jesus was referring to the sense of judicial separation between Him and the Father that took place as a result of Jesus being the sin-bearer. Soon enough, Jesus gave up His spirit.

At Jesus's death, three momentous events occurred. First, the temple curtain was torn from top to bottom, thereby showing that the way of access into God's presence was now available. Second, a great earthquake occurred, showing that Christ's death was an earth-shattering event. And third, a number of righteous people were raised from death to life and went into Jerusalem, where they were recognized by family members and friends.

Matthew 27:57-61; Mark 15:42-47; Luke 23:50-56; John 19:38-42. The bodies of crucified criminals were normally disposed of, not buried. However, Joseph of Arimathea—a rich man and a member of the Sanhedrin—made arrangements to bury Jesus's body in his own tomb. Jesus's body was wrapped in a linen cloth. Then about 75 pounds of aromatic spices were mixed together to form a gummy substance and applied to the wrappings of cloth around His body. After His body was placed in a rock tomb, an extremely large stone was rolled against the entrance by means of levers. This stone would have weighed somewhere around two tons (4000 pounds).

Matthew 27:62-66. Roman guards were then stationed at the tomb. These disciplined men were trained and motivated to be effective guards as assigned by the Roman government. Fear of cruel punishment produced flawless attention to duty, especially in the night watches. These Roman guards would have affixed on the tomb the Roman Seal, a stamp representing Roman power and authority.

Today's Big Ideas

- Jesus died on the cross of Calvary (Matthew 27:45-56; Mark 15:33-41; Luke 23:44-49; John 19:31-37).

- Jesus was buried (Matthew 27:57-61; Mark 15:42-47; Luke 23:50-56; John 19:38-42), and guards were posted at His tomb (Matthew 27:62-66).

Insights on Difficult Verses

Matthew 27:52-53. These individuals did not receive their permanent resurrection bodies at this time but rather were resuscitated from the dead, much like Lazarus in John 11. All these individuals eventually died again and went back into the grave. The reception of their permanent resurrection bodies is yet future (1 Thessalonians 4:13-17; 1 Corinthians 15:50-52).

Mark 15:34. The word "forsaken" carries the idea of abandonment. Jesus's greatest suffering on the cross was not physical, but spiritual. Christ became sin for us (2 Corinthians 5:21). Christ had thus become the object of the Father's displeasure, for He became the sinner's substitute. The sense of abandonment that Jesus sensed was judicial, not relational.

Major Themes

Multiple resuscitations (Matthew 27:52). Scholars have different views on the timing of these resuscitations. Some believe the people were raised at Jesus's death and then went into Jerusalem. Others say that because Jesus is the firstfruits of the dead (1 Corinthians 15:23), they must have been raised after Christ was raised even though their tombs were opened by an earthquake three days earlier. The debate continues.

Darkness (Mark 15:33). The darkness that fell at Jesus's death was a mark of divine judgment. This is borne out in many Old Testament passages, including Isaiah 5:30; 13:10-11; Joel 2:1-2; Amos 5:20; and Zephaniah 1:15.

Digging Deeper with Cross-References

The veil or curtain (Matthew 27:51)—Exodus 26:31-33; Hebrews 10:19-20

Why have you forsaken me? (Mark 15:34)—Psalm 22:1-31; Isaiah 53:10; Mark 14:27; 2 Corinthians 5:21; Galatians 3:13

Life Lessons

Access to God through Jesus (Matthew 27:51). When Jesus died, "the curtain of the temple was torn in two, from top to bottom." This thick curtain blocked everyone (except the high priest once a year) from entering into the Most Holy Place. The tearing of the curtain symbolically indicates that we now have unhindered access to God through Jesus Christ. "Let us then with confidence draw near to the throne of grace, that we may receive mercy and find grace to help in time of need" (Hebrews 4:16).

Changed lives (John 19:38-39). Even in the immediate circumstances of Christ's death, people in the vicinity experienced changed lives. One criminal on the cross became a believer and was promised

Paradise by Christ (Luke 23:39-43). The centurion who witnessed Christ die said, "Truly this man was the Son of God" (Mark 15:39).

Verses to Remember

- "Father, into your hands I commit my spirit!" (Luke 23:46).
- "Truly this man was the Son of God!" (Mark 15:39).

Questions for Reflection and Discussion

1. Why did Jesus say, "My God, my God, why have you forsaken me?"

2. How could a secular Roman guard recognize Jesus's identity when the top religious leaders did not (Mark 15:39)?

3. What do you learn from John 19:26-27 about showing love even in your darkest moment?

My Father, I have learned that as horrible as the crucifixion of Jesus was, You already knew it would happen. In fact, there are prophecies of the crucifixion in the Old Testament. This shows me that the crucifixion of Jesus for my sins was a key component of Your eternal plan of salvation. May You be praised for so great a salvation. In Jesus's name, amen.

The Resurrection of Jesus Christ

In the previous lesson we discussed Jesus's death and burial, and the Roman guards that were posted at the tomb (Matthew 27:45-66; Mark 15:33-47; Luke 23:44-56; John 19:31-42). Today we explore Jesus's resurrection and His appearances to some of His followers.

Begin by reading Matthew 28:1-15; Mark 16:1-13; Luke 24:1-35; and John 20:1-18. As you read, never forget that you can trust everything that is recorded in the Word of God (Matthew 5:18; John 10:35).

Chronological marker. It is resurrection Sunday, April 5, AD 30.

Overview of Today's Scripture Reading

Matthew 28:1-10; Mark 16:1-11; Luke 24:1-12; John 20:1-18. Mary Magdalene, "the other Mary," and Salome visited the tomb to anoint Jesus's body with spices. Upon their arrival, they were told by an angel that Jesus had been resurrected from the dead. They were instructed to go tell the disciples the good news. Jesus made His first resurrection appearance to Mary Magdalene. He then appeared to others. He provided indisputable proof that He was truly risen from the dead.

Matthew 28:11-15. When the chief priests were told what happened, they immediately gave money to the soldiers who were guarding the tomb, instructing them to tell people, "His disciples came by night and stole him away while we were asleep." The soldiers took the money and did as they were instructed.

Mark 16:12-13; Luke 24:13-35. The resurrected Jesus then appeared to two disciples on the road to Emmaus and spoke to them about His true identity. "Beginning with Moses and all the Prophets, he interpreted to them in all the Scriptures the things concerning himself."

Christ's words to the disciples cannot be limited to Old Testament prophecies of His future coming. His words likely also included a recounting of His many preincarnate appearances to the Old Testament patriarchs (see, for example, John 8:56; 1 Corinthians 10:1-4; Hebrews 11:26). After the resurrected Christ departed, the two disciples asked each other, "Did not our hearts burn within us while he talked to us on the road, while he opened to us the Scriptures?" (Luke 24:32).

Today's Big Ideas

- Jesus was resurrected from the dead (Matthew 28:1-10; Mark 16:1-8; Luke 24:1-12; John 20:1-10).

- The Jewish Sanhedrin bribed the guards who were on duty at Jesus's tomb to deny the claims of His resurrection (Matthew 28:11-15).

- Jesus made convincing appearances to His followers (Mark 16:9-13; Luke 24:13-35; John 20:11-18).

Insights on Difficult Verses

Mark 16:9-20. These verses are absent from the two oldest Greek manuscripts in our possession—Codex Alexandrinus and Codex Sinaiticus. This has led some scholars to suggest that these verses do not belong in the Bible. Fortunately, Mark 16:9-20 does not affect a single major doctrine of Christianity.

John 20:17. Jesus indicated to Mary that He had not yet ascended to the Father and would still be on earth for a time prior to the ascension. Therefore, she need not cling to Him. There would still be plenty of opportunity for them to see each other before He went to heaven.

John 20:17. In the Incarnation, Jesus was both God and man. It is thus in His humanity that Christ acknowledged the Father as "my God."

Major Themes

Recognizing the resurrected Jesus (Luke 24:31). There are a number of reasons why Jesus's followers may not have immediately recognized Him after the resurrection. They were evidently slow to believe (Luke

24:25-26; John 20:24-25), blinded by deep grief (John 20:11-15), and probably frightened (Luke 24:36-37). Also, it was dark outside (John 20:1,14-15), and He was sometimes too far away (John 21:4).

Beginning with Moses and all the Prophets (Luke 24:27). In addition to speaking of preincarnate appearances, Jesus likely touched on the more than 100 messianic prophecies in the Old Testament, such as Isaiah 7:14; Micah 5:2; and Zechariah 12:10.

Digging Deeper with Cross-References

Resurrection (John 20:1-10)—Matthew 22:31-32; John 11:25; Acts 1:21-22; 4:2,33; Romans 1:3-4; 6:5; 1 Peter 1:3; 3:21

The resurrection appearances (John 20:11-18)—Matthew 28:8-10; Mark 16:9-14; Luke 24:13-43; John 20:11-18; 1 Corinthians 15:5-7

Life Lessons

The Bible is a Jesus book (Luke 24:27). On five different occasions, Jesus claimed to be the theme of the entire Old Testament: Matthew 5:17; Luke 24:27,44; John 5:39; and Hebrews 10:7. The Old and New Testaments are inseparably connected in the person of Jesus Christ.

Burning hearts (Luke 24:32). The two disciples on the road to Emmaus said to each other, "Did not our hearts burn within us while he talked to us on the road, while he opened to us the Scriptures?" That same burning heart is the birthright of every Christian. Jesus may not be here personally teaching us, as it happened with these two disciples. But John 16:13-15 tells us that the Holy Spirit, whom Jesus sent, continues to teach us about Christ. So stay excited about the Lord.

Verses to Remember

- "The angel said to the women, 'Do not be afraid, for I know that you seek Jesus who was crucified. He is not here, for he has risen, as he said'" (Matthew 28:5).

- "O foolish ones, and slow of heart to believe all that the prophets have spoken! Was it not necessary that the Christ should suffer these things and enter into his glory?" (Luke 24:25-26).

Questions for Reflection and Discussion

1. What do you think is the significance of the statement "He has risen" for Christianity (Matthew 28:6)? What is its significance for humankind?

2. What do you make of the fact that while most of Jesus's male followers remained in hiding, His female followers were both at the cross and at the tomb (Mark 16:1; John 19:25)?

3. What difference does it make to you personally that the Jesus of Christianity is alive and well?

My Father, glory, glory, glory! With the pain of the previous few lessons regarding Jesus's suffering, the account of the resurrection is wonderful beyond description. I serve a living Jesus. Praise be to the Lord! In Jesus's name, amen.

The Great Commission

Yesterday we focused on Christ's resurrection and His appearance to some of His followers (Matthew 28:1-15; Mark 16:1-13; Luke 24:1-35; John 20:1-18). Today we zero in on Jesus's Great Commission and further appearances to His followers.

Begin by reading Matthew 28:16-20; Mark 16:14-20; Luke 24:36-53; and John 20:19–21:25. As you read, trust God to open your eyes so you can discover wondrous things from His Word (Psalm 119:18).

Chronological marker. It is AD 30, shortly after the resurrection.

Overview of Today's Scripture Reading

Matthew 28:16-20; Mark 16:14-18; Luke 24:36-49; John 20:19-23. The resurrected Jesus met with His disciples in Galilee and charged them with the Great Commission. They were to make disciples of all nations and baptize them in the name of the Father, the Son, and the Holy Spirit. Jesus—who, as God, is omnipresent—promised to be with His followers until the end of the age.

John 20:24-31. The disciples told Thomas about Christ's appearance to them. Thomas refused to believe. He demanded not only to see Christ's wounds but to actually touch them before he would believe that Christ had risen from the dead. When the risen Jesus appeared the following week, He had a special word for Thomas, inviting him to see and touch—thereby revealing that He knew what Thomas had said to the others the previous week. The evidence of eye and ear was sufficient. Thomas responded worshipfully.

John 21:1-14. Jesus then appeared to seven of His disciples at the Sea of Galilee. He ate a meal with them to prove the reality and the physicality of His resurrection.

John 21:15-19. Jesus had forgiven Peter for his threefold denial. Though Peter was still smarting, Jesus's gentle words reinstated him to full service. Jesus charged him, "Feed my sheep." Jesus also revealed to him that he would ultimately die in service to Him.

John 21:20-25. Peter was inquisitive about the Lord's plans for John and how long John would live. Jesus told Peter that this was His concern alone.

Mark 16:19-20; Luke 24:50-53. The Lord then ascended into heaven. The disciples were filled with joy. They then went out to preach the good news of salvation to any who would listen.

Today's Big Ideas

- The resurrected Jesus appeared to His gathered disciples (Luke 24:36-49; John 20:19-23), to doubting Thomas (John 20:24-29), and to seven disciples (John 21:1-14).

- The resurrected Jesus reinstated Peter (John 21:15-19).

- The resurrected Jesus gave His followers the Great Commission (Matthew 28:16-20; Mark 16:14-20).

- Jesus ascended into heaven (Luke 24:50-53).

Insights on Difficult Verses

Mark 16:16. This verse does not demand baptism for salvation. The latter part of the verse reads, "Whoever does not believe will be condemned." Unbelief, not a lack of baptism, brings damnation (1 Corinthians 1:17).

John 20:19. Just because the resurrected Jesus could get into a room with a closed door does not mean His resurrection body was immaterial. Jesus asserted that His resurrection body had flesh and bones and was not merely spiritual (Luke 24:39). Jesus can do any miracle He wants, including getting into a closed room. For Jesus, it's as easy as walking on water (John 6:16-20).

Major Themes

Three persons with one name (Matthew 28:19). This verse supports the doctrine of the Trinity. The word "name" is singular in the Greek, indicating one God. However, there are three distinct persons within the Godhead—the Father, the Son, and the Holy Spirit.

The end of the age (Matthew 28:20). This likely refers to the second coming of Christ, after which Christ will set up His millennial kingdom on earth (Revelation 20).

Digging Deeper with Cross-References

All authority is given to Jesus (Matthew 28:18)—Daniel 7:13-14; John 3:35; 13:3; 17:2; Ephesians 1:20-22; Philippians 2:9-10
The Great Commission (Matthew 28:19-20)—Mark 1:17; 16:15-20; Acts 1:8; 14:21-22; Colossians 1:28-29

Life Lessons

You can be sure you are saved (John 20:30-31). The last chapter of John's Gospel affirms, "Now Jesus did many other signs in the presence of the disciples, which are not written in this book; but these are written so that you may believe that Jesus is the Christ, the Son of God, and that by believing you may have life in his name." The word "believe" occurs almost 100 times in this Gospel. If you believe in Jesus, you're in the family of God!

Peter's restoration (John 21:15-19). Peter denied Jesus three times. But Jesus sought Peter out to restore him. In the process He asked Peter three times if he loved Him, and Peter obviously did (see verse 7). The book of Acts reveals that Peter went on to become a powerful leader in the early church.

Verses to Remember

- "Go therefore and make disciples of all nations, baptizing them in the name of the Father and of the Son and of the Holy Spirit, teaching them to observe all that I have commanded you. And behold, I am with you always, to the end of the age" (Matthew 28:19-20).

- "See my hands and my feet, that it is I myself. Touch me, and see. For a spirit does not have flesh and bones as you see that I have" (Luke 24:39).

- "He parted from them and was carried up into heaven" (Luke 24:51).

Questions for Reflection and Discussion

1. Have you ever had any doubts about the resurrection? How does John 20:24-29 help you in this regard?

2. What role do you want to play in Jesus's Great Commission?

3. Are you convinced that "Jesus is the Christ, the Son of God, and that by believing you may have life in his name" (John 20:31)?

My Father, thank You for the Gospel accounts, which inform me of the coming of Jesus Christ into the world. I will next study the book of Acts, where I will learn more about the activities of the risen Christ and the Holy Spirit, whom Christ sent. In Jesus's name, amen.

CHAPTER 4

The Church Is Born and the Gospel Spreads

DAY 47

Jesus Ascends and the Holy Spirit Descends

In yesterday's lesson we explored Jesus's resurrection appearances (Matthew 28:16-20; Mark 16:14-20; Luke 24:36-53; John 20:19–21:25). Now we give consideration to Jesus's ascension into heaven and the descent of the Holy Spirit on believers.

Begin by reading Acts 1–3. As you read, allow the Word of God to bring revival to your soul (Psalm 119:25,93,107).

Chronological marker. Christ's ascension in Acts 1 occurred on Thursday, May 14, AD 30. The Day of Pentecost was May 24, AD 30.

Introduction to Acts

Author: Luke, a close companion of the apostle Paul. The book of Acts may be considered part 2 of Luke's Gospel.

Date: written in AD 61, about a year after Luke wrote his Gospel

Fast facts:

- Luke's Gospel contains an orderly account of the accomplishments of Jesus during His earthly life. The book of Acts contains an orderly account of the resurrected Jesus's accomplishments, through the Holy Spirit, in the 30 years following His resurrection and ascension.

- The book chronicles how Christianity miraculously spread

among both Jews and Gentiles around the northern Mediterranean, including Samaria (Acts 8:5-25); Phoenicia, Cyprus, and Antioch (9:32–12:25); Phrygia and Galatia (13:1–15:35), Macedonia (15:36–21:16); and Rome (21:17–22:29).

- Acts is a book of transitions—from Judaism to Christianity, from law to grace, and from Jews alone as the people of God to Jews and Gentiles as the people of God.

Key words in Acts (and the number of times they appear):

Holy Spirit (42)	witness (27)
believe (38)	church (24)
pray/prayer (32)	persecution/affliction (21)
apostle (30)	good news/gospel (17)
baptize/baptism (27)	repent/repentance (11)

Overview of Today's Scripture Reading

Acts 1–2. Acts picks up where the Gospels left off. The Gospel accounts portray Jesus as appearing to His followers to prove His resurrection, and the book of Acts records that these appearances lasted 40 days (1:3).

The risen Lord instructed His followers to stay in Jerusalem so that the promise concerning the Holy Spirit would be fulfilled. It occurred a week and a half later, and the disciples became supernaturally empowered by the Holy Spirit.

Filled with new courage, the disciples boldly proclaimed the message of the resurrected Lord. Peter's sermon, focusing largely on Jesus's resurrection, led to 3000 conversions. The Christian church was born that day.

Acts 3. A lame man was instantly healed at Peter's command, thereby adding further credence to the truth that the divine Messiah, Jesus Christ, was now risen and exercising His omnipotence in mighty miracles through the apostles. Peter delivered another sermon to the nation of Israel, calling on the nation to repent of its rejection of Jesus Christ. Had the nation repented, times of restoration and renewal would have come. But Peter's words fell on deaf ears.

Today's Big Ideas

- Jesus ascended into heaven (1:6-11).
- The Holy Spirit fell on believers on the Day of Pentecost (2:1-13).
- Peter preached a sermon on the Day of Pentecost (2:14-41).

Insights on Difficult Verses

Acts 2:38. The Greek text can be understood in two different ways: (1) Repent and be baptized *in order to obtain* the remission of sins, or (2) repent and be baptized because your sins *have been remitted.* (I believe the second option is correct.)

Acts 3:20-21. This may refer to either the new heavens and new earth (Revelation 21:1-5) or to Israel's restoration (Isaiah 40:9-11; Jeremiah 32:42-44).

Major Themes

Apostles (Acts 1:2). The apostles were chosen messengers of Christ, handpicked by the Lord (Matthew 10:1-4; Acts 1:26). They were the special recipients of God's self-revelation (1 Corinthians 2:13). They recognized their divine authority (1 Corinthians 7:10; 11:23) and were authenticated by miracles (Acts 2:43; 3:3-11; 5:12; 9:32-42; 20:6-12).

Names and titles mean something (Acts 3:15). In Bible times, knowing a person's title amounted to knowing his character. Jesus, the Author of life, is the source of life (John 1:4; 11:15; 14:6).

Digging Deeper with Cross-References

The promise of His coming (Acts 1:9-11)—1 Thessalonians 3:13; 2 Thessalonians 1:6-10; 2:8; 1 Peter 4:12-13; 2 Peter 3:1-14; Jude 14-15; Revelation 19:11–20:6

Ministries of the Holy Spirit (Acts 1:8)—John 16:8-15; Romans 8:26; 12:6-8; 1 Corinthians 2:9–3:2; 6:19; 12:13; Galatians 5:22-23; Ephesians 4:30; 5:18; Titus 3:5; 2 Peter 1:21

Life Lessons

Power from the Holy Spirit (Acts 1:8). The indwelling presence of the Holy Spirit and His empowerment enables Christ's followers to be effective witnesses (Acts 2:4; 1 Corinthians 6:19-20; Ephesians 3:16,20). Ephesians 5:18 instructs that we are to be perpetually filled with the Holy Spirit—controlled by Him.

Prayer and God's sovereignty (Acts 1:12-17). Here we witness both human prayer (Acts 1:14) and God's sovereign actions (Acts 1:16). God is sovereign over all things (Ephesians 1:18-23), but He has sovereignly ordained to accomplish certain things only as a result of prayer. Therefore, we should always pray (Philippians 4:6; James 4:2).

Verses to Remember

- "You will receive power when the Holy Spirit has come upon you, and you will be my witnesses in Jerusalem and in all Judea and Samaria, and to the end of the earth" (Acts 1:8).

- "All who believed were together and had all things in common. And they were selling their possessions and belongings and distributing the proceeds to all, as any had need" (Acts 2:44-45).

Questions for Reflection and Discussion

1. Would you describe yourself as a spirit-filled Christian? How do you know whether you are?

2. Do you think miracles still happen today?

3. Does Acts 1–3 make you want to learn more about the Holy Spirit?

My Father, it seems that the Holy Spirit was so real and so powerful among the Christians in the first century. As I study the book of Acts, please teach me what You want me to know about the Holy Spirit and His various ministries. In Jesus's name, amen.

Day 48

The Ministry of the Apostles

Yesterday we considered Jesus's ascension into heaven and the descent of the Holy Spirit on believers (Acts 1–3). Today we will focus on the early activities of the apostles and the resistance they encountered.

Begin by reading Acts 4–7. As you read, never forget that God urges you to quickly obey His Word in all things (Psalm 119:60).

Chronological marker. The events in today's Scripture reading span AD 30–35.

Overview of Today's Scripture Reading

Acts 4. The Jewish Sanhedrin interrogated Peter and John regarding a man's healing. Peter and John claimed the resurrected Christ healed the man, but this aggravated the Sadducees because they denied the doctrine of the resurrection. There was great concern that this man's healing would point even more people to Jesus Christ and give the Christian movement further momentum. The Sanhedrin warned them to speak no further in Jesus's name. Peter and John replied that they were compelled to obey God rather than men. After Peter and John were released, the believers prayed for continued boldness.

Acts 5. Ananias and Sapphira sold some land and pretended to give all the money to meet needs in the church, but they secretly kept some of the money. They lied to the Spirit and deceived the church community. For this they forfeited their lives—a temporal judgment that caused the church to fear God. At this early stage in the church, such fear of God was a healthy thing.

Meanwhile the apostles performed more and more signs, and the church continued to grow. The apostles were arrested and interrogated.

They repeated the message Peter and John had given earlier—that they must obey God rather than men. A Pharisee named Gamaliel convinced the Sanhedrin to back down for a time in order to evaluate whether what was taking place was of God.

Acts 6:1-7. Not all the needs were being met within the church, particularly among Greek-speaking widows. Deacons were appointed to distribute food to them. Notice that all seven men had Greek names.

Acts 6:8–7:60. Stephen was a powerful preacher and an able debater who performed convincing signs and wonders among the people. He was framed for blasphemy and arrested. He ably defended himself before the Sanhedrin with a lengthy speech that exalted Jesus as the true Messiah. The Jewish leaders responded by stoning him to death.

Today's Big Ideas

- The early believers had everything in common (4:32-37).
- The apostles did signs and wonders among the people (5:12-16).
- The apostles were arrested and freed (5:17-42).
- Stephen was seized, gave a powerful speech, and was stoned to death (6:8–7:60).

Insights on Difficult Verses

Acts 4:12. Some today claim it is too narrow-minded to say that Jesus is the only way of salvation. However, this is the consistent teaching of Scripture. Jesus asserted, "I am the way, and the truth, and the life. No one comes to the Father except through me" (John 14:6). Paul said, "There is one God, and there is one mediator between God and men, the man Christ Jesus" (1 Timothy 2:5).

Acts 5:3-4. The Holy Spirit is God. In this passage, lying to the Holy Spirit is equivalent to lying to God. The Holy Spirit, as God, is everywhere-present (Psalm 139:7), all-knowing (1 Corinthians 2:10), all-powerful (Romans 15:19), eternal (Hebrews 9:14), and of course, holy (John 16:7-14).

Major Themes

The resurrection of Christ (Acts 4:33). Christ's resurrection is the foundation stone of Christianity. Paul said, "If Christ has not been raised, your faith is futile" (1 Corinthians 15:17). Jesus proved His resurrection by making many appearances to many people over many days (Acts 1:3; see 1 Corinthians 15:6).

The significance of signs (Acts 5:12). The Greek word *semeion* ("sign") refers to a miracle with a message. A sign is a miracle that attests to something. The apostles' signs (miracles) attested that they were genuine messengers of God (Hebrews 2:3-4).

Digging Deeper with Cross-References

God answers the prayers of His people (Acts 4:23-31)—Psalms 50:15; 91:15; 99:6; 118:5; 138:3; Isaiah 30:19; 58:9; 65:24; Jeremiah 29:12; Daniel 9:21-23; 10:12; Matthew 7:7

The glory of God (Acts 7:55)—Exodus 24:17; 40:34; 1 Kings 8:11; Psalm 19:1-4; Isaiah 48:11; Ezekiel 10:4; Luke 2:9; 2 Corinthians 3:18

Life Lessons

Standing strong in the face of persecution (Acts 5:41). The apostles suffered for their witness of Christ. Scripture reveals that the godly will suffer persecution (2 Timothy 3:12). We should not be surprised if the world hates us (1 John 3:13). Those persecuted for righteousness are blessed (Matthew 5:10-11). We, too, ought to rejoice in being counted worthy to suffer.

The body is buried, and the spirit is in heaven (Acts 7:59). When Stephen was being stoned to death, he prayed, "Lord Jesus, receive my spirit." At the moment of the Christian's death, the spirit departs the body and goes to be with the Lord. Second Corinthians 5:8 affirms, "We would rather be away from the body and at home with the Lord" (see Philippians 1:23).

Verses to Remember

- "There is salvation in no one else, for there is no other name

under heaven given among men by which we must be saved"
(Acts 4:12).

- "Whether it is right in the sight of God to listen to you rather
  than to God, you must judge, for we cannot but speak of what
  we have seen and heard" (Acts 4:19).

Questions for Reflection and Discussion

1. Like the first-century Pharisees and Sadducees, many today
   reject Jesus despite the powerful evidence that supports the
   veracity of the Bible. Why do you think this is so?

2. Have you ever had to disobey humans in order to obey God?

3. Have you ever been persecuted as a Christian? What have you
   learned in this lesson that can help you to better endure such
   persecution?

*My Father, many people today think Christians are narrow-minded in
believing that Jesus is the only way of salvation. They claim we are arro-
gant. I fear that too many Christians are now shying away from telling the
truth on this matter for fear of offense. Lord, please embolden me. In Jesus's
name, amen.*

DAY 49

Saul's Conversion

Yesterday we gave attention to the apostles' early activities and the resistance they encountered (Acts 4–7). Today we turn our attention to such momentous events as Saul's conversion and Peter's encounter with Cornelius.

Begin by reading Acts 8–11. As you read, ask God to help you understand His Word (Psalm 119:73).

Chronological marker. The events in this lesson took place from AD 36 to the early 40s.

Overview of Today's Scripture Reading

Acts 8. The good news of the gospel was preached to the Samaritans, who were hated by the Jews. Many Samaritans became believers. Through the apostles, the Holy Spirit was imparted to these new members of the body of Christ, just as the Spirit had earlier been imparted to Jewish believers in Christ on the day of Pentecost. All are one in Christ.

Acts 9. Soon after this, God brought Saul to faith in Christ. After his conversion, he quickly became a powerful and bold witness to Jesus Christ. (Saul later started using the Greco-Roman version of his name, Paul [Acts 13:9]—a wise move because he became an apostle to the Gentiles.) Meanwhile, the apostles continued to perform mighty miracles in attesting to the truth about Jesus (verses 32-43).

Acts 10:1–11:18. Meanwhile, the Lord taught the apostle Peter that the barrier between Jews and Gentiles had been brought down. The Gentiles were thus welcome to God's salvation. Peter initially met with resistance from other church leaders and believers on this. But after explaining his vision—as well as the Holy Spirit's falling on the Gentiles—it was clear God Himself was behind all of this.

Acts 11:19-30. The persecution against the church worsened. There was no sign of it letting up. Things were getting intense. Still, the church continued to explode throughout the Roman Empire. Despite the Roman sword being against the church's throat, the church grew...and grew...and grew. This in itself was a mighty miracle of God.

Today's Big Ideas

- Saul became a believer, proclaimed Jesus, and was persecuted (9).

- Peter met with the household of Cornelius, a Gentile, to explain the gospel (10).

- Peter reported to the church about Gentile conversions (11:18).

Insights on Difficult Verses

Acts 8:26. God's angels are sometimes used in evangelism. In this case an angel guided the evangelist Philip to a sinner—an Ethiopian treasurer. In another case an angel guided a sinner (Cornelius) to an evangelist (Peter) (Acts 10:1-8). God's motivation: He is "not wishing that any should perish, but that all should reach repentance" (2 Peter 3:9).

Acts 11:26. The "-ian" ending in the word "Christian" literally means "belonging to the party of." We might loosely translate the term Christian, "those belonging to Christ," "Christ-ones," or perhaps "Christpeople." They are ones who follow the Christ. The people of Antioch likely called the followers of Jesus "Christians" as a derogatory term. But Jesus's followers eventually came to use the term as a badge of honor. The collective movement of Christians soon came to be known as Christianity.

Major Themes

Burial in Bible times (Acts 8:2). As soon as Stephen died, he was immediately buried. Funerals in biblical times were performed very quickly. This is for the practical reason that the hot climate would rapidly cause decay and odor.

Saul's transformation (Acts 9:1-2). Years after becoming a Christian, Paul (formerly Saul) acknowledged to God, "When the blood of Stephen your witness was being shed, I myself was standing by and approving and watching over the garments of those who killed him" (22:20). He later acknowledged, "I not only locked up many of the saints in prison after receiving authority from the chief priests, but when they were put to death I cast my vote against them" (26:10). The greatest persecutor of the church became the greatest missionary of the church.

Digging Deeper with Cross-References

Martyrdom (Acts 8:1-3)—Matthew 10:21,39; Acts 21:13; 1 Corinthians 13:3; Revelation 6:9; 11:7; 16:6; 20:4

Magic (Acts 8:9-25)—Isaiah 47:12; Ezekiel 13:18; Revelation 9:21

Gentile conversions (Acts 10)—Acts 11:1; 13:48; 15:7; 18:6; 28:28; Romans 9:24; 15:9; Galatians 3:14; Revelation 11:15; 15:4

Life Lessons

The danger of magic (Acts 8:9-25). Magic was used in biblical times for selfish purposes, to harness personal power. God condemns all forms of occultism, including magic (Exodus 22:18; Leviticus 19:31; Deuteronomy 18:9-13; Ezekiel 13:18,20; Acts 19:19-20; Galatians 5:20; Revelation 9:21; 21:8).

Fearing God (Acts 10:35). Christians are called to live in reverent fear of God (1 Samuel 12:14,24; 2 Chronicles 19:9; 1 Peter 1:17; 2:17). Fear of the Lord motivates one to be obedient to God (Deuteronomy 5:29; Ecclesiastes 12:13) and to serve Him (Deuteronomy 6:13). It also motivates one to avoid evil (Proverbs 3:7; 8:13; 16:6). Fear of the Lord is true wisdom (Job 28:28; Psalm 111:10) and the beginning of knowledge (Proverbs 1:7).

Verses to Remember

- "The church throughout all Judea and Galilee and Samaria had peace and was being built up. And walking in the fear of the Lord and in the comfort of the Holy Spirit, it multiplied" (Acts 9:31).

- "Peter opened his mouth and said: 'Truly I understand that God shows no partiality, but in every nation anyone who fears him and does what is right is acceptable to him'" (Acts 10:34-35).

- "To the Gentiles also God has granted repentance that leads to life" (Acts 11:18).

- "In Antioch the disciples were first called Christians" (Acts 11:26).

Questions for Reflection and Discussion

1. Do you think you sufficiently fear God?

2. Do you think believers can be forgiven after committing a serious sin (Acts 8:18-24)? What is the basis for your answer?

3. Do you think your conversion to Christ has radically changed your life? Why or why not?

My Father, Your Word says that two key outgrowths of fearing You are obedience and avoiding evil. Sometimes I fail in these areas. I am not consistent. Please enable me by Your Spirit to reverence You the way I'm supposed to. In Jesus's name, amen.

DAY 50

Paul and Barnabas Spread the Gospel

In the previous lesson we discussed such momentous events as Saul's conversion and Peter's encounter with Cornelius (Acts 8–11). Today we explore the ministry of Paul and Barnabas and consider the deliberations of the Jerusalem Council.

Begin by reading Acts 12–15:35. As you read, remember that God's Word is the true source of hope (Psalm 119:81).

Chronological marker. This lesson considers events that occurred in AD 44–49.

Overview of Today's Scripture Reading

Acts 12. Herod Agrippa I sought to destroy the infant church (12:1). The apostles became targets of persecution. James (the brother of John) was executed, and Peter was thrown in jail. The church immediately prayed for Peter's deliverance, and God sent an angel to lead Peter out of prison. Peter then went to the house of John Mark's mother and knocked on the door. Disbelief eventually gave way to relief as those within the house realized that Peter really had returned safely. The guards who were assigned to watch over Peter were executed at Herod's command. Meanwhile, Paul and Barnabas continued their work as traveling missionaries.

Acts 13–14. Paul and Barnabas were officially set apart by the Holy Spirit for what would be Paul's first missionary tour. The church fasted and prayed and laid hands on them. Paul and Barnabas were accompanied by John Mark, though John Mark would leave the team early in the mission. The team ended up ministering in Cyprus, Pisidian Antioch, Iconium, and Lystra (where Paul was stoned). The team finally returned to Syrian Antioch.

Note that in each city, Paul first preached at the local Jewish synagogue, where he typically met with resistance and sometimes attempts on his life. After speaking to the Jews, he spoke to the Gentiles in each city.

Acts 15. The Jerusalem Council was convened to consider whether Gentile converts should be required to adopt the ceremonial requirements of Judaism in order to become Christians. James (half-brother of Jesus and president of the council) discouraged the others from burdening the Gentile converts with anything beyond a few simple points. The apostles and elders agreed that Gentiles did not have to get circumcised.

Today's Big Ideas

- An angel broke Peter out of jail (12:6-20).

- Herod gave a self-exalting speech and was subsequently executed by an angel (12:20-25).

- Paul and Barnabas spread the gospel in various cities (13:4–14:28).

- The Jerusalem Council declared that Gentile believers did not need to be circumcised (15:1-35).

Insights on Difficult Verses

Acts 15:28-29. Some cults claim this passage prohibits blood transfusions, arguing that ingesting blood by the mouth is no different from ingesting blood intravenously. Of course, eating blood is not the same as a blood transfusion. A transfusion treats blood not with disrespect but with reverence. A transfusion replenishes the supply of essential, life-sustaining fluid that has in some way been drained away or has become incapable of performing its God-intended tasks in the body. A transfusion uses blood for the same purpose God intended—as a life-giving agent in the bloodstream.

Major Themes

God and judgment (Acts 12:21-23). The God of love, grace, and mercy is also a God of judgment and wrath in the face of unrepentant sin. Three examples: Judgment fell on the Jews for rejecting Christ (Matthew 21:43), on Ananias and Sapphira for lying to God (Acts 5), and on Herod (through an angel) for self-exalting pride.

Angels execute judgments (Acts 12:22-23). Angels not only announce God's impending judgments but also sometimes execute them. Herod's experience is a prime example. In the future tribulation period, angels will unleash the seven trumpet judgments (Revelation 8).

Digging Deeper with Cross-References

Angels used in judgment (Acts 12:23)—Numbers 22:22; Judges 5:23; 2 Samuel 24:16; 2 Kings 19:35; 1 Chronicles 21:15; 2 Chronicles 32:21; Psalms 35:5; 78:49; Isaiah 37:36

Men worshipped (Acts 12:22)—Acts 14:11; 28:6; compare with Exodus 20:1-10; Romans 1:25

Give God glory (Acts 12:23)—Joshua 7:19; Isaiah 24:15; Jeremiah 13:16; Revelation 14:7

Life Lessons

Guardian angels for Christians (Acts 12:15). Acts 12:15 refers to Peter's angel. Does this mean each Christian has his or her own private guardian angel? Maybe. But other verses reveal that multiple angels watch over us. For example, Psalm 91:9-11 says, "Because you have made the LORD your dwelling place...he will command his angels concerning you to guard you in all your ways" (see also 2 Kings 6:17; Matthew 26:53; Luke 16:22). Take joy in God's provision of angels among us!

Strategic missionary work (Acts 13–14). Paul went on three missionary tours. One of Paul's strategies was to visit major Roman capitals on existing trade routes, a strategy that resulted in the gospel spreading out to other areas through these routes. You and I can be missionaries in our neighborhoods, at our workplaces, and even on our own doorsteps when cultists ring the doorbell (1 Peter 3:15).

Verses to Remember

- "Let it be known to you therefore, brothers, that through this man forgiveness of sins is proclaimed to you, and by him everyone who believes is freed from everything from which you could not be freed by the law of Moses" (Acts 13:38).

- "Through many tribulations we must enter the kingdom of God" (Acts 14:22).

Questions for Reflection and Discussion

1. Why do you suppose persecution and martyrdom couldn't slow the growth of the Christian church?

2. Do you think Christians should fast today (Acts 13:2-3; 14:23)? Why or why not?

3. Why do you suppose so many more Gentiles responded to the gospel than Jews in the book of Acts?

My Father, it is sobering to ponder that You are not just a God of love but also a God of judgment. Your Word teaches that I will one day stand before the judgment seat of Christ to have my life evaluated and either receive or lose rewards. I want to live now in view of then. Please help me keep my priorities right. In Jesus's name, amen.

DAY 51

Doing God's Word

Yesterday we focused on the ministry of Paul and Barnabas and the deliberations of the Jerusalem Council (Acts 12–15:35). Today we zero in on tests of our faith and practical aspects of doing what God's Word says.

Begin by reading through James. As you read, keep in mind that God desires you not only to hear His Word but also to do it (James 1:22).

Chronological marker. The Jerusalem Council (which we studied yesterday) met about AD 49. The book of James was also written in AD 49. It is therefore appropriate that we study the book of James at this juncture.

Introduction to James

Author: James

Fast facts:

- James was the oldest half brother of Jesus and the leader of the Jerusalem church (Acts 12:17; Galatians 2:9).

- James was writing to Jewish Christians ("the twelve tribes"—1:1), who were in danger of giving nothing but lip service to Jesus. This situation may have arisen as a result of the persecution of Herod Agrippa I (Acts 12). Perhaps some of these Jewish Christians had become gun-shy about living the Christian life.

- James's intent, therefore, is to distinguish true faith from false faith. He shows that true faith results in outward works.

Key words in James (and the number of times they appear):
deeds/works (15)
faith (15)
law (10)
judge/judgment (8)
doer (4)

Overview of Today's Scripture Reading

James 1:1-18. Everyone has trials and temptations. These constitute tests of our faith (verses 2-12). James argued that God allows us to encounter these trials because they mature our faith and increase our patient endurance as we depend upon God.

James 1:19–5:6. James stressed the importance of righteous conduct that grows out of a living faith. It is not enough to be a hearer of God's Word; one must be a doer of God's Word (1:22-25). Faith without works is dead (2:14-26), meaning that one's faith in Christ must show itself in the way one lives.

True faith not only causes one to obey the Word of God (1:19-27) but also shows itself in the way one treats other people. For example, a person of faith does not discriminate against others (2:1-13). Nor does a person of faith misuse his or her tongue with others (3:1-12). A person of true faith grows in wisdom (3:13-18), is humble in his or her interactions, avoids lust and licentious living (4:1-12), and openly depends on and submits to God (4:13–5:6).

James 5:7-20. James closes by encouraging readers to patiently endure their sufferings because the Lord is coming (verses 7-12). Regardless of the trials that inevitably surface in life, believers can rest assured that God has a purpose for allowing them.

Today's Big Ideas

- Be joyful whenever your faith is tested (1:1-18).
- Be a doer of God's Word, not just a hearer (1:19-27).

- Faith without works is dead (2:14-26).
- Faith shows itself in concrete ways (3–5).

Insights on Difficult Verses

James 2:16-17. A person is saved by faith alone, but not by a faith that is alone. Genuine faith will always result in good works in the saved person's life.

James 2:21. James is not talking in this verse about justification before God but rather justification before men. We know this to be true because James stressed that we should "show" (verse 18) our faith (compare with verse 23).

Major Themes

James draws from Jesus. James drew much of his material from his half brother, Jesus. This includes James's words about humility (4:10; see Matthew 5:5), judging (4:11-12; see Matthew 7:1), and swearing (5:12; see Matthew 5:34-37).

Trials can benefit us. James said our trials can produce steadfastness in us (1:3). Afflictions can also motivate us to obey God's Word (Psalm 119:67). As well, trials that come our way as a form of divine discipline produce in us the "peaceful fruit of righteousness" (Hebrews 12:11).

Digging Deeper with Cross-References

Faith (James 2:14,17-18)—Luke 17:5; 18:8; Romans 10:17; 14:23; 2 Corinthians 5:7; Galatians 5:6; 1 Timothy 1:5; Hebrews 11:1,39; 1 John 5:4

Good works (James 2:14,17)—Matthew 5:16; Colossians 1:10; 1 Timothy 6:18; Titus 2:7,14; 3:8; Hebrews 10:24; 1 Peter 2:12

Life Lessons

Faith manifests itself. James's big point is that while faith alone saves a person, that faith ought to show itself in the way one lives life. In James's theology, faith has very practical effects. Our faith should impact how we relate to God, how we relate to other people, our sense of social justice, and our commitment to personal ethics.

Being a doer of God's Word. It is all too easy to be a mere hearer of God's Word without letting it change the way we live every day. May it never be, James says (1:19-27). We ought to approach Scripture with a predetermined attitude of obedience. We should resolve that whatever we discover in God's Word, we will do it (Matthew 4:20; 7:24; 9:9; 21:6; 26:19; Luke 5:5; 6:47; John 2:7).

Verses to Remember

- "Count it all joy, my brothers, when you meet trials of various kinds, for you know that the testing of your faith produces steadfastness" (James 1:2).

- "Be doers of the word, and not hearers only, deceiving yourselves" (James 1:22).

- "Faith by itself, if it does not have works, is dead" (James 2:17).

Questions for Reflection and Discussion

1. The teaching that we are to be doers of God's Word and not just hearers can be very convicting. How do you assess yourself in this regard?

2. Have you been injured recently by someone's harsh tongue? Have you injured anyone recently with your tongue?

3. What is your attitude toward the poor?

My Father, I desire to be a doer of Your Word and not just a hearer. I don't want to be selective in my obedience to You. By Your divine enabling, I want to obey You in my public life as well as in my private life. In Jesus's name, amen.

Day 52

The True Gospel

In yesterday's lesson we explored tests of our faith, being a doer of God's Word, and practical applications of doing what God's Word says (James). Now we give consideration to the true gospel—more specifically, to justification and how it relates to grace versus the law.

Begin by reading Galatians 1–3. As you read, remember that great spiritual wisdom comes from studying God's Word (Psalm 119:98-104).

Chronological marker. The Jerusalem Council met in AD 49 (see Acts 15). The book of James—the focus of our previous lesson—was written in AD 49. It is therefore appropriate that we now examine Galatians, written in AD 50.

Introduction to Galatians

Author: the apostle Paul

Fast facts:

- Judaizers who had infiltrated some of Paul's congregations claimed Paul made the gospel more appealing to Gentiles by removing Jewish legal requirements. They taught that after believing in Christ, Gentiles must take an additional step and become Jews through circumcision, eat only the right kinds of foods, and participate in certain Jewish feast days (Acts 15:24; 20:29-30).

- This added works to grace, and Paul would not have it (4:20).

- Salvation is a gift that is received solely by faith in Christ (3:6-9). Paul warned that anyone who delivered a different gospel (including a gospel from Judaizers) was accursed before God (1:8).

Key words in Galatians (and the number of times they appear):

Christ (41)   good news/gospel (13)
law (33)   circumcise/circumcision (13)
believe/faith (26)   grace (7)
spirit (18)

Overview of Today's Scripture Reading

Galatians 1:1-10. Paul begins by affirming he is an apostle by divine appointment (1:1-5). Apparently the Judaizers who had infiltrated the church at Galatia challenged his apostleship. Paul expressed dismay because the Galatians had departed from the gospel of grace (1:6-10) and had given some credence to the false teachings of the Judaizers.

Galatians 1:11–2:21. Because Paul was an apostle by divine appointment, his gospel of justification—a gospel in which the believing sinner is made right with God by grace through faith—came not from men but from God (1:11-24). This message of justification was backed by the other apostles in Jerusalem (2:1-10). However, Paul had to publicly correct Peter on the issue of law versus grace (2:11-21).

Galatians 3. Paul argued that the Galatians must continue their spiritual journey the way they began it—by faith (3:1-5). Abraham was justified by faith, as are all believers (3:6-9). Believers have been redeemed from the curse of the law (3:10-18). The law was never intended to save people but rather to drive them to faith (3:19-22). Therefore the teachings of the Judaizers are false, man-made teachings. The Judaizers' gospel brings bondage, but the true gospel of grace brings liberty and freedom.

Today's Big Ideas

- Do not fall for a false gospel of works (1:6-10).
- We are justified by faith (2:15-21).
- The righteous shall live by faith (3:10-14).

Insights on Difficult Verses

Galatians 1:8. Those who bring a different gospel are "accursed." This comes from the Greek word *anathema*, which refers to devoting the offending person to eternal hell (Romans 9:3; 1 Corinthians 12:3; 16:22).

Galatians 1:20. Paul's declaration "I do not lie" is a clear indication that the Judaizers accused Paul of being a liar.

Major Themes

Good news (Galatians 1:6). The word "gospel" means "good news." By trusting in Christ, people are justified (Romans 3:24), reconciled to God (2 Corinthians 5:19), forgiven of sins (Colossians 2:14), and adopted into God's family (Romans 8:14). That's very good news!

Justification (Galatians 2:16). The word "justification" is a legal term. Negatively, the word means that one is forever pronounced not guilty before God. Positively, the word means that one is forever pronounced righteous (Romans 3:20,23-24,28).

Digging Deeper with Cross-References

Paul's apostleship (Galatians 1:11–2:10)—Romans 1:1; 11:13; 1 Corinthians 9:1; 15:9; 2 Corinthians 1:1; 11:5; Ephesians 1:1; Colossians 1:1; 1 Timothy 1:1; 2 Timothy 1:1

Justification (Galatians 2:15-21)—Genesis 15:6; Acts 13:39; Romans 3:20,23-24,28; 5:1; 1 Corinthians 6:11 (see also Habakkuk 2:4; Galatians 3:6; Philippians 3:9; Hebrews 10:38; 11:4)

Life Lessons

The danger of a false gospel (Galatians 1:8). The false gospel of which Paul spoke was a gospel of legalism that added works to faith. Don't ever fall into the trap of thinking that you need to do this or that to ensure your salvation. You are saved by grace alone through faith alone (see Ephesians 2:8-9).

Grace and peace (Galatians 1:3). Paul often greeted the recipients of his letters with "Grace to you and peace from God our Father and the Lord Jesus Christ." These are important words for people engulfed in legalism (such as the Galatians). The word "grace" literally means "unmerited favor." It is because of God's unmerited favor that human beings can have peace with God (Romans 5:1-2).

Verses to Remember

- "Even if we or an angel from heaven should preach to you a gospel contrary to the one we preached to you, let him be accursed" (Galatians 1:8).

- "I have been crucified with Christ. It is no longer I who live, but Christ who lives in me. And the life I now live in the flesh I live by faith in the Son of God, who loved me and gave himself for me" (Galatians 2:20).

Questions for Reflection and Discussion

1. What false gospels are common today?

2. Have you pondered the significance of Paul's statement, "It is no longer I who live, but Christ who lives in me"? In what ways is this verse liberating?

3. Can you think of at least three ways that the gospel is good news?

My Father, how I rejoice that I have believed the true gospel, which brings salvation. How I rejoice that Christ lives in me. How I rejoice at the grace and peace that have been bestowed on me from heaven. I am grateful. In Jesus's name, amen.

DAY 53

Freed from the Yoke of Slavery

Yesterday we considered justification, and how it relates to grace versus the law (Galatians 1–3). Today we will focus on the nature of Christian liberty.

Begin by reading Galatians 4–6. As you read, remember that reading Scripture can strengthen your faith in God (Romans 10:17).

Chronological marker. Paul wrote Galatians in AD 50.

Overview of Today's Scripture Reading

Galatians 4. Believers are no longer bound by the law (4:1-7). We are not slaves to the law, but have been adopted into God's family as sons. For this reason, we now have intimacy with God. We must not forget that the law conflicts with the freedom we have in Christ (4:8-31).

Paul affirmed that the Galatians started out just fine. They trusted in the gospel of grace. But somehow, they became ensnared by the idea that they must observe certain Jewish festivals to please God. Paul instructed them to put this kind of thinking out of their minds.

Paul used an allegory to illustrate his point. Ishmael represents a works-based solution to the problem of Sarah's barrenness. Isaac represents God's provision of a son based on His unconditional promise to Abraham. Hagar (Ishmael's mother) represents the Law of Moses and corresponds to the Jerusalem of Paul's day. Sarah (Isaac's mother) represents freedom and liberty. Now, just as Sarah urged Abraham to drive out Ishmael, so the Galatians ought to drive out the works-based Law and hold on to God's unconditional grace. After all, Paul says, "We are not children of the slave but of the free woman" (4:31).

229

Galatians 5:1–6:10. The greatest enemy to Christian liberty is legalism (5:1-12). Paul did not want his readers to fall from grace (seeking justification by the law). Paul expressed confidence that his readers would not do this.

Of course, believers must also be cautious not to fall into lawlessness (5:13–6:10). Christians are set free not only from bondage to the law but also from bondage to sin. Our liberty in Christ should never be used as an excuse to engage in sin.

Paul emphasized the importance of walking in the Spirit—that is, perpetually depending on the Holy Spirit. This enables believers to enjoy victory over sin and have the fruit of the Spirit grow in their lives.

Galatians 6:11-18. The only thing that matters is that Christians are new creations in Jesus Christ. Engaging in legalistic works, such as circumcision, counts for nothing. Therefore the Galatians should not fall for the false teachings of the Judaizers.

Today's Big Ideas

- Paul has great concern for the Galatians (4:8-20).

- Christ has set us free from all yokes of slavery (5:1-15).

- Dependence on the Holy Spirit leads to victory over the flesh and the manifestation of the fruit of the Spirit in our lives (5:16-26).

Insights on Difficult Verses

Galatians 4:3. "The elementary principles of the world" apparently refers to the bondage of man-made legalistic practices.

Galatians 4:4. "The fullness of time" refers to God's sovereign timetable in the outworking of His divine plan of salvation.

Galatians 4:10. "Days and months and seasons and years" refers to the festivals of the Jewish calendar.

Galatians 5:2. By "no advantage," Paul means that law and grace do not mix. It's one or the other.

Major Themes

"Abba! Father!" (Galatians 4:6). Christians are privileged to call God Abba and Father. "Abba" is an Aramaic term of affection and intimacy—similar to the English word "daddy" or "papa." Formerly we were alienated from God. But now, through Jesus, we enjoy great intimacy with God.

The fruit of the Holy Spirit (Galatians 5:22-23). As we depend on the Spirit, He produces fruit in our lives. The qualities listed here actually provide an accurate profile of Jesus Himself. The character of our Lord is reproduced in our lives as we daily walk in dependence on the Spirit.

Digging Deeper with Cross-References

Sexual immorality (Galatians 5:19)—Acts 15:20; 1 Corinthians 5:9-10; 10:8; Colossians 3:5; 1 Thessalonians 4:3; 2 Peter 2:14; Jude 7

Self-deception (Galatians 6:3)—Psalm 36:2; Isaiah 44:20; James 1:22,26; 1 John 1:8

Life Lessons

Walking in dependence on the Holy Spirit (Galatians 5:16). We can have victory over sin by walking in dependence on the Holy Spirit. The word "walk" in this verse is a present-tense verb, indicating continuing action. We are to persistently and continually walk in dependence on the Holy Spirit. As we do this, we will live in a way that is pleasing to God.

Bear one another's burdens (Galatians 6:2). We were never intended to traverse this life alone. We not only need God, we also need each other. Do you know someone who needs some help? Why not reach out? A powerful motivation is found in Christ's Golden Rule: "Whatever you wish that others would do to you, do also to them" (Matthew 7:12).

Verses to Remember

- "For freedom Christ has set us free; stand firm therefore, and do not submit again to a yoke of slavery" (Galatians 5:1).

- "Walk by the Spirit, and you will not gratify the desires of the flesh. For the desires of the flesh are against the Spirit, and the desires of the Spirit are against the flesh, for these are opposed to each other, to keep you from doing the things you want to do" (Galatians 5:16-17).

- "The fruit of the Spirit is love, joy, peace, patience, kindness, goodness, faithfulness, gentleness, self-control; against such things there is no law" (Galatians 5:22-23).

Questions for Reflection and Discussion

1. Are there any "yokes of slavery" in your life right now?

2. Do you ever find yourself trying to resist fleshly temptations in your own strength?

3. How do you think one actually goes about walking in the Spirit?

My Father, I praise You for the ministry of the Holy Spirit in my life. I thank You that He empowers me to overcome sin. I thank You that He produces Christ's likeness in me. Please help me continue learning about the Holy Spirit. In Jesus's name, amen.

CHAPTER 5

Paul's Second and Third Missionary Tours

DAY 54

Paul the Evangelist

Yesterday we gave attention to the nature of Christian liberty (Galatians 4–6). Today we turn our attention to the continued missionary work of the apostle Paul and his associates.

Begin by reading Acts 15:36–18:11. As you read, stop and meditate on any verses that speak to your heart (Joshua 1:8; Psalm 1:1-3).

Chronological marker. We took a brief detour from Acts to study James (written AD 49) and Galatians (written AD 50). We now return to the book of Acts with events that took place in AD 50 and 51.

Overview of Today's Scripture Reading

Acts 15:36-41. Paul was about to go on his second missionary tour. The plan was for Barnabas to accompany him, as he had on the first tour. The two men debated whether to bring John Mark with them. Barnabas said yes. Paul said no because John Mark deserted them at the beginning of the first missionary tour. Barnabas and John Mark left for Cyprus, and Paul and Silas traveled through Syria and Cilicia.

Acts 16. Paul and Silas went to Derbe and Lystra. Paul had visited these cities during his first missionary tour, so now he revisited them to strengthen them. While there, Paul and Silas met young Timothy, whom Paul enlisted for missionary work (verses 1-3).

Paul and Silas continued their traveling. The Holy Spirit prevented them from going to Asia and Bithynia. A vision directed them to Macedonia (verses 4-10). While in Philippi, a businesswoman named Lydia became a believer, as did the rest of her family (verses 11-15).

Paul also exorcised a spirit of divination from a slave girl. The girl's owner was enraged, for he lost the income he made from her fortune-telling abilities. Paul and Silas got tossed in jail but were supernaturally released by an earthquake. The jailer and his family become believers, so this was a win-win event (16:16-34).

Acts 17. Paul then preached in a synagogue in Thessalonica. The local Jews were greatly angered, but there were some Gentile conversions (verses 1-9). The next city, Berea, had a more receptive audience. They listened to Paul and compared what he said to the Scriptures. But some hostile Jews from Thessalonica followed Paul and Silas and had them ousted from the city (verses 10-14).

Paul then went to Athens and preached to local intellectuals. Most remained unconvinced by Paul's words, but a few were open-minded and turned to the Lord (verses 15-34).

Acts 18:1-11. Paul then traveled from Athens to Corinth, where he met up with Aquila and his wife, Priscilla. They supported themselves as tent makers as they engaged in evangelism. Silas and Timothy soon arrived. As Paul preached, many resisted, but some were converted.

Today's Big Ideas

Paul evangelized in...
    Philippi (16:16-40)
    Thessalonica (17:1-9)
    Berea (17:10-15)
    Athens (17:16-34)
    Corinth (18:1-11)

Insights on Difficult Verses

Acts 17:28. This verse does not mean the writings of a pagan poet belong in the Bible. Paul quoted him because he said something worthy of inclusion regarding the point Paul was making.

Acts 17:28-29. In one sense, all human beings on earth are the off-spring of God since we were all created by Him (Genesis 1:26-27; Malachi 2:10). However, only believers in the Lord Jesus are in God's eternal family (Romans 8:16; Philippians 2:15; 1 John 3:10).

Major Themes

All races are equal (Acts 17:26). All humans are equal in terms of their creation (Genesis 1:28), the sin problem (Romans 3:23), God's love for them (John 3:16), and God's provision of salvation for them (Matthew 28:19). God's redeemed will be from "every tribe and language and people and nation" (Revelation 5:9).

God providentially controls our circumstances (Acts 17:28). God controls the circumstances of our lives, for "in him we live and move and have our being." "A man's steps are from the LORD" (Proverbs 20:24; see also Proverbs 16:9; Jeremiah 10:23).

Digging Deeper with Cross-References

Christ judges in righteousness (Acts 17:31)—Matthew 25:31-46; John 5:25-30; Revelation 20:11-15

God's work of preservation (Acts 17:28)—Genesis 45:7; Deuteronomy 4:4; 6:24; Joshua 14:10; 24:17; 1 Samuel 30:23; Nehemiah 9:6,21; Job 10:12; Psalms 3:5; 12:7; 16:1; Proverbs 2:8; 22:12; Isaiah 43:2; 49:8; Daniel 3:25; 6:23; Jonah 1:17

Life Lessons

Don't sweat bad circumstances (Acts 16:16-24). God remains on the throne, bringing about His eternal purposes even when bad things happen—like being tossed in jail. Consider these verses: Deuteronomy 10:14; 1 Chronicles 29:12; 2 Chronicles 20:6; Psalm 33:8-11; Isaiah 46:10; Ephesians 1:20-22; and John 14:1-3.

Test all things (Acts 17:11). We ought to follow the example of the Bereans by testing all things against Scripture. Believers can be deceived (Acts 20:28-30; 2 Corinthians 11:2-3), but we guard ourselves from false doctrine by consulting Scripture (Acts 17:11; 1 Thessalonians 5:21).

Verses to Remember

- "They received the word with all eagerness, examining the Scriptures daily to see if these things were so" (Acts 17:11).

- "The God who made the world and everything in it, being Lord of heaven and earth, does not live in temples made by man, nor is he served by human hands, as though he needed anything, since he himself gives to all mankind life and breath and everything" (Acts 17:24-25).

Questions for Reflection and Discussion

1. Does Paul's evangelism from city to city motivate you to get more involved in sharing the gospel with others?

2. In these days of spiritual deception, do you want to make a resolution to be like the Bereans, testing all things against Scripture (Acts 17:11)?

3. What impacted you most in this lesson?

My Father, I'm no apostle, but I desire to follow Paul's example in sharing the gospel with others. My problem is that I'm not nearly as bold as Paul was. I fear rejection. I fear ridicule. Please teach me and strengthen me. Help me grow. In Jesus's name, amen.

Awaiting Christ's Coming for Us

In the previous lesson we discussed the apostle Paul's missionary work in various cities (Acts 15:36–18:11). Today we explore Paul's ministry among the Thessalonians.

Begin by reading through 1 Thessalonians. As you read, notice how the Word of God is purifying your life (John 17:17-18).

Chronological marker. Yesterday we studied events that took place AD 50 to 51. First Thessalonians was written in early AD 51.

Introduction to 1 Thessalonians

Author: the apostle Paul

Fast facts:

- The church at Thessalonica was founded around AD 50.

- Thessalonica was a capital of the Roman province of Macedonia in northern Greece. It was a prosperous port.

- Paul visited Thessalonica for a short time. He would have stayed longer, but Jewish resistance shortened his stay. The Jews didn't appreciate Paul winning converts to Christianity from among their own. For Paul's safety, the Christians in Thessalonica sent him to Berea (Acts 17:1-10).

Key words in 1 Thessalonians (and the number of times they appear):

faith (8)	coming (4)
love (8)	hope (4)
gospel (6)	

Overview of Today's Scripture Reading

1 Thessalonians 1–3. Paul expressed thanks for how the Thessalonian Christians had been spiritually transformed, with a firm and eternal hope, full of faith and love (1). However, Paul also found it necessary to answer false charges of troublemakers who had attacked his character and message. He reminded the Thessalonians about what he had accomplished among them and how he had refused financial support so no one could impugn his motives (2). Meanwhile, Paul sent Timothy to minister among them. He was comforted to hear Timothy's report that the Thessalonians had grown in their faith and love (2:17–3:10).

1 Thessalonians 4–5. Paul now sought to answer the Thessalonians' questions on various issues. He taught them that in contrast to the pagans, they ought to seek sexual purity (4:1-8). He also urged that there should be no idlers in the church, sitting around awaiting the Lord's coming. Everyone should work instead of sponging on the generosity of fellow Christians (4:9-12).

The Thessalonians were also concerned about fellow believers who had died and how this might relate to the rapture of the church. Paul informed them that the dead in Christ will rise first, and then the living will be transformed into their resurrection bodies to meet them in the air (4:13-18).

Paul also provided instructions on the eschatological day of the Lord (5:1-11). He closed with a few instructions on holy living (5:12-22).

Today's Big Ideas

- At the rapture we will experience a reunion with all our Christian loved ones (4:13-18).

- The day of the Lord will bring God's judgment and wrath (5:1-11).

- Christians should seek to please the Lord, especially in view of the reality that the Lord could come for us at any time (4:1-12; 5:12-28).

Insights on Difficult Verses

1 Thessalonians 4:13. This verse does not teach that at death the soul goes to sleep so that it is unconscious (see Mark 9:43-48; Luke 16:22-23; Philippians 1:23; Revelation 19:20). Rather, "sleep" is a reference to the physical body.

1 Thessalonians 4:16. The angels will accompany Jesus at the rapture just as they will at the second coming (2 Thessalonians 1:7). The "voice of an archangel" refers to the archangel Michael's voice.

Major Themes

Sanctification (1 Thessalonians 4:3). There are three aspects of sanctification: positional sanctification (being "positionally set apart" from sin—1 Corinthians 6:11), progressive sanctification (growing in holiness daily—1 Peter 1:16), and ultimate sanctification (heavenly perfection—1 John 3:2).

The rapture (1 Thessalonians 4:13-17). The rapture is that glorious event in which the dead in Christ will be resurrected and living Christians will be instantly translated into their resurrection bodies (John 14:1-3; 1 Corinthians 15:51-54; 1 Thessalonians 4:13-17).

Digging Deeper with Cross-References

The rapture (1 Thessalonians 4:13-17)—John 14:1-3; 1 Corinthians 15:51-53; Philippians 3:20-21; 4:5; Colossians 3:4; 1 Thessalonians 1:10; 2:19; 5:9,23; 2 Thessalonians 2:1,3; Titus 2:13

The second coming (1 Thessalonians 3:13)—Matthew 24:15-31; 26:64; Mark 13:14-27; 14:62; Luke 21:25-28; Acts 1:9-11; 2 Thessalonians 1:6-10; 2:8; 1 Peter 4:12-13; Revelation 19:11–20:6

Life Lessons

The blessed hope (1 Thessalonians 4:17). The term "blessed hope" (Titus 2:13) refers to the rapture. It is blessed in the sense that it brings blessedness to believers (Romans 8:22-23; Philippians 3:20-21; 1 Thessalonians 4:13-18; 1 John 3:2-3).

Prophecy and purity (see 1 Thessalonians 4:1-12). The imminence of the rapture should motivate us to live in purity and righteousness (Romans 13:11-14; 2 Peter 3:10-14; 1 John 3:2-3).

Verses to Remember

- "This is the will of God, your sanctification: that you abstain from sexual immorality; that each one of you know how to control his own body in holiness and honor, not in the passion of lust like the Gentiles who do not know God; that no one transgress and wrong his brother in this matter, because the Lord is an avenger in all these things, as we told you beforehand and solemnly warned you" (1 Thessalonians 4:3-7).

- "You are all children of light, children of the day. We are not of the night or of the darkness…Since we belong to the day, let us be sober, having put on the breastplate of faith and love, and for a helmet the hope of salvation" (1 Thessalonians 5:5,8).

Questions for Reflection and Discussion

1. Does prophecy make a difference in how you live your life day to day?

2. On a scale of one to ten, how committed would you say you are to being set apart from sin and set apart to God?

3. Is sexual purity a high priority in your life?

My Father, I am thankful that You have included prophecy in the Word of God. It not only gives me strong confidence that the Bible is the Word of God but also motivates me to live as You would have me live. I'm appreciative. In Jesus's name, amen.

Instructions on the Day of the Lord

Yesterday we focused on the coming of the Lord and how to please God during the interim (1 Thessalonians). Today we zero in on the punishment of the wicked, the emergence of the antichrist, standing firm in the faith, and avoiding idleness.

Begin by reading through 2 Thessalonians. As you read, keep in mind that the Word of God brings spiritual maturity (1 Corinthians 3:1-2; Hebrews 5:12-14).

Chronological marker. Paul wrote 1 Thessalonians in early AD 51. He followed up with 2 Thessalonians a bit later that same year.

Introduction to 2 Thessalonians

Author: the apostle Paul

Fast facts:

- Several months had passed since Paul wrote 1 Thessalonians.

- He now wrote 2 Thessalonians to further explain and clarify God's program of events relating to the day of the Lord and Christ's second coming.

- He also wanted to encourage the Thessalonians to correct the disorders remaining among them.

Key words in 2 Thessalonians (and the number of times they appear):

love (7)	coming of Jesus Christ (3)
faith (5)	truth (3)
glory/glorify (4)	

Overview of Today's Scripture Reading

2 Thessalonians 1. Paul begins with thanks to God for the Thessalonians' faith and love as well as their firm stand for Christ in the face of persecution (verses 1-4). They were setting a great example for other Christians. He assured them that those who were presently causing them suffering would one day be irrevocably punished at the second coming of Christ (verses 5-12).

2 Thessalonians 2. Some of the Thessalonians were apparently concerned that the day of the Lord had already come, for some phony epistles had surfaced teaching this idea. Paul responded that certain noticeable events would take place before this eschatological day comes, including the emergence of the antichrist and various social upheavals (verses 1-12).

2 Thessalonians 3. Paul closes by exhorting the Thessalonians to pray on his behalf as they continued to wait patiently for the coming of the Lord (verses 1-5). He also deals with the proper attitude one should have while waiting for the Lord's coming. On one hand, believers should be constantly ready for Christ's coming (by living righteously). On the other hand, people who were so caught up in prophetic excitement that they stopped working and lived off of others were to be rebuked (verses 6-13). Balance is necessary in the Christian life.

Today's Big Ideas

- Unbelievers will be judged (1:5-12).
- The antichrist will be a man of lawlessness (2:1-12).
- Christians must stand firm in the faith (2:13-17).
- We are not to be idle as we await the Lord's coming (3:6-15).

Insights on Difficult Verses

2 Thessalonians 1:9. The Greek word translated "destruction" carries the idea of a continual and perpetual state of ruination, which the wicked will consciously experience for all eternity (Matthew 8:12; 22:13; 24:51; 25:30; Luke 16:22-28).

2 Thessalonians 2:9. Satan can do grade-B supernormal signs. But he cannot perform grade-A supernatural miracles, which only God can do (see, for example, Exodus 8:19).

2 Thessalonians 2:15. The Greek word translated "traditions" (*paradosis*) refers to that which has been passed down. Paul had passed down apostolic teachings orally that were later recorded in the pages of Scriptures (see 2 Timothy 3:15-17).

Major Themes

The antichrist (2 Thessalonians 2:1-12). This "man of lawlessness" will perform counterfeit signs. He is called "the beast" in Revelation 13:1-10. He will eventually rule the whole world (Revelation 13:7).

The day of the Lord (2 Thessalonians 2:1-12). This phrase is generally used of the judgment that will climax in the future seven-year tribulation period (Revelation 4–18; see also Isaiah 65:17-19; 66:22; 2 Peter 3:10-13; Revelation 21:1).

Digging Deeper with Cross-References

The antichrist (2 Thessalonians 2:1-12)—1 John 2:18; 4:3; 2 John 1:7; Revelation 13:1-10; 19:20

Satanic power (2 Thessalonians 2:9)—Job 1:12; Luke 4:6; Acts 26:18; Ephesians 6:12

Life Lessons

Avoid idleness (2 Thessalonians 3:6-13). Believers are exhorted to avoid idleness and be committed to work as they await the Lord's coming. Hebrews 6:12 likewise urges believers not to be sluggish. Romans 12:11 urges believers not to be "slothful in zeal." Proverbs 18:9 speaks against the person who is "slack in his work."

Protection from the devil (2 Thessalonians 3:3). The Lord will "guard you against the evil one." One way the Lord does this is through the spiritual armor God provides for us (Ephesians 6:10-20). You and I must choose to put on this armor. God doesn't force us to dress in it. Wearing this armor means that our lives will be characterized by such things as righteousness, obedience to the will of God, faith in God, and an effective use of the Word of God (see Matthew 4). We must also remember Peter's exhortation regarding the devil: "Resist him, firm in your faith" (1 Peter 5:9).

Verses to Remember

- "Now may our Lord Jesus Christ himself, and God our Father, who loved us and gave us eternal comfort and good hope through grace, comfort your hearts and establish them in every good work and word" (2 Thessalonians 2:16).
- "The Lord is faithful. He will establish you and guard you against the evil one" (2 Thessalonians 3:3).

Questions for Reflection and Discussion

1. Do you take spiritual warfare seriously? Can you think of a time you sensed demonic forces working against you?
2. Would you say you are a hard worker? Are there any changes you want to make in this regard, especially since being a hard worker is biblical?
3. Do you feel it important to ask others to pray for you, as Paul did in 2 Thessalonians 3:1?

My Father, though the prophetic future sometimes seems frightful, I take comfort in knowing that You are in sovereign control of the world, guiding history toward its culmination at the second coming of Christ. I want to be ready for the day of the rapture. Please enable me by Your Spirit to consistently live a life pleasing to You. In Jesus's name, amen.

Alleviating Divisions in the Church

In yesterday's lesson we explored the punishment of the wicked, the emergence of the antichrist, standing firm in the faith, and avoiding idleness (2 Thessalonians). Now we give consideration to alleviating divisions in the church.

Begin by reading Acts 18:12–19:22 and 1 Corinthians 1–4. As you read, remember that the Word of God can help you be spiritually fruitful (Psalm 1:1-3).

Chronological marker. The events described in Acts 18:12–19:22 occurred around AD 53. Paul wrote 1 Corinthians in AD 55.

ACTS

Overview of Today's Scripture Reading

Acts 18:12–19:22. Apollos was a powerful speaker and defender of Jesus, but he was a bit deficient in doctrinal accuracy. Priscilla and Aquila therefore trained him. Apollos then ministered among the Corinthians (Acts 18:12–19:1).

Meanwhile, Paul went to Ephesus where he encountered followers of John the Baptist. He told them about Jesus, and they believed and were baptized. Paul continued speaking about the kingdom of God to any who would listen (Acts 19:1-10).

Today's Big Ideas

- Priscilla and Aquila trained Apollos (18:12-28).
- Paul evangelized in Ephesus (19:1-10).

Insights on Difficult Verses

Acts 19:11-12. Only the apostles were given the special "signs of an apostle" (2 Corinthians 12:12). Once they passed off the scene, their unique sign-gifts passed with them (Hebrews 2:3-4).

1 CORINTHIANS

Introduction to 1 Corinthians

Author: the apostle Paul

Fast facts:

- Corinth was a strategic center in Greece. It was a hub of commerce. A gospel message proclaimed in Corinth might find its way to the distant regions of the inhabited earth.

- Corinth's moral character also made it a fertile field for the gospel. The city contained the Temple of Aphrodite, the Greek goddess of love, where 1000 sacred prostitutes (priestesses) were made available to its cultists. This led to sexual debauchery throughout the city.

Key words in 1 Corinthians (and the number of times they appear):

body (44)	raise us/resurrection (20)
Spirit (41)	power (15)
wisdom/wise (26)	spiritual/spiritually (15)
church (22)	authority (13)
world (21)	

Overview of Today's Scripture Reading

1 Corinthians 1. A significant division riddled the Corinthian church. Distinct cliques followed Paul, Apollos, Cephas, or Christ. Paul urged them to stop following mere human desires, which are selfish. They should instead seek wisdom from God, which brings unity.

1 Corinthians 2. The Corinthian believers were ill-equipped to discover God's wisdom on their own. They needed to understand God's Word. The Holy Spirit helps Christians understand God's Word.

1 Corinthians 3. Following different human leaders is an indicator of spiritual immaturity. God's wisdom reveals that we must build on the foundation of Jesus alone (see Matthew 7:24-27).

1 Corinthians 4. Human leaders in the church must find their true purpose—not to build their own little empires, but to teach about Christ. Christians should use their spiritual gifts to serve Christ alone (4:1-13).

As their spiritual father, Paul urged the Corinthians to follow his example in being faithful to Christ and living in unity with others (4:14-21).

Today's Big Ideas

- Divisions had erupted in the Corinthian church (1:10-17; 3:1-23).

- Believers will face Christ at the judgment seat of Christ (3:10-23).

- Paul set an example for the Corinthians (4).

Insights on Difficult Verses

1 Corinthians 1:10. The word "united" comes from a Greek word used of setting broken bones. Paul wanted hurtful fractures and divisions in the church to end.

1 Corinthians 1:17. Baptism is not required for salvation. There is a distinction between baptism and the gospel that saves (1 Corinthians 15:1-4).

Major Themes

Spirits are often not named (Acts 19:12-16). Spirits are often not named in Scripture but rather are identified by their character ("evil spirits"). Scripture also mentions "deceitful spirits" (1 Timothy 4:1) and "unclean spirits" (Revelation 16:13).

God in us (1 Corinthians 3:16). God walked with Adam and Eve (Genesis 3:8-10), dwelt among the Israelites in the temple (2 Samuel

22:7), and dwelt (or "tabernacled") among humans in the person of Jesus (John 1:14). Today, Christians are the temple of the Holy Spirit.

Digging Deeper with Cross-References

Fellowship with Christ (1 Corinthians 1:9)—Matthew 18:20; Luke 24:15,32; Acts 4:13; 1 John 1:3; Revelation 3:20

Exhortations to unity (1 Corinthians 1:10-17; 3:1-23)—2 Corinthians 13:11; Ephesians 4:3; Philippians 1:27; 4:2; Colossians 2:2; 1 Peter 3:8

Life Lessons

Don't fear appearing foolish (1 Corinthians 1:23-31). The teaching that Jesus died for our sins sounds foolish to unbelievers. But don't ever shy away from sharing the gospel. You simply need to tell the truth about Jesus and then leave the results with God. Some people may surprise you by converting on the spot.

Building a God-honoring life (1 Corinthians 3:10-15). At the judgment seat of Christ, our works will be examined and tested against the fire of His holiness. If our works are built with good materials—Christ-honoring motives, godly obedience, and integrity—our works will stand. If our works are built with worthless materials—carnal attitudes, sinful motives, prideful actions, and selfish ambition—they will burn up.

Verses to Remember

- "The natural person does not accept the things of the Spirit of God, for they are folly to him, and he is not able to understand them because they are spiritually discerned" (1 Corinthians 2:14).

- "No one can lay a foundation other than that which is laid, which is Jesus Christ" (1 Corinthians 3:11).

Questions for Reflection and Discussion

1. Is the future judgment seat of Christ a strong motivator for you?

2. After briefly assessing your life, would you say that overall you are building your life with good materials (1 Corinthians 3:11-15)?

3. Have you ever been a member of a church where there was significant disunity? What did you learn from the experience?

My Father, I am so thankful that Jesus is my rock-solid foundation. I desire to build my life on Christ-honoring motives, godly obedience, and integrity, not on carnal attitudes, sinful motives, pride-filled actions, and selfish ambition. Please enable me! In Jesus's name, amen.

Day 58

Paul's Instructions on Ethical Issues

Yesterday we considered divisions in the church (1 Corinthians 1–4). Today we will focus on Paul's instructions on sexual immorality, lawsuits in the church, and principles of marriage.

Begin by reading 1 Corinthians 5–7. Read with the anticipation that the Holy Spirit has something important to teach you today (see Psalm 119:105).

Chronological marker. Paul wrote 1 Corinthians in AD 55.

Overview of Today's Scripture Reading

1 Corinthians 5. A case of incest erupted in the church (a man was having relations with his father's wife—perhaps a stepmother). Paul chastised the church for its failure to take disciplinary action. He ordered the church to oust the unrepentant sexual offender from fellowship until he repented and could be restored to fellowship.

Paul then made an important qualification. He drew a distinction between how we relate to unbelievers outside the church and believers in the church. Paul was not telling the Corinthians to avoid all fellowship with unbelievers, for we need to evangelize them. But Christians must separate from believers who engage in willful sin and refuse to repent. This separation is a form of discipline intended to lead the sinner to repentance.

1 Corinthians 6. Paul urged church members to stop taking legal action against each other in secular civil courts. It is better to settle differences within the Christian community—for example, by consulting one or more respected Christians.

Paul then quickly revisited the issue of sexual immorality. This was important for the Corinthians, for Corinth was a city brimming with sexual sin due to the temple prostitutes associated with pagan religion. Paul instructed that all sexual relationships outside of marriage violate God's holy will. Sexual immorality is a sin against one's own body as well as a defiling of the temple of the Holy Spirit (the body).

1 Corinthians 7. Paul then answered the Corinthians' various questions about marriage, celibacy, divorce, and remarriage. He provided two guiding principles—maintain sexual purity, and maintain commitment to the Lord.

Today's Big Ideas

- Sexually immoral believers must repent or be put out of the church (5).
- Believers ought not file lawsuits against other believers (6:1-11).
- Believers must flee sexual immorality (6:12-20).

Insights on Difficult Verses

1 Corinthians 5:5. The sexual offender should be put out of the church and into the world, where Satan rules. This will hopefully lead to repentance so the person can be restored to the church.

1 Corinthians 7:12. Paul was not saying this part of 1 Corinthians was not inspired by God. He was saying that Jesus did not say anything about the matter during His three-year ministry on earth. Because Paul was an apostle, his words were divinely sourced and thus divinely authoritative (1 Corinthians 2:4,13).

1 Corinthians 7:14. The overflowing grace in a believing marriage partner spills over onto his or her spouse as well as the children in the family—possibly leading to their salvation if they themselves turn to Christ.

Major Themes

Believers will judge angels (1 Corinthians 6:3). The fact that believers will judge angels in the afterlife forever dispels the notion that humans *become* angels. Colossians 1:16 tells us that God created the angels *as* angels (they were not formerly humans). Psalm 8:5 indicates that man was created lower than the angels. First Corinthians 13:1 draws a distinction between the languages of human beings and those of angels.

One husband for one wife (1 Corinthians 7:2). This is one of many verses teaching monogamy. From the very beginning, God set the pattern by creating a monogamous marriage relationship with one man and one woman, Adam and Eve (Genesis 1:27; 2:21-25; Matthew 19:4; see also Deuteronomy 17:17).

Digging Deeper with Cross-References

Christ, our Passover Lamb (1 Corinthians 5:7)—Isaiah 53:7; John 1:29; 1 Peter 1:19; Revelation 7:9

Marriage (1 Corinthians 7)—Proverbs 18:22; Jeremiah 29:6; Matthew 19:10; 1 Timothy 3:12; 4:3; 5:14; Hebrews 13:4; Revelation 14:4

Life Lessons

Avoid sexual immorality (1 Corinthians 6:13,18). Paul instructed that all Christians should flee fornication. The word "fornication" refers to all forms of sexual immorality (Acts 15:20). Fornication should not be even once named or spoken of among Christians (Ephesians 5:3).

Sexuality in marriage (1 Corinthians 7:1-5). A sexual relationship can only be engaged in within the confines of marriage between a man and woman (verse 2). Sex within marriage is good (Genesis 2:24; Matthew 19:5; 1 Corinthians 6:16; Ephesians 5:31). Sexual intercourse was actually one of God's first commands to Adam and Eve: "Be fruitful and multiply and fill the earth" (Genesis 1:28). Husbands and wives must always be sexually available to each other (1 Corinthians 7:1-5).

Verses to Remember

- "'All things are lawful for me,' but not all things are helpful. 'All things are lawful for me,' but I will not be enslaved by anything" (1 Corinthians 6:12).

- "Flee from sexual immorality. Every other sin a person

commits is outside the body, but the sexually immoral person sins against his own body" (1 Corinthians 6:18).

- "Do you not know that your body is a temple of the Holy Spirit within you, whom you have from God? You are not your own, for you were bought with a price. So glorify God in your body" (1 Corinthians 6:19-20).

Questions for Reflection and Discussion

1. Does the fact that your body is a temple of the Holy Spirit motivate you to avoid sexual immorality?

2. Does the fact that you were "bought with a price" (the blood of Christ) motivate you to avoid sexual immorality?

3. What strategies can you put in place to follow Paul's instruction to "flee immorality"?

My Father, it often seems hard to walk the straight and narrow way in our sexually dysfunctional society. I thank You for the teachings in 1 Corinthians about why we as Christians must pursue sexual purity. Don't let me forget. In Jesus's name, amen.

Day 59

Avoiding Offense

Yesterday we gave attention to sexual immorality and lawsuits in the church, as well as principles of marriage (1 Corinthians 5–7). Today we turn our attention to avoiding offense among Christians in the church.

Begin by reading 1 Corinthians 8–11:1. As you read, remember that the Word of God is alive and working in you (Hebrews 4:12).

Chronological marker. Paul wrote 1 Corinthians in AD 55.

Overview of Today's Scripture Reading

1 Corinthians 8. Some believers in Corinth thought it was no problem to eat meat that had been sacrificed to idols and then sold in the markets. Others were offended by the idea, considering it as participating in idolatry. Though Paul agreed in principle that it was fine to eat such meat, he urged believers to avoid doing so if it would injure other people's conscience. He indicated it is sometimes best to limit personal liberty to avoid the possibility of offending a weaker brother over a minor matter.

1 Corinthians 9. Paul speaks of his modus operandi in ministry. He accommodated himself to the needs and characteristics of others in order to evangelize among them more effectively. To the Jew he became as a Jew in order to win the Jew for Christ. To the weak he became weak that he might win the weak for Christ. He sums it up this way: "I have become all things to all people, that by all means I might save some" (1 Corinthians 9:22).

1 Corinthians 10–11:1. Paul warned that Christians must stay away from the worship of idols. Spiritual compromise has taken place among

God's people in the past. During the wilderness experience, the Israelites succumbed to worshipping pagan gods (Numbers 25).

Paul closed out this section by briefly returning to the issue of eating meat that had been sacrificed to idols, perhaps as a way of clarifying his warning against idolatry. If we truly seek to do all things for the glory of God, then we will seek to avoid any action that might injure the conscience of another.

Today's Big Ideas

- Christians must try not to offend the consciences of weaker brothers and sisters (1 Corinthians 8; 10:23–11:1).

- Paul accommodated himself to the needs of others in order to evangelize them effectively (9).

- Believers must avoid all forms of idolatry (10:1-22).

Insights on Difficult Verses

1 Corinthians 8:5. Paul is referring to false pagan entities of Greek and Roman mythology—so-called gods and lords. They are *false* gods and lords.

1 Corinthians 8:6. The Father, as the one God, does not mean Jesus is not God. Jesus, as the one Lord, does not mean the Father is not Lord. Both the Father and Jesus are God and Lord (see Matthew 11:25; John 20:28; Romans 10:9; Hebrews 1:8; 1 Peter 1:2).

1 Corinthians 10:8. Paul's statement that 23,000 died in the incident of the golden calf does not contradict the statement in Exodus 32:28 that 3000 died. Exodus 32 reports only those killed by the sword. First Corinthians 10 includes those killed both by the sword and a plague.

Major Themes

Beware of becoming a stumbling block (1 Corinthians 8:9-13). The warning against being a stumbling block for other Christians is a common New Testament theme. Paul exhorted Christians to "decide never to put a stumbling block or hindrance in the way of a brother"

(Romans 14:13)—especially a new convert, who can easily be bent out of shape.

Ministerial pay (1 Corinthians 9:1-15). Clergy have a right to make their living by their service in the church (Galatians 6:6; 1 Timothy 5:17-18). Paul chose not to avail himself of this right because he wanted to avoid bringing any offense to the Corinthian believers.

Digging Deeper with Cross-References

God the Creator (1 Corinthians 8:6)—Genesis 1–2; Exodus 20:11; Psalm 33:6,9; Isaiah 44:24; Jeremiah 32:17; John 1:3; Colossians 1:16; Hebrews 1:2; 11:3

The worship of evil spirits (1 Corinthians 10:20)—Leviticus 17:7; Deuteronomy 32:17; 2 Chronicles 11:15; Psalm 106:37; Revelation 9:20

Life Lessons

Receiving the prize (1 Corinthians 9:24-27). Believers will one day stand before the judgment seat of Christ (Romans 14:8-10; 1 Corinthians 3:11-15; 9:24-27). Believers are eternally secure in their salvation (John 10:28-30; Romans 8:29-39; Ephesians 1:13; 4:30; Hebrews 7:25), but they may receive or lose rewards at the judgment seat of Christ based on whether they've been faithful or unfaithful (2 Timothy 4:8; James 1:12; 1 Peter 5:4; Revelation 2:10).

Avoid idolatry (1 Corinthians 10:1-22). Idolatry involves worshipping other things in the place of God. These things can include money, materialism, fame, sexual immorality, and much more. The New Testament consistently urges Christians to avoid all forms of idolatry (1 Corinthians 5:11; 2 Corinthians 6:16; Galatians 5:20; Colossians 3:5; 1 John 5:21).

Verses to Remember

- "I have become all things to all people, that by all means I might save some" (1 Corinthians 9:22).

- "No temptation has overtaken you that is not common to man. God is faithful, and he will not let you be tempted beyond your ability, but with the temptation he will also provide the way of escape, that you may be able to endure it" (1 Corinthians 10:13).

- "Whether you eat or drink, or whatever you do, do all to the glory of God" (1 Corinthians 10:31).

Questions for Reflection and Discussion

1. What do you think Paul means when he says God will "provide the way of escape" so that we can endure temptations (1 Corinthians 10:13)?

2. Is it possible there may be some inadvertent idols in your life (1 Corinthians 10:1-22)?

3. How might you "become all things to all people" to win people to Christ today (1 Corinthians 9:22)?

My Father, this passage of Scripture seems convicting to me. I know I have done many things for my own glory instead of for Your glory. I know I give in to temptation all too often. But I thank You for this instruction because I want to implement what I have learned. Please help me. In Jesus's name, amen.

Day 60

Spiritual Gifts

In the previous lesson we discussed liberty in the church (1 Corinthians 8–11:1). Today we explore proper worship in the church, the exercise of spiritual gifts, and the resurrection.

Begin by reading 1 Corinthians 11:2–16:24. As you read, remember that those who obey the Word of God are truly blessed (Psalm 119:2; Luke 11:28; Revelation 1:3).

Chronological marker. Paul wrote 1 Corinthians in AD 55.

Overview of Today's Scripture Reading

1 Corinthians 11:2-34. Paul spoke of several issues related to proper church worship. Women were to have their heads covered, and the Lord's Supper was to be celebrated with respect and honor, not as a gluttonous feast.

1 Corinthians 12. The Holy Spirit gives one or more spiritual gifts to believers so they can mutually edify the body of Christ. Every individual part of the body is necessary.

1 Corinthians 13. All the spiritual gifts must be exercised according to love. Regardless of how gifted a person may be, he is nothing but a "clanging cymbal" if he does not have love.

1 Corinthians 14. Some of the Corinthians were making too big a deal over speaking in tongues. Paul said the gift of prophecy was the more important gift because it served to edify the church with sound doctrine. A person should not speak in tongues during church unless an interpreter is present. Paul wanted church services to be orderly.

1 Corinthians 15. The resurrection of Christ is the cornerstone of Christianity. Paul not only provided evidence that the event occurred but also spoke of the nature of the resurrection body. Because Christ was resurrected, we too shall be resurrected. The resurrection body will be ideally suited for existence in heaven. Death will be defeated.

1 Corinthians 16. Paul ended his letter by providing instructions for a collection he intended to make for the poor church at Jerusalem (verses 1-4). He then closed with a few exhortations and greetings (verses 5-24).

Today's Big Ideas

- Christians are to celebrate the Lord's Supper in a respectful and honorable way (11:17-34).

- Members of the body of Christ bless each other with their unique spiritual gifts (12).

- We ought to follow the way of love (13).

- The spiritual gift of prophecy is the most beneficial gift (14:1-25).

- Church services ought to be orderly (14:26-40).

- As Christ was resurrected from the dead, so Christians will be resurrected from the dead (15).

Insights on Difficult Verses

1 Corinthians 11:3. The Father and Jesus are equally divine (John 10:30) even though the Father is in authority over Jesus.

1 Corinthians 15:29. Some commentators think baptism for the dead was a false belief held by some Corinthians. Others suggest that newly baptized converts were replenishing the depleted ranks of believers who had died.

1 Corinthians 15:44-50. "Spiritual body" carries the idea of a supernatural, spirit-dominated body. It is nevertheless a physical body (Luke 24:37).

1 Corinthians 15:50. "Flesh and blood" is an idiom referring to mortal humanity.

Major Themes

Varying uses of trumpets (1 Corinthians 15:52). Trumpets serve multiple purposes in the Bible. They can signal the gathering of the Lord's people (Numbers 10:7-8), the assembling of the Lord's army (Numbers 10:9), the announcement of a new king (1 Kings 1:34-39), and our summons at the rapture (1 Thessalonians 4:16).

Death as a judgment (1 Corinthians 11:30). Some of the Corinthians got sick and died as a result of partaking of the Lord's Supper while remaining in sin (see 1 John 5:16). By contrast, righteousness leads to long life (Deuteronomy 4:40; 2 Kings 20:1-6; Proverbs 10:27; Ephesians 6:2-3).

Digging Deeper with Cross-References

The rapture (1 Corinthians 15:51-53)—John 14:1-3; Philippians 3:20-21; Colossians 3:4; 1 Thessalonians 1:9-10; 4:13-17; 5:9,23; 2 Thessalonians 2:1,3; Titus 2:13; Hebrews 9:28; James 5:7-9; 1 Peter 5:4; 1 John 2:28–3:2; Jude 21

Resurrection (1 Corinthians 15:12-21)—Isaiah 25:8; John 5:25, 28-29; 6:39-40,44,54; 11:24-25; Acts 24:15; 2 Corinthians 5:1; Philippians 3:21

Life Lessons

Christians and spiritual gifts (1 Corinthians 12:1-11). Spiritual gifts are special abilities bestowed sovereignly by the Holy Spirit upon individual believers for the purpose of edifying the church. These gifts include teaching, pastoring, evangelizing, the message of wisdom, the message of knowledge, faith, healing, miraculous powers, prophecy, distinguishing between spirits, speaking in different tongues, and the interpretation of tongues (Romans 12:3-8; Ephesians 4:7-13).

The imminence of the rapture (1 Corinthians 15:51-52). The term "imminent" literally means "ready to take place" or "impending." The rapture is imminent (1 Thessalonians 1:9-10; 4:13-17; Titus 2:13). This reality ought to motivate us to live in purity (Romans 13:11-14; 2 Peter 3:10-14; 1 John 3:2-3).

Verses to Remember

Behold! I tell you a mystery. We shall not all sleep, but we shall all be changed, in a moment, in the twinkling of an eye, at the last trumpet. For the trumpet will sound, and the dead will be raised imperishable, and we shall be changed. For this perishable body must put on the imperishable, and this mortal body must put on immortality. When the perishable puts on the imperishable, and the mortal puts on immortality, then shall come to pass the saying that is written: "Death is swallowed up in victory." "O death, where is your victory? O death, where is your sting?" (1 Corinthians 15:51-55).

Questions for Reflection and Discussion

1. Do you want to make any changes in your life in view of the biblical teaching, "If we judged ourselves truly, we would not be judged" (1 Corinthians 11:31)?

2. Is it possible you might fall short of the kind of love described in 1 Corinthians 13:4-7?

3. Do you know what your spiritual gift is? (If not, the best way to discover it is to get involved in some form of ministry at your church.)

My Father, how I yearn to be a living manifestation of the love described in today's passage. And how I yearn for the day of the rapture, when my perishable body will be made imperishable. Please help me to maintain an eternal perspective. In Jesus's name, amen.

DAY 61

The God of All Comfort

Yesterday we focused on issues of worship in the church and resurrection (1 Corinthians 11:2–16:24). Today we zero in on persecution and the God of all comfort.

Begin by reading Acts 19:23–20:1 and 2 Corinthians 1:1–2:13. As you read, keep in mind that just as we eat food for physical nourishment, so we need the Word of God for spiritual nourishment (1 Corinthians 3:2; Hebrews 5:12; 1 Peter 2:2).

Chronological marker. Yesterday we completed our study of 1 Corinthians, written in AD 55. The events in Acts 19:23-41 take place around AD 55–56. Paul wrote 2 Corinthians in AD 56.

ACTS

Overview of Today's Scripture Reading

Acts 19:23–20:1. The gospel of Jesus Christ cut into the profits of businessmen who sold miniature replicas of the pagan goddess Diana. These businessmen got very angry at Paul.

2 CORINTHIANS

Introduction to 2 Corinthians

Author: the apostle Paul

Fast facts:

- False prophets had penetrated the Corinthian church and assaulted Paul's character and authority. Some of the Corinthians apparently believed their lies and rebelled against Paul.
- Paul intervened and made a "painful visit" to them (2:1). He

followed up this visit with a severe letter (no longer in our possession—2:4).

- Later, Titus reported to Paul that the majority of Corinthian believers had repented of their rebellion against him (7:7).

- Grieved at past strained relations, Paul wrote this letter to the Corinthians to clarify his ministry, calling, and authority as an apostle.

Key words in 2 Corinthians (and the number of times they appear):

know (29)	love (13)
comfort (27)	joy/rejoice (13)
glory (19)	weak/weakness (12)
grace (18)	heart (11)
sorrow (18)	death (9)
affliction/suffering (15)	

Overview of Today's Scripture Reading

2 Corinthians 1:1-11. Paul opened by giving thanks to God. He then revealed that God comforted him in his afflictions so he could be a channel of comfort to the Corinthians in their afflictions. Likewise, God's comfort to the Corinthians through Paul could then enable them to become channels of comfort to others who were suffering.

2 Corinthians 1:12–2:4. Paul explained to the Corinthians why his visit to them had been delayed. It was not for any lack of desire. Rather, he wanted them to have plenty of time to engage in needed repentance. (False teachers had stirred up some of the people against Paul.)

2 Corinthians 2:5-13. Paul also requested that they graciously restore a repentant man to fellowship who had sinned sexually and had evidently been especially antagonistic toward Paul.

Today's Big Ideas

- God comforts us in our afflictions so that we may comfort others (1:3-11).

- The Corinthians were to forgive a man who had engaged in incest but who had now repented (2:5-13; see 1 Corinthians 5:1-13).

Insights on Difficult Verses

2 Corinthians 2:4. Paul apparently wrote a painful letter between 1 and 2 Corinthians that God did not intend to be part of the Bible.

2 Corinthians 2:10. Apparently the person under church discipline had verbally attacked Paul. Paul personally forgave the offense directed at him, and then he urged the Corinthian believers to forgive the person and restore him to fellowship. The man had repented of his sexual sin.

Major Themes

Rely on God's strength (2 Corinthians 1:8-9). Things were so difficult for Paul and his associates in Asia that they despaired even of life. They did not trust in themselves but in God. Paul elsewhere affirmed, "I can do all things through him who strengthens me" (Philippians 4:13; see John 15:5).

Satan the arch-deceiver (2 Corinthians 2:11). Satan distorts the Scriptures (Genesis 3:4-5; Matthew 4:6), schemes to outwit humans (2 Corinthians 2:11), masks himself by appearing as an angel of light (2 Corinthians 11:14), and is a master "deceiver of the whole world" (Revelation 12:9).

Digging Deeper with Cross-References

Forgiveness (2 Corinthians 2:5-11)—Genesis 50:17; Matthew 6:14; Mark 11:25; Luke 6:27,37; Romans 12:17,19; Ephesians 4:32; Colossians 3:13

Comfort from God (2 Corinthians 1:3-4)—Psalms 71:21; 86:17; Isaiah 12:1; 51:3,12; 66:13

Life Lessons

Comforting others (2 Corinthians 1:3-4). God's comforting presence can flow through each of us to suffering brothers or sisters. The church is full of people who are hurting, so church members who have experienced pain are admonished to help others who are enduring similar hurts. We need each other!

Beware of peddlers of God's Word (2 Corinthians 2:17). The Greek word translated "peddler" means "to corrupt." It refers to corrupt hucksters or con men who deceptively offer inferior products and cheap imitations (such as a false gospel). Apparently, these peddlers mixed God's Word with paganism and Jewish tradition. We have peddlers today too. Christian beware!

Verses to Remember

- "Blessed be the God and Father of our Lord Jesus Christ, the Father of mercies and God of all comfort, who comforts us in all our affliction, so that we may be able to comfort those who are in any affliction, with the comfort with which we ourselves are comforted by God" (2 Corinthians 1:3-4).

- "We felt that we had received the sentence of death. But that was to make us rely not on ourselves but on God who raises the dead" (2 Corinthians 1:9).

Questions for Reflection and Discussion

1. Has God comforted you during a particular trial? How can you share that comfort with others going through a similar trial?

2. Are you presently facing any difficult circumstances in which you can follow Paul's example of relying entirely on God and not on yourself?

3. Have you seen any peddlers of God's Word on TV recently? What kind of doctrines do they teach?

My Father, I thank You for the comfort You've given me during my various trials. I also thank You for the opportunity to be a channel of comfort to my brothers and sisters who are experiencing similar trials. You are an awesome God worthy of praise. In Jesus's name, amen.

The Glory of the Gospel

In yesterday's lesson we explored persecution and the God of all comfort (Acts 19:23–20:1; 2 Corinthians 1:1–2:13). Now we give consideration to the new covenant and the glory of the gospel.

Begin by reading 2 Corinthians 2:14–7:16. As you read, remember that storing God's Word in your heart can help you to avoid sinning (Psalm 119:9,11).

Chronological marker. Paul wrote 2 Corinthians in AD 56.

Overview of Today's Scripture Reading

2 Corinthians 2:14-17. Paul said that the Corinthians' favorable response to his corrective instructions was like a sweet fragrance.

2 Corinthians 3. Some of the Corinthian believers, however, were apparently still questioning Paul's credentials and authority. He responded that the lives that were changed as a result of his ministry were more than enough to vindicate his character. The church itself constituted his letter of approval.

Paul then emphasized that his ministry centered on the new covenant of grace, which is far superior to the old covenant (Hebrews 8:1–10:18). One is engraved on the heart, the other on stone. One focuses on the Spirit, the other on the letter of the law. One brings righteousness, the other condemnation.

2 Corinthians 4. Paul compared himself to a clay pot filled with a treasure—the glory of the gospel. Though Paul had experienced significant suffering in his work of ministry (as Jesus said he would—Acts 9:16), it was nothing in comparison with the glory he would experience in the afterlife.

2 Corinthians 5. Though the earthly body is temporal and frail (like a tent), the future resurrection body will be eternal and strong (like a building). The Holy Spirit in our lives is a down payment, guaranteeing what is to come. Meanwhile, we seek to please God, for we will all appear before the judgment seat of Christ.

The good news is that God sent His beloved Son Jesus Christ into the world to reconcile believing sinners to Himself through Jesus's sacrifice at Calvary. In the outworking of God's plan of salvation, Paul was an ambassador of Christ, reaching as many as possible with this good news.

2 Corinthians 6. Paul reminded the Corinthians of the trials and tribulations he had experienced in the work of ministry. Such was to be expected in serving Christ. As for the Corinthians, Paul urged them to avoid evil and unbelief, and not to be unequally yoked with unbelievers.

2 Corinthians 7. Titus brought Paul the news that the Corinthians had responded favorably to Paul's rebuke. Paul expressed joy at their repentance.

Today's Big Ideas

- Paul was a minister of the new covenant of grace (3).

- Paul compared himself to a clay pot filled with a treasure—the glory of the gospel (4).

- Our resurrection bodies will be powerful and permanent (5:1-10).

- God sent Jesus to reconcile sinners to Himself (5:11-21).

Insights on Difficult Verses

2 Corinthians 3:17. This does not mean Jesus is the Holy Spirit. The Holy Spirit is Lord in the sense of being Yahweh (the Lord God). Jesus and the Holy Spirit are distinct persons in the Trinity (John 14:16; 15:26; 16:7,13-14).

2 Corinthians 5:19. God desires to save all (2 Peter 3:9), but not all will be saved (Matthew 7:13-14; Revelation 20:11-15). Reconciliation is only for those who are "in Christ" (verse 17).

Major Themes

Satan, the "god of this world" (2 Corinthians 4:4). Satan is the "ruler of this world" (John 12:31), who deceives the whole world (Revelation 12:9; 20:3). He has power in the governmental realm (Matthew 4:8-9; 2 Corinthians 4:4), the physical realm (Luke 13:11,16; Acts 10:38), and the ecclesiastical realm (Revelation 2:9; 3:9).

Death of the physical body (2 Corinthians 5:1). When humans physically die, their spirit departs from their material body (or "tent"). They will receive their resurrection body ("building") on the future day of the rapture (1 Thessalonians 4:13-17).

Digging Deeper with Cross-References

God rewards faithful believers (2 Corinthians 5:9-11)—Romans 14:8-10; 1 Corinthians 3:10-15; 4:5; 9:24-27; Ephesians 6:7-8; 2 Timothy 4:8; 1 Peter 5:4; James 1:12; 1 John 2:28; 2 John 8; Revelation 1:14; 2:10,23

Confidence in God's response (2 Corinthians 3:4; 4:14)—Psalm 20:7; Proverbs 3:26; Romans 8:31; Philippians 1:6; 2 Timothy 4:18; Hebrews 13:6

Life Lessons

A possible forfeiture of rewards (2 Corinthians 5:9-11). Some may lose rewards at the judgment seat of Christ (1 Corinthians 3:15). They may even experience a sense of shame at the judgment (2 John 1:8). Jonathan Edwards (1703–1758) urged, "Resolved, never to do anything, which I should be afraid to do, if it were the last hour of my life."

Come out and be separate (2 Corinthians 6:14-15). Christians are not to be unequally yoked with unbelievers. In 1 Timothy 5:22, Paul urges his young protégé not to "take part in the sins of others; keep yourself pure." Ephesians 5:11 exhorts us, "Take no part in the unfruitful works of darkness, but instead expose them."

Verses to Remember

- "We look not to the things that are seen but to the things that are unseen. For the things that are seen are transient, but the things that are unseen are eternal" (2 Corinthians 4:18).

- "We know that while we are at home in the body we are away from the Lord, for we walk by faith, not by sight. Yes, we are of good courage, and we would rather be away from the body and at home with the Lord" (2 Corinthians 5:6-8).

- "If anyone is in Christ, he is a new creation" (2 Corinthians 5:17).

Questions for Reflection and Discussion

1. Is there any sense in which you are "unequally yoked"?

2. Do you find it difficult to walk by faith and not by sight? Why?

3. Do you think Jonathan Edwards's resolution might be a workable philosophy for your life? Why or why not?

My Father, I ask that You work in my life in such a way that I can honestly resolve never to do anything that I would be afraid to do in the last hour of my life. Please strengthen my resolve. In Jesus's name, amen.

Day 63

Generous Giving

Yesterday we considered the new covenant and the glory of the gospel (2 Corinthians 2:14–7:16). Today we will focus on generosity in giving and Paul's vindication of his apostleship.

Begin by reading 2 Corinthians 8–13. As you read, remember that the Word of God teaches us, trains us, and corrects us (2 Timothy 3:15-17).

Chronological marker. Paul wrote 2 Corinthians in AD 56.

Overview of Today's Scripture Reading

2 Corinthians 8–9. The Macedonian Christians had been giving liberally to the needy brethren in Jerusalem, who were experiencing something of a famine (8:1-6). Paul desired that the Corinthian believers do the same (8:7–9:15). He assured them that God would reward their generosity. As a motivation for giving, Paul reminded them how Jesus gave Himself on their behalf. He also reminded them that God loves a cheerful giver.

2 Corinthians 10–12. Paul provided a defense of his apostolic authority and his credentials. This was apparently aimed at a small minority of church members that remained in rebellion against him and resisted his authority (10). In establishing his credentials as an apostle, Paul spoke of his knowledge, personal integrity, visions from the Lord, and miraculous acts, and he answered the charge that he was a weak and timid leader.

Paul was not about to get into a mudslinging match or play one-upmanship. He had no interest in arguing about whose leadership abilities were superior to whose. He emphasized that the only thing that matters is God's revealed will.

Paul warned the Corinthians that these rabble-rousers were intent on getting church members to follow them rather than Christ. He exposed the underhanded and deceitful tactics they were using to undermine him. He observed that he suffered as a true apostle of Christ, completely unlike these troublemakers in the church (11).

As a true apostle, Paul received exceedingly great revelations in a vision. To keep him humble, God allowed him to suffer a thorn in the flesh. Through this experience, he learned that God's power is made perfect in human weakness (12).

2 Corinthians 13. Paul closed the letter with exhortations, personal greetings, and a trinitarian benediction (13:11-14).

Today's Big Ideas

- Paul gave instructions regarding a collection for the Jerusalem church (8–9).

- Paul manifested the authority of an apostle (10).

- Paul conducted himself as an apostle (11:1-15).

- Paul suffered as an apostle (11:16-33).

- Paul had a vision as an apostle (12:1-10).

- Paul was selfless as an apostle (12:11-18).

Insights on Difficult Verses

2 Corinthians 8:9. Paul is speaking about spiritual prosperity, not financial prosperity (see 1 Corinthians 4:11).

2 Corinthians 12:2. The three heavens in Scripture are the earth's atmosphere (Job 35:5), the interstellar universe (Genesis 1:17; Deuteronomy 17:3), and God's dwelling place (2 Corinthians 12:2).

2 Corinthians 12:7. Paul's "thorn" was apparently physical. Some scholars have suggested the possibility of a severe eye disease.

Major Themes

God is triune (2 Corinthians 13:14). The doctrine of the Trinity is based on three lines of evidence:

- There is one true God (Isaiah 44:6; 46:9).

- Three persons are recognized as God—the Father (1 Peter 1:2), Jesus (Hebrews 1:8), and the Holy Spirit (Acts 5:3-4).

- There is three-in-oneness in God (Matthew 28:19).

The weapons of our warfare (2 Corinthians 10:3-4). We live on a physical planet, but the weapons of our warfare are not physical. Paul urged, "Take up the whole armor of God, that you may be able to withstand in the evil day, and having done all, to stand firm" (Ephesians 6:13). You and I are in a spiritual battle.

Digging Deeper with Cross-References

The work of Satan (2 Corinthians 11:14)—Genesis 3:1-5; John 8:44; Acts 5:3; 1 Corinthians 7:5; 1 Timothy 3:6; 1 Peter 5:8; James 3:13-16; Revelation 12:10

Visions in Bible times (2 Corinthians 12:1)—Genesis 46:2; Numbers 12:6; Psalm 89:19; Daniel 2:19; 4:5,13; Hosea 12:10; Joel 2:28; Luke 1:22; Acts 2:17; 10:3; 11:5; 16:9; 18:9

Life Lessons

Beware of Satan's masquerade (2 Corinthians 11:14). Satan has his own church (Revelation 2:9), his own ministers (2 Corinthians 11:4-5), his own system of theology (1 Timothy 4:1; Revelation 2:24), his own counterfeit gospel (Galatians 1:7-8), and his own throne (Revelation 13:2). He inspires false Christs (Matthew 24:4-5), false teachers (2 Peter 2:1), false prophets (Matthew 24:11), and false apostles (2 Corinthians 11:13). Satan is a master deceiver.

God's power is made perfect in human weakness (1 Corinthians 12:8). In God's economy, the weaker the human vessel, the more God's strength and grace shines forth. Paul had already affirmed, "We have this treasure in jars of clay, to show that the surpassing power belongs to God and not to us" (2 Corinthians 4:7). We need not be dismayed by our weaknesses. They provide opportunity for God's great power to work!

Verses to Remember

- "Though we walk in the flesh, we are not waging war according to the flesh. For the weapons of our warfare are not of the flesh but have divine power to destroy strongholds. We destroy arguments and every lofty opinion raised against the knowledge of God, and take every thought captive to obey Christ" (2 Corinthians 10:3-5).

- "My grace is sufficient for you, for my power is made perfect in weakness" (2 Corinthians 12:9).

Questions for Reflection and Discussion

1. Are you facing any difficult circumstances that seem beyond your ability to fix? What have you learned in this lesson that might help you in this regard?

2. Can you think of any current examples of Satan masquerading as an angel of light?

3. When was the last time you gave yourself a thorough spiritual examination to assess your relationship with God? There's no time like the present!

My Father, how wonderful it is that Your power is made perfect in human weakness, for I am weak. How wonderful it is that no matter what I face in life, Your grace will be sufficient for me. I am grateful. In Jesus's name, amen.

All Stand Guilty Before God

Yesterday we gave attention to Paul's instructions on giving generously and cheerfully, as well as other matters of concern to the Corinthian church (2 Corinthians 8–13). Today we turn our attention to Paul's teaching about how all people are guilty before God.

Begin by reading Romans 1:1–3:20. As you read, never forget that you can trust everything that is recorded in the Word of God (Matthew 5:18; John 10:35).

Chronological marker. Yesterday we completed our study of 2 Corinthians, written in AD 56. The next book chronologically is Romans, written in AD 57.

Introduction to Romans

Author: the apostle Paul

Fast facts:

- Rome was a hub city connected by road to numerous other cities in the ancient world. It was thus a strategic city in the spread of the gospel.

- The church at Rome was predominantly made up of Gentile believers (1:5,13; 11:13; 15:15-16). However, there was also a strong minority of Jewish believers (2:17; 9–11; 14).

- Paul had a strong desire to visit the church of Rome (1:10-15). He apparently wrote this letter to prepare the way for his eventual visit to the city (15:14-17).

Key words in Romans (and the number of times they appear):

law (75)	Gentiles (28)
justified/righteous (57)	flesh (27)
sin (48)	grace (25)
die/death (45)	judge/judgment (22)
faith (40)	believe (21)
Spirit (35)	count/impute/reckon (21)

Overview of Today's Scripture Reading

Preface. Romans is the most theological of all of Paul's letters. Paul spoke of...

- humankind's sin problem and the universal need for righteousness (1:18–3:20)

- salvation and justification by faith (3:21–5:21)

- how a believer experientially grows in righteousness in daily life, how he is freed from the power of sin, and how he is freed from the domination of the law (6–8)

- Jews' special place in God's plan (9–11)

- spiritual gifts (12:3-8)

- respect for the government (13:1-7)

- unity between Jews and Gentiles (15:5-13)

Romans 1:1-17. The apostle Paul expressed his desire to minister in Rome. He also stated the theme of the book—the gospel of salvation.

Romans 1:18-32. The Gentiles stand condemned because they suppressed the knowledge of God they gained from "general revelation"— that is, revelation available to all humanity in the world of nature (the starry universe—see Psalm 19) and the inner conscience. The Gentiles ultimately turned to idolatry and paganism.

Romans 2:1–3:8. The Jews also stand condemned because they failed to live up to God's infinitely righteous standards. Paul, himself a

Jew, provided a reality check for his fellow Jews by reminding them that they haven't obeyed God's law (2:17-29) or believed His Word (3:1-8).

Romans 3:9-20. The conclusion is obvious: All stand guilty before God. Paul clearly defines humanity's sin problem. He will also clearly define God's solution: Salvation in Jesus Christ.

Today's Big Ideas

- The Gentiles are guilty before God (1:18-32).
- The Jews are guilty before God (2:1–3:8).
- Conclusion: All are guilty before God (3:9-20).

Insights on Difficult Verses

Romans 1:7. A saint is not a person canonized by a church. Rather, believers are saints in the biblical sense of being set apart to God.

Romans 2:6-8. A person who habitually does good works reveals that his heart has been regenerated by God (verse 7). A person who habitually does evil shows his alienation from God (verse 8).

Major Themes

The sin of homosexuality (Romans 1:26). Homosexuals will not inherit God's kingdom (1 Corinthians 6:9-10). Homosexual practices are condemned (Leviticus 18:22; Romans 1:26). Paul, however, speaks of the possibility of complete liberation from homosexual sin (1 Corinthians 6:9-11).

All have sinned (Romans 3:9-18). "Surely there is not a righteous man on earth who does good and never sins" (Ecclesiastes 7:20). "All we like sheep have gone astray; we have turned—every one—to his own way" (Isaiah 53:6; see also 1 John 1:8).

Digging Deeper with Cross-References

Servants of God (Romans 1:1)—1 Kings 18:36; 1 Chronicles 6:49; Ezra 5:11; Daniel 3:26; 2 Timothy 1:3; James 1:1; 1 Peter 2:16

God judges evil (Romans 2:6)—Psalm 62:12; Proverbs 24:12; Matthew 16:27; 2 Corinthians 5:10; Revelation 2:23

Life Lessons

Not ashamed of the gospel (Romans 1:16-17). Paul asserted, "I am not ashamed of the gospel, for it is the power of God for salvation to everyone who believes." Far from being something to be ashamed about, the gospel ought to be shouted from every rooftop. After all, the word "gospel" means "good news," and everyone needs to hear it.

God has no favorites (Romans 2:11). Our text tells us, "God shows no partiality" (see also Acts 10:34; Galatians 2:6; Ephesians 6:9; Colossians 3:25; 1 Peter 1:17). God is no respecter of persons. We are all on the same level before God, regardless of our personal position, wealth, influence, popularity, ethnicity, or outward appearance.

Verses to Remember

- "His eternal power and divine nature, have been clearly perceived, ever since the creation of the world, in the things that have been made" (Romans 1:20).

- "By works of the law no human being will be justified in his sight, since through the law comes knowledge of sin" (Romans 3:20).

Questions for Reflection and Discussion

1. Have you ever felt ashamed of the gospel? (Do you prefer not to bring up the gospel in the presence of other people?)

2. Why do you suppose people tend to gravitate toward doing good works to attempt earning favor with God?

3. How does Romans 1:1–3:20 make you all the more appreciative of the grace of God?

My Father, more than ever I sense my complete unworthiness to be saved. My sinfulness abounds. Nothing I do is good enough to merit salvation. I am so very appreciate of Your wondrous, amazing grace. Thank You for showering this grace on me. In Jesus's name, amen.

Christ's Righteousness in Us

In the previous lesson we discussed Paul's teaching about righteousness, unrighteousness, and judgment (Romans 1:1–3:20). Today we explore what Paul says about the imputation and impartation of righteousness.

Begin by reading Romans 3:21–8:39. As you read, trust God to open your eyes so you can discover wondrous things from His Word (Psalm 119:18).

Chronological marker. Paul wrote Romans in AD 57.

Overview of Today's Scripture Reading

Romans 3:21–5:21. Since no one—Jew or Gentile—can produce the righteousness that leads to salvation, God's solution is to impute righteousness to those who believe in Christ. This is the doctrine of justification. Justification involves not just acquitting the believing sinner of all sin but also imputing the very righteousness of Christ to his or her account. This justification is not something that can be earned but rather is given entirely by God's grace (3:21-24) and based on the blood sacrifice of Jesus (3:25-26). This gift is received by faith alone (3:27-31).

This principle of justification apart from works is illustrated in the life of Abraham (4). The wonderful thing about justification is that it brings reconciliation between God and man (5:1-11). Condemnation results from the first Adam's sin, but the imputation of righteousness is found in the second Adam, Jesus Christ (5:12-21).

Romans 6–8. Paul speaks not only about the imputation of righteousness but also the impartation of righteousness. More specifically, Paul revealed that positionally speaking, the believer is dead to the principle of sin (6:1-14) as well as the practice of sin (6:15-23). Union with

Jesus Christ makes the sanctified life possible. Because of what Christ has accomplished, the Christian has been set free from the law (7). As well, the Holy Spirit indwells and empowers every believer so that the sanctified life becomes possible in this life (8:1-17). Better yet, one day Christians will be entirely set free from the presence of sin when they are glorified in heaven (8:18-39).

Today's Big Ideas

- Believers are justified by faith (3:21-31; 4:25).
- We have peace with God through faith (5:1-11).
- We die in Adam but come alive in Christ (5:12-21).
- We are dead to sin but alive to God (6:1-14).
- We have died to the law through Christ (7:1-6).
- We are set free by the Spirit (8:1-11).
- We are more than conquerors through Him who loved us (8:31-39).

Insights on Difficult Verses

Romans 5:18-19. Romans is clear that not all will be saved, but only those who are justified by faith (5:1). Paul conceded that not even all his Jewish kinsmen will be saved (11:5,7-10), but some would be "accursed" (9:3). Provision has been made for all to be saved, but that provision becomes a reality only for those who trust in Christ (5:18-19).

Romans 8:14. Believers become "sons of God" in the sense that they are adopted into God's forever family.

Romans 8:16-17. Believers inherit all spiritual blessings in this life (Ephesians 1:3). In the life to come, they will share with the Lord Jesus in all the riches of God's glorious kingdom (1 Corinthians 3:21-23).

Major Themes

Sin: missing the target (Romans 3:23). The word "sin" means "to miss the target." Sin is failure to live up to God's standards. All of us miss the target. There is not one person who is capable of fulfilling all of God's laws at all times.

Salvation is a free gift (Romans 6:23). Scripture portrays salvation as a free gift. Revelation 22:17 refers to the water of life "without price." Ephesians 2:8-9 tells us that salvation is by grace, meaning it comes by God's unmerited favor. "Unmerited" means this favor cannot be earned.

Digging Deeper with Cross-References

The blood of the Lamb (Romans 5:9)—Matthew 26:28; Mark 14:24; John 6:53; Acts 20:28; 1 Corinthians 11:25; Colossians 1:14; 1 John 1:7; Revelation 1:5; 5:9

Human death (Romans 5:12; 6:23)—Genesis 2:16-17; 3:19; 49:33; Deuteronomy 31:16; Job 18:14; 30:23; Psalms 23:4; 116:15; Ecclesiastes 3:1-2; 7:2; 8:8; Isaiah 25:8; Ezekiel 18:23; 33:11; Luke 12:20; 1 Corinthians 15:26,56; Philippians 1:21; Hebrews 9:27; Revelation 1:18; 21:3-4

Life Lessons

Justification by faith (Romans 4:1-12). Negatively, justification means that one is once and for all pronounced not guilty before God. Positively, the word means that one is once and for all pronounced righteous. It happens the moment a person trusts in Christ for salvation. It is a singular and instantaneous judicial act of God (Romans 3:25,28,30; 8:33-34). Let the reality that you are justified motivate you to live righteously out of thanksgiving for what Christ has done for you.

God brings good out of evil (Romans 8:28). This passage tells us, "We know that for those who love God all things work together for good, for those who are called according to his purpose." We should always be watching for how our sovereign God might bring good out of the evil circumstances we sometimes face.

Verses to Remember

- "Do not present your members to sin as instruments for unrighteousness, but present yourselves to God as those who have been brought from death to life, and your members to God as instruments for righteousness" (Romans 6:13).

- "There is therefore now no condemnation for those who are in Christ Jesus. For the law of the Spirit of life has set you free in Christ Jesus from the law of sin and death" (Romans 8:1-2).

Questions for Reflection and Discussion

1. When was the last time God brought good out of evil in your life?

2. Do you ever feel a sense of condemnation after you sin? What have you learned in this lesson that will help you see this in right perspective?

3. What have you learned about salvation in this chapter that excites you?

My Father, what a release it is to know that there is no more condemnation for me—ever! You have pronounced me not guilty and have imputed the very righteousness of Christ to me. I don't think I'm capable of understanding how awesomely great that is. I thank You. In Jesus's name, amen.

God's Sovereign Plan for the Jews

Yesterday we focused on Paul's words on the imputation and impartation of righteousness (Romans 3:21–8:39). Today we zero in on God's sovereign plan for the Jews and Gentiles.

Begin by reading Romans 9–11. As you read, allow the Word of God to bring revival to your soul (Psalm 119:25,93,107).

Chronological marker. Paul wrote Romans in AD 57.

Overview of Today's Scripture Reading

Preface. In these chapters, Paul turns his attention to the salvation of the Jews, God's chosen people. He speaks of Israel's past election and spiritual privileges (9), Israel's present state of unbelief (10), and Israel's future prospect of restoration and salvation (11). Israel as a nation was set aside for its unbelief, yet Israel has a future and will be grafted back into their place of promised blessing, thus fulfilling God's covenant promises.

Romans 9:1-29. Paul first turns to the question of Israel so he can vindicate God's righteousness in His sovereign dealings with the Jews. He points out that there is no inconsistency between God's election of—and promises to—the Jewish people in the Old Testament and God's current rejection of the Jews in their state of unbelief (9:6-13). After all, God never promised that every physical descendant of Abraham would be saved.

Romans 9:30–10:21. Jewish guilt is rooted in their attempt to accomplish their own righteousness (at which they failed) instead of God's plan of righteousness by faith (9:30–10:4). Paul points out that salvation by faith was always available (10:5-13). All the Jews needed to do in

New Testament times was turn to Christ the Savior in faith, but most refused and hardened themselves against Christ (10:9-10). The Jewish people heard the gospel (10:18) and understood it (10:19-20) but chose to reject it. God is therefore righteous in condemning them.

Romans 11. The good news, however, is that God is not yet finished with the Jews. Israel's rejection by God is neither complete nor final (11:1-10). It is not complete because there has always been a believing remnant (of which Paul was a part). It is temporary because Israel will one day gloriously turn to the true Messiah, and blessing will be restored to the nation (11:25-27). Meanwhile, God is bringing good out of Israel's hardness, for it opens the door for Him to pour out blessings on the Gentiles (11:11-15).

Today's Big Ideas

- God sovereignly elected Israel in the past (9:1-29).
- Israel is currently in a state of unbelief (9:30–10:21).
- There is a future salvation for Israel (11).

Insights on Difficult Verses

Romans 9:6. Not all of Abraham's physical descendants are true heirs of the promise.

Romans 9:13. In context, the word "hate" is a Hebrew idiom meaning "to love less" (Genesis 29:30-33; Luke 14:26). We might paraphrase the verse this way: "In comparison to my great love for Jacob, my feeling for Esau, whom I love less, may seem like hatred."

Romans 9:18. Ten times Exodus reports that Pharaoh hardened his own heart (Exodus 7:13-14,22; 8:15,19,32; 9:7,34-35; 13:15), and ten times it says God hardened Pharaoh's heart (4:21; 7:3; 9:12; 10:1,20,27; 11:10; 14:4,8,17). Pharaoh hardened his own heart seven times before God first hardened it, though the prediction that God would do it preceded all.

Major Themes

God is absolutely sovereign (Romans 9:14-18). Romans portrays God as absolutely sovereign over all things in the universe. God asserts, "My counsel shall stand, and I will accomplish all my purpose" (Isaiah 46:10). He promises, "As I have planned, so shall it be, and as I have purposed, so shall it stand" (Isaiah 14:24).

Israel will be saved (Romans 11:25-29). Israel will finally convert at the end of the future tribulation period (Zechariah 12:2–13:1). The restoration of Israel will include the confession of Israel's national sin (Leviticus 26:40-42; Jeremiah 3:11-18; Hosea 5:15), following which Israel will be saved, thereby fulfilling Paul's prophecy in Romans 11:25-29.

Digging Deeper with Cross-References

Wisdom of God (Romans 11:33; 16:27)—Job 12:13; Psalm 104:24; Proverbs 3:19; James 3:17

Truthfulness (Romans 9:1)—Mark 5:33; John 21:24; Acts 26:25; 2 Corinthians 1:18; 4:2; 11:31; Galatians 4:16; Ephesians 4:15,25; 6:14; Philippians 4:8; James 5:12

Life Lessons

Loving others enough to die for them (Romans 9:1-3). Paul loved his fellow Jews so much that he was willing to give up his life on their behalf. This reminds us of Jesus's words: "Greater love has no one than this, that someone lay down his life for his friends" (John 15:13). Jesus, of course, demonstrated His great love for us by dying on our behalf (Isaiah 53:7; John 3:16-17; 10:11-18; 1 Timothy 2:5-6; 1 Peter 2:24; 1 John 2:2; Revelation 5:9).

Zeal without knowledge (Romans 10:1-3). Paul conceded that the Jews had a great zeal for God but not according to knowledge. They desperately needed to hear and receive the true gospel of grace. Paul himself was once an unsaved Jew—he too had zeal without knowledge.

Verses to Remember

- "Christ is the end of the law for righteousness to everyone who believes" (Romans 10:4).

- "If you confess with your mouth that Jesus is Lord and believe in your heart that God raised him from the dead, you will be saved" (Romans 10:9).

- "Oh, the depth of the riches and wisdom and knowledge of God! How unsearchable are his judgments and how inscrutable his ways" (Romans 11:33).

Questions for Reflection and Discussion

1. Do you know any unbelievers who have "zeal without knowledge"? How might you reach them with the truth?

2. Are there any circumstances in which you would show supreme love by giving your life for another?

3. Does it comfort you to know that God is sovereign over all things?

My Father, I am so thankful that Jesus loved me enough to die for me. His love—Your love—is supreme, beyond what I can comprehend. Please grant me the ability to demonstrate my love for You by consistent obedience to Your Word. In Jesus's name, amen.

Day 67

The Practice of Righteousness

In yesterday's lesson we explored God's sovereign plan for the Jews and Gentiles (Romans 9–11). Now we give consideration to the actual practice of righteousness among God's people.

Begin by reading Romans 12–16. As you read, never forget that God urges you to quickly obey His Word in all things (Psalm 119:60).

Chronological marker. Paul wrote Romans in AD 57.

Overview of Today's Scripture Reading

Preface. Romans closes with an extended exhortation for believers to live out their salvation. Paul speaks of the Christian's duty to God (12), to the governmental authorities (13), and to other people (14–16).

Romans 12. Foundationally, the believer must surrender himself or herself to God as a living sacrifice and experience true transformation through the renewing of the mind. Only then will Christian conduct become a daily reality. This daily reality should include living in humility, demonstrating love for others, and using one's spiritual gifts to bless others.

Romans 13. All authority comes from God, so believers must submit to their government. After all, government serves to punish evildoers (13:1-7). Believers must also show love to their neighbors, for love comes from God. Such love fulfills the requirements of the law. Further, as we walk with Christ, our daily conduct ought to conform to the conduct of Christ (13:11-14). In other words, we should begin to take on the family likeness.

Romans 14:1–15:13. Strong Christians need to consider their weaker brothers and sisters (that is, weak in the faith) so that they do not offend or injure them. Paul said the strong and the weak should accept each other (14:1-12). The strong should be cautious not to cause the weak to stumble (14:13-18) and should make efforts to help them (15:1-6). The strong and weak should accept each other just as Christ accepted both Jews and Gentiles (15:7-13).

Romans 15:14–16:27. Paul concludes by reaffirming his ministry to the Gentiles, and he expresses his desire to visit the Romans soon.

Today's Big Ideas

- Submit to authority (13:1-7).
- Love fulfills the Law (13:8-14).
- Avoid judging others (14:1-12).
- Avoid causing others to stumble (14:13-23).
- Christ is our example (15:1-7).

Insights on Difficult Verses

Romans 13:12. The day that is "at hand" is the day of the Lord's second coming (1 Thessalonians 5:2-4).

Romans 14:10. The idea of a judgment seat goes back to the athletic games of Paul's day. After the races and games concluded, the emperor took his seat on an elevated throne, and one by one, the winning athletes came up to the throne to receive a reward. This reward was usually a wreath of leaves, a "victor's crown." Similarly, each Christian will stand before Christ the Judge and receive (or lose) rewards (see Psalm 62:12; Jeremiah 17:10; Matthew 16:27; 1 Corinthians 4:5; Ephesians 6:7-8).

Major Themes

Character and clothing (Romans 13:14). Paul exhorted Christians to "put on the Lord Jesus Christ." Such language surfaces often in the New Testament. First Peter 5:5 exhorts, "Clothe yourselves...with humility toward one another." Colossians 3:12 says, "Put on...compassion, kindness, humility, meekness, and patience."

The origin of human government (Romans 13:1-6). God is a God of order. This order is evident in the authority structures He set up among human beings. God first set up human government in Genesis 9:6, and a primary purpose of government is to restrain evil among the populace. Other authority structures God set up include the family unit (1 Corinthians 11:3; Ephesians 6:1) and church leadership (1 Timothy 5:17).

Digging Deeper with Cross-References

Universal worship (Romans 14:11)—Psalm 22:27-28; Isaiah 45:22-23; 66:23; Philippians 2:9-11

The death of the righteous (Romans 14:8)—Genesis 25:8; 49:33; 50:26; Numbers 23:10; Deuteronomy 34:5; Joshua 24:29,33; 1 Samuel 25:1; 2 Kings 13:20; Psalm 23:4; Proverbs 14:32; Luke 2:29; 16:22; 2 Corinthians 5:1; Philippians 1:21; Hebrews 11:13; Revelation 14:13

Life Lessons

Don't be conformed to this world (Romans 12:2). Our text tells us, "Do not be conformed to this world, but be transformed by the renewal of your mind." Some of Paul's Roman readers had apparently already succumbed to being transformed by the world—not planet Earth, but an anti-God, satanic philosophy. The renewing of minds can happen only through the ministry of the Holy Spirit as believers read and digest God's Word (Psalm 119:11; Colossians 1:28; 3:10,16; Philippians 4:8).

The marks of a Christian (Romans 12:9-21). Christians ought to show genuine love, honor others, serve the Lord, pray ceaselessly, be hospitable, bless people, avoid pride, and live peaceably with others. The more our minds are renewed through the Holy Spirit and God's Word (see verse 2), the more these behaviors will surface and flourish in our daily lives.

Verses to Remember

- "I appeal to you therefore, brothers, by the mercies of God, to present your bodies as a living sacrifice, holy and acceptable to God, which is your spiritual worship" (Romans 12:1).

- "The night is far gone; the day is at hand. So then let us cast off the works of darkness and put on the armor of light" (Romans 13:12).

- "Put on the Lord Jesus Christ, and make no provision for the flesh, to gratify its desires" (Romans 13:14).

Questions for Reflection and Discussion

1. What behavior changes do you think might be involved in presenting your body to God as a living sacrifice?

2. Do you think your mind has been conformed to any elements of the world? Do you want to make any changes?

3. In view of the clothing metaphors in the New Testament, how can you "dress for success" in your life as a Christian?

My Father, I fear there may be some elements of the world that have tainted my thinking. I desire my mind to be renewed by Your Word and by Your Spirit. Please mold me and make me into the person You want me to be. I give myself to You as a living sacrifice. In Jesus's name, amen.

CHAPTER 6

Paul in Prison

Day 68

Paul Continues Evangelizing

Yesterday we considered the practice of righteousness among God's people (Romans 12–16). Today we will focus on Paul's continued evangelism and the persecution he suffered.

Begin by reading Acts 20–24. As you read, ask God to help you understand His Word (Psalm 119:73).

Chronological marker. Yesterday we completed our study of Romans, written in AD 57. The events in Acts 20–24 are dated around late AD 57 and early 58.

Overview of Today's Scripture Reading

Acts 20. Paul traveled through several provinces with some ministry associates, preaching along the way. In Troas, Paul preached a late-night sermon in an upstairs room, and a young man named Eutychus fell asleep and fell out the window. Paul promptly revived him.

Paul then headed to Jerusalem, timing his visit to be there for the Feast of Pentecost. While en route, Paul stopped at Miletus to visit with elders of the church at Ephesus. He urged them to stand for the truth of the gospel and resist the advances of false teachers.

Acts 21. As Paul continued traveling by ship toward Jerusalem, he was warned by the prophet Agabus that the Jews would arrest him there. He pressed on anyway and finally arrived.

Paul first greeted the leadership at the church in Jerusalem. He conceded to their request to sponsor several men undergoing purification rituals at a Jewish temple. Soon enough, however, Paul was apprehended by a mob of angry Jews who jumped to the conclusion that he committed blasphemy by bringing a Gentile into the holy sanctuary. Paul was providentially rescued by some Roman soldiers.

Acts 22. Paul attempted to give his testimony to the crowd. They listened initially, but soon enough they shouted him down, demanding that he die for his blasphemy. The Roman soldiers put him in a Roman jail to protect him from the Jews. He was about to be "examined by flogging" (tortured until he offered information) when he revealed he was a Roman citizen. This necessitated that he be treated fairly while in Roman custody. (Roman citizens were guaranteed a fair trial.)

Acts 23. Paul then appeared before the Jewish Sanhedrin. He received a bad reaction when he affirmed Jesus's resurrection, so the Romans again jailed him for protection. Not long after, the Lord appeared to Paul and informed him he would be His witness in Rome. Jewish zealots plotted to kill Paul, but his nephew tipped off the Roman guards. The Roman commander promptly sent Paul to Caesarea to stand trial before the governor, Felix.

Acts 24. Jews from Jerusalem traveled to Caesarea to appear before Felix and charge Paul with blasphemy. Paul then demonstrated the falsity of the charges. He ended up in a Caesarian prison.

Today's Big Ideas

- Paul continued his ministry of evangelism (20:1–21:26).
- Paul traveled to Jerusalem, was arrested for blasphemy, and defended himself (21:27–24:27).

Insights on Difficult Verses

Acts 20:20. In the early days of Christianity, there was no centralized church building where believers could congregate. Rather, there were many small house-churches scattered throughout the city (Acts 2:46; 5:42; 12:12; Colossians 4:15; 1 Corinthians 16:19). The apostle Paul's ministry in Acts 20:20 was actually from house-church to house-church.

Acts 20:28. This verse should not be taken to mean that God in His divine nature has blood. The verse is referring to Jesus in the Incarnation. Jesus in His human nature shed His blood on the cross.

Major Themes

The Lord's day (Acts 20:7). Our text tells us that "the disciples came together to break bread" on the "first day of the week" (Sunday). This would seem to indicate that the early church was even now meeting on Sundays, having transitioned away from meeting on Saturday (the Sabbath day) (see Romans 6:14; 14:5; Galatians 3:24-25; Colossians 2:16).

Warnings from heaven (Acts 22:18). When Paul was in Jerusalem, the Lord suddenly spoke to him: "Make haste and get out of Jerusalem quickly, because they will not accept your testimony about me." We witness such warnings from heaven in other parts of Scripture (see, for example, Genesis 19:12; Matthew 2:13).

Digging Deeper with Cross-References

Plots (Acts 23:12-22)—Genesis 37:18; Numbers 16:3; Judges 9:1; 2 Kings 12:20; 14:19; Daniel 6:4; Matthew 12:14

Conscience (Acts 24:16)—Psalm 51:7; Proverbs 30:20; Matthew 27:3; Romans 9:1; 2 Corinthians 1:12; 1 Timothy 4:2; Titus 1:15; Hebrews 10:22

Life Lessons

Serve the Lord in humility (Acts 20:19). God uses humble servants, just as He used the apostle Paul. Scripture exhorts us to be clothed with humility (Colossians 3:12; 1 Peter 5:5-6), to be humble and gentle (Ephesians 4:2), and to walk humbly with our God (Micah 6:8).

It is more blessed to give (Acts 20:35). Our text quotes the words of Jesus: "It is more blessed to give than to receive." This goes along with an attitude of humility. Prideful people are self-focused. Humble people are other-focused. Prideful people seek blessing. Humble people seek to bless others. Which kind of person do you aspire to be?

Verses to Remember

- "Pay careful attention to yourselves and to all the flock, in which the Holy Spirit has made you overseers, to care for the church of God, which he obtained with his own blood. I know that after my departure fierce wolves will come in among you, not sparing the flock; and from among your own selves will arise men speaking twisted things, to draw away the disciples after them" (Acts 20:28-30).

- "I always take pains to have a clear conscience toward both God and man" (Acts 24:16).

Questions for Reflection and Discussion

1. Can you think of some examples of false teachers who have emerged from within the Christian church?

2. How important is it to you to maintain a clear conscience?

3. Is it your goal to serve the Lord in humility?

My Father, I am appreciative for the example set for us by Paul. He served You in humility, maintained a clear conscience, and was committed to standing against false doctrine. Please enable me to follow his example. In Jesus's name, amen.

Paul in Trouble with the Authorities

Yesterday we gave attention to Paul's continued evangelism and the persecution he suffered (Acts 20–24). Today we see even more of Paul's trouble with the authorities.

Begin by reading Acts 25–28. As you read, remember that great spiritual wisdom comes from studying God's Word (Psalm 119:98-104).

Chronological marker. The events in Acts 25–28 take place around AD 59–60.

Overview of Today's Scripture Reading

Acts 25. Paul defended himself before Festus, the Roman provincial governor of Judea. Festus asked Paul if he was willing to be tried before the Jewish Sanhedrin. Because of Jewish hostilities, Paul knew he'd never receive a fair trial that way. So as a Roman citizen with Roman rights, he appealed his case to Caesar.

Before Paul left for Rome, another Roman ruler—Herod Agrippa II—expressed interest to Festus about hearing Paul's story firsthand. Festus said he'd arrange it. He hoped that perhaps Agrippa would be able to clarify charges against Paul before sending Paul on to Rome.

Acts 26. Paul made a powerful plea on his own behalf before Festus and Agrippa. He effectively testified that the Lord Jesus had personally commissioned him to be an apostle to the Gentiles. Festus and Agrippa were in agreement that Paul was innocent of Jewish charges against him. And now, since Paul appealed to Caesar, his next destiny would be Rome.

Acts 27. Paul set sail for Rome as a prisoner. While en route, the ship encountered a violent storm with threatening waves. The ship drifted off course. Concerned that the ship would soon sink, the crew tossed tackle overboard in hopes of increasing stability on rough seas.

During the storm crisis, Paul received a vision from the Lord. Paul then assured the ship's crew—based on the vision—that everyone would survive, even though the ship itself would be wrecked as it ran aground on an island. As it happened, the ship indeed was torn apart by violent waves when it hit land, but the entire crew survived.

Acts 28. The island they ended up on was Malta. After arriving, Paul was bitten by a poisonous snake, but he miraculously survived, to the thrill of local islanders. (They assumed he must be a god.) This set the stage for Paul to carry out a ministry of miracles on the island for the next three months.

Finally, after this brief detour on Malta, Paul was able to set sail for Rome again. Upon arriving, Paul preached to local Jews about Jesus. Some received his message. Others rejected it.

Over the next two years, Paul was under house arrest in Rome. All who came to visit him at the house received a free sermon about Jesus.

Today's Big Ideas

- Paul defended himself before Festus (25) and Agrippa (26).
- Paul set sail for Rome and was shipwrecked on the island of Malta (27).
- Paul traveled from Malta to Rome (28).

Major Themes

Jesus lives (Acts 25:19). The risen Christ had appeared to Paul and called him to ministry (Acts 9). Paul was later caught up to heaven with the Lord (2 Corinthians 12:1-4). Paul knew that if he died, he'd go straight to be with the Lord in heaven (2 Corinthians 5:8; Philippians 1:21-23).

Repentance shows itself in deeds (Acts 26:20). John the Baptist urged Jewish leaders to "bear fruit in keeping with repentance" (Matthew 3:8). People are urged to "repent and turn to God, performing deeds in keeping with...repentance" (Acts 26:20; see also 2 Chronicles 7:14; Proverbs 28:13; 2 Corinthians 7:10).

Digging Deeper with Cross-References

> *Persecution (Acts 26:15)*—Matthew 5:10-11; Luke 6:22-23; Acts 5:41; Romans 8:17; 2 Timothy 3:12; 1 John 3:13; Revelation 2:10
>
> *"Witness" in the book of Acts (Acts 26:16)*—Acts 1:22; 2:40; 7:44; 10:43; 14:3,17; 15:8; 22:5,15,20

Life Lessons

Making a defense (Acts 26:2). Paul gave an answer for his faith before King Agrippa. First Peter 3:15 urges, "Always [be] prepared to make a defense to anyone who asks you for a reason for the hope that is in you; yet do it with gentleness and respect." Notice that it is not just a matter of what you say ("make a defense") but also how you say it ("with gentleness and respect").

Bringing good out of evil in Paul's life (Acts 28:30). At the close of Acts, Paul was confined to his rented house, not free to go about as he desired. Even here God brought good out of evil. During this time of confinement, Paul wrote Ephesians, Philippians, Colossians, and Philemon. He also preached the Word of God to any who were around him. God can bring good out of evil in our lives too (Romans 8:28).

Verses to Remember

> I am Jesus whom you are persecuting. But rise and stand upon your feet, for I have appeared to you for this purpose, to appoint you as a servant and witness to the things in which you have seen me and to those in which I will appear to you, delivering you from your people and from the Gentiles—to whom I am sending you to open their eyes, so that they may turn from darkness to light and from the power of Satan to God, that they may receive forgiveness of sins and a place among those who are sanctified by faith in me (Acts 26:15-18).

Questions for Reflection and Discussion

1. How does the reality that Jesus lives affect your daily routine?

2. Do you consider yourself always prepared to give an answer for the hope that is within you?

3. Have you ever been guilty of lip-service repentance before God—that is, verbalizing repentance in prayer without following through by "performing deeds in keeping with repentance"?

My Father, help me to be true to my word when I repent before You. Enable me to perform deeds in keeping with my repentance. Enable me to bear fruit in keeping with repentance. I want to please You. In Jesus's name, amen.

Christ Is Fully Sufficient

In the previous lesson we discussed Paul's appeal to Caesar, his defense before Agrippa, and his sea journey to Rome (Acts 25–28). Today we explore forgiveness and Christ's full sufficiency in all things.

Begin by reading through Colossians; Philemon. As you read, remember that reading Scripture can strengthen your faith in God (Romans 10:17).

Chronological marker. In the previous lesson we concluded our study of events in Acts 25–28, dated AD 59–60. Today we explore Philemon and Colossians, both written in AD 61.

PHILEMON

Introduction to Philemon

Author: the apostle Paul

Fast facts:

- Philemon was Paul's friend and the leader of the Colossian church.

- He was a prominent man whose slave Onesimus escaped, became a believer, and was now returning under Paul's counsel.

Key words in Philemon (and the number of times they appear):

accept/receive back (3)	grace (3)
love (3)	appeal (2)

Overview of Today's Scripture Reading

Philemon 1-7. Paul was thankful for Philemon's Christian faith and love.

Philemon 8-16. Onesimus had escaped from Philemon's household and probably fled to Rome. He met Paul in prison (we are not told how this happened). Under Paul's leading, Onesimus became a Christian.

Paul came to love young Onesimus. He was aware that under Roman law, Onesimus could be executed as a runaway slave. Paul sent Onesimus back to Philemon with a letter urging him to set Onesimus free as a brother in Christ so that he could return to help Paul in ministry. Paul urged Philemon to forgive Onesimus just as Christ had forgiven Philemon.

Philemon 17-25. Paul placed any debt Onesimus might have to his own account. He trusted that Philemon would do the right thing before the Lord.

Today's Big Ideas

- Philemon was a faithful Christian (4-7).

- Paul appealed to Philemon to receive back his escaped slave—now a Christian convert—without penalty (8-22).

COLOSSIANS

Introduction to Colossians

Author: the apostle Paul

Fast facts:

- Colossae was about 100 miles east of Ephesus.

- Paul had never been to the city, but he had heard about the church from his associate Epaphras (1:7-8).

- Some of the news he heard bothered him, so he wrote this epistle while in prison.

Key words in Colossians (and the number of times they appear):
  faith/faithful (9)
  wisdom (6)
  complete/full (5)
  knowledge (4)

Overview of Today's Scripture Reading

Colossians 1–2. Within the Colossian church were both Greeks and Jews. Some of the Jews brought preconceived religious ideas with them to incorporate into Christianity. By holding on to Jewish food laws and festivals (2:16), circumcision (2:11), mysticism (2:18), and an inflated view of angels (2:18), they brought un-Christian elements into the church.

Paul thus urged the Colossians not to let anyone judge them concerning laws about food or holy days (2:16). He said we have a spiritual circumcision in Christ and do not need a physical circumcision (2:11). He warned believers against the "idle notions" that can result from mysticism (2:18). He argued for the supremacy of Christ over all things (1:15), including the world of angels.

Colossians 3–4. The foundation for the spiritual life is not Jewish legalism (3:1-4). Rather, because of the believer's union with Christ's death, he must regard himself as dead to sin (3:5-11). And because of the believer's union with Christ in His resurrection, he must count himself as alive to righteousness (3:12-17). This righteousness should show itself in one's relationships (3:18–4:6).

Today's Big Ideas

- Christ is preeminent over all (1:15-23).
- Christ is fully sufficient for our needs (2:6-15).
- We should maintain an eternal perspective (3:1-17).

Insights on Difficult Verses

Colossians 1:15. Jesus is "firstborn over all creation" in the sense of being preeminent over creation.

Colossians 1:16. Thrones, dominions, rulers, authorities—these are various ranks of angels.

Colossians 1:24. Paul followed Christ's footsteps in suffering, as you and I do (1 Corinthians 12:26; Philippians 1:29).

Major Themes

Forgive others (Philemon 17). God has forgiven us, so we should forgive others (Matthew 18:22,35; Luke 17:4). Our forgiveness should be without limit (Matthew 18:21-22).

The Bible does not condone slavery (Philemon 16). Scripture does not approve of slavery. Rather, it simply alludes to the de facto situation of that day. Biblically, there is neither slave nor free in Jesus Christ (Acts 17:26,29; Galatians 3:28).

Digging Deeper with Cross-References

The supremacy of Christ (Colossians 1:15-23)—Matthew 3:11; John 3:31; 13:13; Acts 2:36; Romans 14:9; Hebrews 1:4; 3:3; 8:6; Revelation 1:11

A heavenly perspective (Colossians 3:1-2)—Psalm 16:11; 1 Corinthians 15:55; 2 Corinthians 5:8; Philippians 1:23; 1 Peter 1:4

Life Lessons

The transformative power of the gospel (Philemon 16). Onesimus became a believer. He was transformed by the power of the gospel. You and I also become transformed. Paul urges, "Do not be conformed to this world, but be transformed by the renewal of your mind" (Romans 12:2).

Total sufficiency in Jesus Christ (Colossians 2:6-15). False teachers infiltrated the Colossian church, claiming that believers must follow legalistic religious traditions. Paul countered that Christ is totally sufficient for salvation and the Christian life. We submit to Christ alone (Colossians 2:8-23).

Verses to Remember

- "As you received Christ Jesus the Lord, so walk in him, rooted and built up in him and established in the faith, just as you were taught, abounding in thanksgiving" (Colossians 2:6).

- "Set your minds on things that are above, not on things that are on earth" (Colossians 3:2).

Questions for Reflection and Discussion

1. What have you learned in this lesson about why you should forgive even though it's not always easy?

2. Do you truly consider Christ to be sufficient for your every need?

3. Why is it important to remember that God does the transforming in our lives, not we ourselves?

My Father, please enable me to walk daily in Jesus Christ, rooted in Him and built up in Him. Please also enable me to maintain an eternal perspective, keeping my eyes on the things of heaven. In Jesus's name, amen.

Day 71

Blessings in Christ

Yesterday we focused on Christ's preeminence and His sufficiency for all our needs (Philemon; Colossians). Today we zero in on the salvation, inheritance, and resources we have in Jesus Christ.

Begin by reading Ephesians 1–3. As you read, keep in mind that God desires you not only to hear His Word but also to do it (James 1:22).

Chronological marker. Yesterday we studied Philemon and Colossians, both written in AD 61. Today we study Ephesians, written a bit later in AD 61.

Introduction to Ephesians

Author: the apostle Paul

Fast facts:

- Ephesus was well known for its temple of the Roman goddess Diana, considered one of the seven wonders of the world. The city was brimming with pagans.

- During his third missionary tour, Paul spent three years there building up the church (Acts 19). When he left, Paul's young associate Timothy pastored there for another year, seeking to establish the believers in sound doctrine (1 Timothy 1:3,20).

- Paul later wrote Ephesians while a prisoner in Rome in AD 61. He intended it to be a circular letter to be read not just in the church at Ephesus but in other churches as well.

Key words in Ephesians (and the number of times they appear):

in Christ/in him (32)	grace (12)
love (20)	church (9)
spirit (15)	walk (8)

Overview of Today's Scripture Reading

Preface. There are no commands in chapters 1–3 but more than 30 commands in chapters 4–6. Paul provides the doctrinal basis for living in chapters 1–3 and then draws the practical application of that doctrine in chapters 4–6.

Ephesians 1:1-14. God's eternal purposes include the redemption, adoption, forgiveness, and sealing of a special people (Christians), who will live forever with Him.

Ephesians 1:15-23. Paul prayed for his readers. He gave thanks to God for them and prayed especially that they would come to understand the awesome eternal blessings that are theirs in Jesus Christ.

Ephesians 2:1-10. Our salvation, from beginning to end, is a result of God's amazing grace, His unmerited favor toward us. We can do nothing to earn such salvation.

Ephesians 2:11-22. In this wondrous salvation, Jews and Gentiles become one in the body of Christ. People from every tribe and nation are a collective unity in the body of Christ.

Ephesians 3:1-13. Paul emphasizes a truth hidden in Old Testament times but now revealed in New Testament times: The church includes both Jews and Gentiles, all under the headship of Christ.

Ephesians 3:14-21. Paul prayed that the Ephesians believers would come to truly know the immeasurable love of Christ.

Today's Big Ideas

- We have rich spiritual blessings in Jesus Christ (1:3-14).
- Our salvation is rooted in God's amazing grace (2:1-10).
- Christians have unity in Christ (2:11-22).
- All believers are equal in the body of Christ (3).

Insights on Difficult Verses

Ephesians 1:10. This verse does not mean that Paul taught universalism, the idea that all people will be saved. Rather Paul was referring to the grand unity that will exist in Christ's future kingdom (see 1 Corinthians 15:27-28; Philippians 2:10-11). Paul emphasized elsewhere in Scripture that some will go to their eternal destiny without Christ (for example, 2 Thessalonians 1:7-9).

Ephesians 1:14. The presence of the Holy Spirit in our lives constitutes God's pledge that our salvation will absolutely be consummated.

Major Themes

Mystery (Ephesians 3:1-9). A mystery is a truth that cannot be discerned simply by human investigation, but requires special revelation from God. The mystery in Ephesians 3 is that Jews and Gentiles are equal heirs in the body of Christ.

God's eternal purpose (Ephesians 3:11). What has happened in the past, what is happening today, and what will happen in the future all provide evidence of the unfolding of God's eternal purposes.

Digging Deeper with Cross-References

Adoption into God's eternal family (Ephesians 1:5; 2:19; 3:6)— Romans 8:14,29; Galatians 3:26; 4:5; Philippians 2:15; Hebrews 12:6-9; 1 John 3:1

God's sovereignty (Ephesians 1:20-22)—Exodus 15:18; Deuteronomy 4:39; 10:14; 2 Chronicles 20:6; Psalms 9:7; 29:10; 33:8-11; Isaiah 40:21-26; 46:10; Romans 14:11

Life Lessons

Your heavenly citizenship (Ephesians 3:19). You and I, even though we live in cities on earth, are more fundamentally citizens of heaven. Paul said that we are "fellow citizens with the saints and members of the household of God" (see also Philippians 3:20). And we are to behave here below as citizens of heaven above.

Answered prayer (Ephesians 1:16). Here are six principles of prayer:

- Our prayers are subject to God's sovereign will (1 John 5:14).
    - Prayer should be continual (1 Thessalonians 5:17).
    - Sin hinders answers to prayer (Psalm 66:18).
    - Righteousness opens the door to prayers being answered (Proverbs 15:29).
    - We should pray in faith (Mark 11:22-24).
    - We should pray in Jesus's name (John 14:13-14).

Verses to Remember

- "By grace you have been saved through faith. And this is not your own doing; it is the gift of God, not a result of works, so that no one may boast" (Ephesians 2:8-9).
- "Now to him who is able to do far more abundantly than all that we ask or think, according to the power at work within us, to him be glory in the church and in Christ Jesus throughout all generations, forever and ever" (Ephesians 3:20-21).

Questions for Reflection and Discussion

1. Is your behavior on earth motivated by your citizenship in heaven?
2. How's your prayer life? What have you learned about prayer in this lesson that might help you?
3. Does your adoption into God's eternal family spiritually motivate you?

My Father, I can't thank You enough for adopting me into Your eternal family. In myself, I could never earn entrance into Your family. But by Your amazing grace, I not only am a member of Your family but also have an eternal inheritance awaiting me. You are awesome! In Jesus's name, amen.

New Life in Christ

In yesterday's lesson we explored the salvation, inheritance, and resources we have in Jesus Christ (Ephesians 1–3). Now we consider some applications to our new life in Christ.

Begin by reading Ephesians 4–6. As you read, stop and meditate on any verses that speak to your heart (Joshua 1:8; Psalm 1:1-3).

Chronological marker. Paul wrote Ephesians in AD 61.

Overview of Today's Scripture Reading

Preface. Paul now demonstrates how doctrine affects duty. In view of what we learned in chapters 1–3 (we are positionally "in Christ"), we are now to walk *for* Christ as we continue to live on earth. We must walk in unity (4:1-16), in holiness (4:17-32), in love (5:1-6), in the light (5:7-14), in wisdom (5:15–6:9), and in victory (6:10-20).

Ephesians 4:1-16. The church is a single organism that is composed of many parts (that is, many Christians). Each part has a specific and important function. The parts work together in perfect harmony as they exhibit humility, gentleness, and mutual support. Christ is the head of this organism.

Ephesians 4:17-32. Because the church is made up of many individual members, each member must be considerate of the others. They are to put off the old sinful self and put on the new, Christ-submitting self.

Ephesians 5:1-21. Believers must seek to avoid the sins that characterize their sinful natures—things like sexual immorality, impurity, and crude speech. Instead, believers ought to be controlled by the Holy Spirit, who produces the likeness of Christ in our lives.

Ephesians 5:22–6:9. Being in Christ ought to affect all our relationships. Husbands are to love their wives as Christ loved the church, and wives are to submit to their husbands (5:22-33). Children must obey their parents (6:1-4). Bondservants ought to obey their masters (6:5-9).

Ephesians 6:10-24. Paul closes by exhorting believers to put on the whole armor of God to protect themselves from the powers of darkness (6:10-20). A strategic part of this armor is the Word of God. (See Main Themes.)

Today's Big Ideas

- We ought to maintain unity in the body of Christ (4:1-16).

- We ought to put on the new self, created after the likeness of God (4:17-32).

- We should walk in love (5:1-21).

- One's walk with Christ affects all personal relationships (5:22–6:9).

- God's armor protects us from the evil one (6:10-20).

Insights on Difficult Verses

Ephesians 4:11. There are no apostles today. The church was built on the foundation of the apostles and prophets (Ephesians 2:20). Such apostles had to be eyewitnesses of the risen Christ (Luke 1:1-4; Acts 1:21-26; 5:32; 1 Corinthians 9:1).

Ephesians 5:18. To be filled with the Holy Spirit means that one's life will be controlled no longer by self but by the Holy Spirit. It is not a matter of acquiring more of the Spirit but rather of the Spirit acquiring all of the individual.

Ephesians 5:19. The reference to singing should not be taken to mean that musical instruments cannot be used in worship (see 2 Samuel 6:5,21; 1 Chronicles 23:5; 2 Chronicles 7:6; 29:25; Psalms 43:4; 71:22; 150:3-5; Revelation 5:8).

Major Themes

God's ordered universe (Ephesians 5:22–6:4). God has set up many authority structures. God set up human government in authority over society (Romans 13:1). He placed the husband in authority over the wife (Ephesians 5:22-33). God placed parents in authority over children (Ephesians 6:1-4). He placed elders in authority over churches (Titus 1:5).

Wearing spiritual armor (Ephesians 6:11-18). "Wearing" this armor means that our lives will be characterized by such things as righteousness, obedience to the will of God, faith in God, and an effective use of the Word of God. These are what spell defeat for the devil in your life.

Digging Deeper with Cross-References

Worship and singing (Ephesians 5:19)—Exodus 15:1-21; Judges 5:1-12; Isaiah 12:5-6; 27:2; 30:29; 42:10-11; 44:23; Psalms 33:3; 40:3; Colossians 3:16

The devil's power (Ephesians 6:12)—Job 1:12; Luke 4:6; Acts 26:18; 2 Thessalonians 2:9

Life Lessons

God seals His people (Ephesians 1:13; 4:30). Believers are sealed by the Holy Spirit for the day of redemption. This seal guarantees that you and I will be delivered into eternal life on "the day of redemption." Because our salvation is secure, we can now live in joyful anticipation of heaven (Psalm 100:4; Philippians 4:6).

Satan's attack against Christians (Ephesians 6:11-18). God reveals how we can be victorious over the devil. As noted previously, God provides spiritual armor for our defense. In addition, Scripture instructs us, "Resist the devil, and he will flee from you" (James 4:7). We are to stand firm against the devil (Ephesians 6:13-14). We should be aware of Satan's strategies (2 Corinthians 2:11; 1 Peter 5:8). We should depend on the Holy Spirit, all the while remembering, "He who is in you is greater than he who is in the world" (1 John 4:4).

Verses to Remember

- "Do not grieve the Holy Spirit of God, by whom you were sealed for the day of redemption" (Ephesians 4:30).

- "Walk as children of light" (Ephesians 5:8).

- "Look carefully then how you walk, not as unwise but as wise, making the best use of the time, because the days are evil" (Ephesians 5:15-16).

- "Be strong in the Lord and in the strength of his might" (Ephesians 6:10).

Questions for Reflection and Discussion

1. What do you think it means to "walk as children of light"?

2. Do you make a conscious effort every day to submit yourself to the control of the Holy Spirit in your life?

3. How seriously do you take spiritual warfare? What have you learned today that might help you here?

My Father, today I am making the deliberate choice to submit my life to the control of the Holy Spirit. My fallen human self will fight me on this, but I seek to be controlled by the Spirit every single day. Please guide me and enable me so this can become a reality in my life. In Jesus's name, amen.

Day 73

Joy in Christ

Yesterday we considered truths that we are to apply to our new life in Christ (Ephesians 4–6). Today we will focus on Paul's joy despite being imprisoned.

Begin by reading through Philippians. As you read, remember that God's Word is the true source of hope (Psalm 119:81).

Chronological marker. After Ephesians, Paul wrote Philippians, dated at AD 63.

Introduction to Philippians

Author: the apostle Paul

Fast facts:

- In Philippi, a Roman colony, there apparently weren't enough Jews to establish a synagogue, which required a minimum of ten adult Jewish men. The Jews therefore met for prayer by the river Gangites on the Sabbath. This was where Paul addressed the first converts of Philippi during his second missionary tour.

- The Philippian church eventually experienced some problems. There were intense rivalries (2:3-4), legalistic disturbances caused by Judaizers (3:1-3), and some who were flirting with worldliness (3:18-19). Because of these internal problems, Paul wrote this letter as a corrective measure.

Key words in Philippians (and the number of times they appear):

Christ (38)	gospel (9)
know/knowledge (18)	imprisonment (4)
joy/rejoice (14)	fellowship (3)

Overview of Today's Scripture Reading

Philippians 1. Paul expressed thanks for the Philippians' continued support of his ministry (verses 1-11). He was presently in prison but nevertheless rejoiced because of the continued spread of the gospel (verses 12-26). He was eager to depart this life and be with Christ in heaven (verses 21-23). But he also recognized the need to remain on earth to continue ministering (verses 27-30).

Philippians 2. The church was experiencing disunity and rivalry, so Paul urged the Philippians to pursue humility, which is foundational to unity (verses 1-4). Christ Himself is our greatest example of humility (verses 5-11). Such humility leads to self-sacrificial living (verses 12-30).

Philippians 3. The apostle Paul, before his conversion to Christ, was committed to a life of legalism. He was a Hebrew of Hebrews. Now, however, Paul said such legalistic pursuits were as nothing when compared to knowing Christ. He said true righteousness is not rooted in external obedience to the law, but is received through faith in Christ.

Philippians 4. Paul urged the Philippians to live in unity with each other, to pursue holiness, and to prayerfully depend on God. As we cast our cares on God, we experience His indescribable peace. Paul boasted he could do all things through Christ (verses 10-20).

Today's Big Ideas

- Paul's imprisonment served to further spread the gospel (1:12-18).
- To live is Christ and to die is gain (1:19-30).
- Christians should be humble (2:1-11).
- Christians should shine as lights (2:12-18).
- Our righteousness is through faith in Christ (3:1-11).
- We ought to press toward the goal that lies ahead (3:12-21).
- Pray about your needs and be at peace (4:4-7).

Insights on Difficult Verses

Philippians 2:6-9. Christ did not give up His deity in the Incarnation. Rather, He veiled His preincarnate glory, submitted to a voluntary nonuse of some of His divine attributes on some occasions, and condescended by taking on the likeness of human beings.

Philippians 2:12. Working out salvation in this context refers to the corporate salvation of the Philippian church. Church members needed to avoid rivalries (2:3-4; 4:2), withstand Judaizers (3:1-3), and avoid worldliness (3:18-19).

Major Themes

Christ is supreme (Philippians 1:21). Christ is our life—our example (2:5), our goal (3:14), and our strength, regardless of what we face in life (4:13).

Live in humility (Philippians 2:5-11). Christians ought to live in humility, just as Christ did. James 4:10 tells us, "Humble yourselves before the Lord, and he will exalt you." By contrast, "The Lord tears down the house of the proud" (Proverbs 15:25).

Digging Deeper with Cross-References

Humility (Philippians 2:5-11)—Micah 6:8; Luke 14:10; 22:26; Romans 11:20; 12:3; James 4:10; 1 Peter 5:5

Joy (Philippians 4:4)—Nehemiah 8:10; Psalms 16:11; 30:5; 89:16; 126:5; 132:16; Isaiah 12:3; 35:10; Luke 2:10; John 15:11; 16:24; 17:13; Romans 14:17

Life Lessons

Five components of prayer (Philippians 4:5-7). Prayer includes...

- thanksgiving (Psalms 95:2; 100:4; Ephesians 5:20)

- praise (Psalms 34:1; 103:1-5,20-22; Hebrews 13:15)

- worship (Exodus 20:3-5; Deuteronomy 5:7; Psalm 95:6; Hebrews 12:28; Revelation 14:7)

- confession (Proverbs 28:13; 1 John 1:9)

- requests to God for specific things (Matthew 6:11; Philippians 4:6-7)

Joy in every circumstance (Philippians 4:4). Like Paul, we can experience joy in every circumstance. This type of joy is not simply a smile on the face, but involves divine peace in the inner heart (4:7).

Verses to Remember

- "For to me to live is Christ, and to die is gain" (Philippians 1:21).

- "Rejoice in the Lord always; again I will say, rejoice" (Philippians 4:4).

- "Do not be anxious about anything, but in everything by prayer and supplication with thanksgiving let your requests be made known to God. And the peace of God, which surpasses all understanding, will guard your hearts and your minds in Christ Jesus" (Philippians 4:6-7).

Questions for Reflection and Discussion

1. When was the last time you remember God coming through for you in answer to prayer? Why not spend a few minutes in personal praise to God for hearing and answering your prayers?

2. Is your Christian life characterized by the kind of joy Paul spoke about? If not, what have you learned in today's lesson that can help you make a change?

3. Do you ever struggle with pride?

My Father, I am so thankful for the apostle Paul's example of how to live as a Christian—not being selfish or ambitious, forgetting the past and pressing toward the future, being humble, maintaining joy in all circumstances, and turning all anxieties over to You. I love You, Lord. I pray in Jesus's name, amen.

Living in Light of God's Awesome Grace

Yesterday we gave attention to Paul's joy despite being imprisoned (Philippians). Today we turn our attention to living in light of God's awesome grace.

Begin by reading 1 Peter. As you read, remember that the Word of God teaches us, trains us, and corrects us (2 Timothy 3:15-17).

Chronological marker. Not long after Paul wrote Philippians, Peter wrote 1 Peter, dated at AD 63.

Introduction to 1 Peter

Author: the apostle Peter

Fast facts:

- Peter and two other fishermen, James and John, saw some of Jesus's greatest miracles and were allowed to see His glory (Mark 9; 2 Peter 1:16-18).

- First Peter was sent to scattered groups of Christians in the five Roman provinces that covered the greater part of modern Turkey. Peter probably wrote from Rome to encourage and strengthen believers facing the Neronian persecution.

- Peter was crucified upside down in Rome during Emperor Nero's persecution in AD 64.

Key words in 1 Peter (and the number of times they appear):

suffer/trial (18)	grace (10)
glory (16)	holy (8)

submissive (7)   call (6)
flesh (7)   chosen (5)

Overview of Today's Scripture Reading

1 Peter 1:1–2:12. Christians enjoy a living hope through the resurrection of Christ from the dead. A wondrous inheritance awaits all believers in heaven (1:1-4). This future hope gives strength to Christians as they suffer trials in the present (1:5-9). The proper response of the Christian to this salvation is a life of holiness (1:13–2:12).

1 Peter 2:13–3:12. Submissiveness is Christlike. Christians testify to their commitment to the Lord by their submission to the government (2:13-17), to masters (2:18-25), and to their marriage partners (3:1-8), even in the face of evil or bad circumstances (3:9-12).

1 Peter 3:13–5:14. Recognizing that his readers will experience increasing opposition to Christianity, Peter exhorted them to be ready to defend their faith and conduct (3:13-16). If they must suffer, Peter said, it ought to be for the sake of righteousness and not because of sin (3:17).

Peter then instructed his readers in how they should live. They are not to pursue the lusts of the flesh (4:1-6). They should show mutual love (4:7-11). If they are slandered for their faith, they should recognize that God will judge persecutors in the end (4:12-19). Meanwhile, church elders must watch over their flocks (5:1-4). All should pursue humility (5:5-7). All should pray, resist the devil, and stay strong in the faith (5:8-14).

Today's Big Ideas

- Believers are born again to a living hope (1:3-12).
- Believers are called to be holy (1:13-25).
- Christ is our cornerstone (2:1-12).
- We are to submit to authority (2:13–3:7).
- We are blessed if we suffer for righteousness' sake (3:8-22).
- Christians may suffer in the present but will experience glory in the future (4:12-19).

Insights on Difficult Verses

1 Peter 3:18. Jesus was not resurrected *as* a spirit, but rather was resurrected *by* the Spirit—the Holy Spirit (Luke 24:39; John 2:19-21; Acts 2:31; Romans 1:4).

1 Peter 3:18-19. Christ may have issued a proclamation of victory to fallen angels (Genesis 6:1-6; 2 Peter 2:4-5; Jude 6). Or perhaps He preached a proclamation of victory to the wicked contemporaries of Noah, whose spirits were now imprisoned (see verse 20).

1 Peter 4:6. This verse refers to those who are now dead but who heard the gospel while they were yet alive. This makes sense in view of the tenses used: The Gospel was preached (in the past) to those who are dead (presently).

Major Themes

Why grace is necessary (1 Peter 1:3,10,13). The word "grace" means "unmerited favor." Romans 5:1-11 reveals that we are given unmerited favor even though we actually merit condemnation. Because of Jesus, we do not receive the punishment we deserve. Rather, we are given a salvation we do not deserve.

Why God allows suffering (1 Peter 1:5-9). God is a master at bringing good out of evil (Romans 8:28). Through suffering, God trains us to obey Him (Hebrews 5:7-8), disciplines us when we go astray (Hebrews 12:3-11), helps us to learn patience (Romans 5:3) and humility (2 Corinthians 12:7-9), and teaches us about His ways (Psalm 119:65-71).

Digging Deeper with Cross-References

> *Trials (1 Peter 1:6)*—Exodus 3:7; Job 14:1; Psalm 119:50,143; Isaiah 63:9; Romans 8:18; 2 Corinthians 4:8
> *Holiness (1 Peter 1:16)*—2 Corinthians 7:1; Ephesians 4:24; Hebrews 12:14; 2 Peter 3:11

Life Lessons

Patiently enduring suffering (1 Peter 1:6). We can choose to *hold up* or *fold up* in the face of suffering. Peter tells us we have to suffer for only a "little while" (during earthly life) in comparison to the long time we'll be in heaven. Suffering tests the genuineness of our faith.

Temporary residents (1 Peter 1:1). Peter refers to Christians as exiles, meaning "temporary residents." "Our citizenship is in heaven" (Philippians 3:20). God's people are "strangers and exiles on the earth," and they "desire a better country, that is, a heavenly one" (Hebrews 11:13-16). We should live our short earthly lives in view of what awaits us in our long heavenly future!

Verses to Remember
- "Keep loving one another earnestly, since love covers a multitude of sins" (1 Peter 4:8).
- "Clothe yourselves, all of you, with humility toward one another, for 'God opposes the proud but gives grace to the humble'" (1 Peter 5:5).
- "Be sober-minded; be watchful. Your adversary the devil prowls around like a roaring lion, seeking someone to devour" (1 Peter 5:8).

Questions for Reflection and Discussion
1. Do you expect God to bring about good from your present evil circumstances?
2. Would you say you have the type of submissive attitude that Peter speaks about in 2:13–3:7?
3. Does your Christian conduct make a consistently positive impact on unbelievers, making Christianity more appealing to them (3:8–5:11)?

My Father, I truly am a temporary resident on this planet. My true home is heaven. Because my time here is short, please enable me to live my life with eternal priorities. In Jesus's name, amen.

Day 75

Pursue Sound Doctrine

In the previous lesson we discussed living in light of God's awesome grace (1 Peter). Today we explore Paul's instructions about choosing elders, teaching sound doctrine, and being ready for every good work.

Begin by reading through Titus. As you read, remember that the Word of God can help you be spiritually fruitful (Psalm 1:1-3).

Chronological marker. Titus was written not long after 1 Peter, in AD 64.

Introduction to Titus

Author: the apostle Paul

Fast facts:

- Titus was a young pastor and leader of the church in Crete. He was one of Paul's trusted inner circle of friends and ministry associates (2 Corinthians 8:23).

- Titus was an uncircumcised Gentile who illustrated one of Paul's teachings: Gentiles need not be circumcised to be saved.

Key words in Titus (and the number of times they appear):

God (13)	doctrine (4)
deed/work (8)	grace (4)
Savior (6)	faithful (3)
be sound (4)	

Overview of Today's Scripture Reading

Titus 1:1-9. Paul charged Titus, a pastor in Crete, to organize the churches there by appointing elders. These elders were to meet certain spiritual qualifications (1:5-9). They were to help protect the flock (God's people in the churches) against the false teachers Paul warns about in the verses that follow.

Titus 1:10-16. Paul focused heavy attention on warning against false teachers (1:10-16). The nature of the false teaching is not entirely clear, though it seems to relate to "Jewish fables," circumcision, genealogies, and Jewish legalism (1:10,14; 3:9-10). The flock must be protected and the false teachers silenced (1:11).

Titus 2:1–3:15. Paul thus urged Titus and his congregations to pursue sound doctrine and good works (1:9; 2:1–3:11). History reveals that the people who lived in Crete were naturally belligerent, argumentative, uncontrolled, and resentful of authority. For this reason, Paul insisted that Titus teach with authority and that the teaching of the Word of God lead to good works. For example, the believers must show respect to civil government (3:1-7), respect each other (3:8-15), and avoid disputes and divisions. Good doctrine naturally leads to good behavior.

Today's Big Ideas

- Elders in the church must meet certain qualifications (1:5-16).
- Sound doctrine must be taught and defended in the church (2).
- Christians need to be ready for every good work (3:1-11).

Insights on Difficult Verses

Titus 2:9. Paul did not condone slavery. He elsewhere declared that God "made from one man every nation of mankind to live on all the face of the earth" and that we are all "God's offspring" (Acts 17:26,29). He emphasized that people of all ethnic backgrounds are positionally equal before God (see Galatians 3:28).

Titus 3:5. The term "washing of regeneration" points to a spiritual washing, not a literal water-baptism kind of washing.

Major Themes

The grace of God (Titus 3:7). "Grace" literally means "unmerited favor." Grace refers to the undeserved, unearned favor of God. Paul tells Titus that we are "justified by his grace." We cannot earn justification. It is the result of God's unmerited favor for those who trust in Christ for salvation (Titus 2:13-14).

Good works and grace (Titus 2:7,14; 3:8,10). Titus speaks of good works that rest on the foundation of God's grace (2:11-13; 3:5-7). Works are not the condition of our salvation, but a consequence of it. We are saved by grace, through faith, for good works.

Digging Deeper with Cross-References

Deceivers (Titus 1:10)—Romans 16:18; 2 Corinthians 11:13; Ephesians 4:14; 2 Timothy 3:13; 2 John 1:7; Revelation 18:23

Doctrine (Titus 1:9-11)—Proverbs 4:2; Matthew 24:5; Mark 16:15-16; 1 Corinthians 1:10-17; 2 Corinthians 4:2; 1 Timothy 4:1-3,6,13; 2 Timothy 2:15; Hebrews 13:9; 2 John 10

Life Lessons

Salvation rests on the foundation of the promises of God (Titus 1:2). Paul informs Titus of the "hope of eternal life, which God, who never lies, promised before the ages began." God is a promise keeper. Prior to his death, an aged Joshua declared, "You know in your hearts and souls, all of you, that not one word has failed of all the good things that the Lord your God promised concerning you. All have come to pass for you; not one of them has failed" (Joshua 23:14; see also Joshua 21:45; Numbers 23:19; 1 Kings 8:56). You can trust God's promises!

Christian conduct (Titus 3). The primary emphasis in Titus 3 is that the Christian should be committed to God-honoring conduct. Titus informs us what such a Christian looks like in real life. He or she is submissive to those in authority, is ready for every good work, avoids speaking evil of another, avoids quarreling, is gentle, and is courteous to others, among other things.

Verses to Remember

When the goodness and loving kindness of God our Savior appeared, he saved us, not because of works done by us in righteousness, but according to his own mercy, by the washing of regeneration and renewal of the Holy Spirit, whom he poured out on us richly through Jesus Christ our Savior, so that being justified by his grace we might become heirs according to the hope of eternal life (Titus 3:4-7).

Questions for Reflection and Discussion

1. Do you ever fall into the trap of thinking you need to do good works to earn God's grace so He will continue to love you? What's the danger of that kind of mindset?

2. Can you think of any televangelists who do not set forth sound doctrine? Why is sound doctrine so critically important?

3. Do you think you could ever be deceived by false doctrine? Can Spirit-filled Christians be deceived?

My Father, I am so grateful that You are a promise-keeping God. I can trust virtually everything found in the Bible. Your Word is an anchor for my life. Your Word protects me from false doctrine. And Your Word gives me an assurance that I am saved. Praise You, Father. In Jesus's name, amen.

Instructions to a Young Pastor

Yesterday we focused on Paul's instructions about choosing elders, teaching sound doctrine, and being ready for every good work (Titus). Today we zero in on issues of concern for a young pastor, including false teachers, prayer, and the qualifications of elders in the church.

Begin by reading 1 Timothy 1–3. As you read, notice how the Word of God is purifying your life (John 17:17-18).

Chronological marker. Paul wrote 1 Timothy in AD 64 to render pastoral advice to his young protégé, Timothy.

Introduction to 1 Timothy

Author: the apostle Paul

Fast facts:

- Timothy was a young and trusted colleague of Paul. He was converted through Paul's ministry in Lystra and grew quickly in his spiritual life.

- Paul trusted Timothy, who helped lead the church in Ephesus and represented Paul to others in various churches (Acts 17:4,15; 1 Corinthians 4:17).

- Paul writes as a mature, experienced pastor to a young, inexperienced pastor.

Key words in 1 Timothy (and the number of times they appear):

faith (19)	faithful (8)
godliness (8)	be sound/well (6)
doctrine (8)	

Overview of Today's Scripture Reading

1 Timothy 1:1-11. Seven years earlier, Paul had warned the Ephesian elders that "fierce wolves" (false teachers) would seek to ravage the church (Acts 20:29-30). Now these false teachers were in full force. Timothy, as a shepherd of the church, was to fight off the wolves. Paul urged Timothy to defend biblical doctrine at all costs.

1 Timothy 1:12-20. Paul's own conversion is an example of God's amazing grace in saving the worst of sinners. Christ not only saved Paul but also called him to ministry. Paul was now passing the mantle of ministry to young Timothy. He was to fight the good fight.

1 Timothy 2. Paul provided brief instructions on praying for rulers (verses 1-8), an important consideration because such rulers could throw Christian pastors in jail (as had happened with Paul). Paul then provided instructions on the role of women in the church (verses 9-15).

1 Timothy 3:1-13. Leaders in the church must have good character. Paul thus instructed Timothy on the specific qualifications for elders (verses 1-7) and deacons (verses 8-13).

1 Timothy 3:14-16. Paul closes this section with a quote from what many believe was an early Christian hymn about Jesus.

Today's Big Ideas

- Beware of false teachers (1:3-11).
- Fight the good fight (1:12-20).
- Pray for everyone (2).
- Elders (3:1-7) and deacons (3:8-13) must be qualified.

Insights on Difficult Verses

1 Timothy 2:3-4. This passage expresses God's desire that all be saved but does not promise that all will be. This divine desire is realized only in those who exercise faith in Christ (Acts 16:31; see also Matthew 13:49; 25:32).

1 Timothy 2:13-15. This may mean the believing woman will be kept safe while bearing children. Or it may mean believing women will be kept safe because of Jesus's birth. Or it may mean that the believing woman will find fulfillment in her God-appointed role as wife and mother.

Major Themes

God's eternality (1 Timothy 1:17). God is the "King of the ages." He alone has immortality (6:16). God "lives forever and ever" (Revelation 15:7). He is "from everlasting to everlasting" (Psalm 90:2). He is enthroned forever (Psalm 102:12) and "inhabits eternity" (Isaiah 57:15).

Women and silence in the church (1 Timothy 2:12). Paul said women are not to be in authority over men as church pastors. However, they are allowed to teach men on an individual basis—as apparently Priscilla, with her husband Aquila, taught Apollos (Acts 18:26). They are permitted to address fellow believers, male and female, to their "upbuilding and encouragement and consolation" (1 Corinthians 14:3). They are permitted to teach women (Titus 2:3-4) and children (2 Timothy 1:5; 3:14) and be involved in other fruitful ministries (Romans 16:3,6,12).

Digging Deeper with Cross-References

Standing for sound doctrine (1 Timothy 1:1-11)—Romans 16:17; Ephesians 4:14; 2 Timothy 4:3-4; Titus 1:9; 2:1

Interceding for others (1 Timothy 2:1-8)—Genesis 20:7,17; Exodus 10:18; Deuteronomy 9:20,26; 1 Samuel 7:5; 2 Samuel 24:17; 1 Chronicles 21:17; 2 Chronicles 30:18; Job 42:10; Psalm 106:23; Jeremiah 18:20; Daniel 9:16; Luke 7:3; Acts 8:15; Romans 15:30; Ephesians 1:16; 2 Timothy 1:18

Life Lessons

Christ empowers us (1 Timothy 1:12). Paul said, "I thank him who has given me strength, Christ Jesus our Lord." Paul elsewhere said, "I can do all things through him who strengthens me" (Philippians 4:13). This is important, for Jesus affirmed, "Apart from me you can do nothing" (John 15:5).

Live to please God (1 Timothy 2:2). Paul urged that each Christian "lead a peaceful and quiet life, godly and dignified in every way." He had earlier written, "We urge you...to live quietly, and to mind your own affairs, and to work with your hands" (1 Thessalonians 4:11). Such a life is pleasing to God.

Verses to Remember

- "The saying is trustworthy and deserving of full acceptance, that Christ Jesus came into the world to save sinners, of whom I am the foremost" (1 Timothy 1:15).
- "There is one God, and there is one mediator between God and men, the man Christ Jesus, who gave himself as a ransom for all" (1 Timothy 2:5-6).

Questions for Reflection and Discussion

1. Does it surprise you that Paul thought of himself as the worst of all sinners? Do you think it's true that the closer our walk is with Christ, the deeper our sense of humility?

2. Can you think of examples in your own life where Christ's strength was manifest in your weakness?

3. Do you think Christians can live peaceful and quiet lives in today's hectic world?

My Father, I rejoice that I can do all things through Christ who strengthens me. After all, as Jesus said, in myself I can do nothing. I praise You for sending Jesus into the world to be my Savior and Mediator. I am thankful. In Jesus's name, amen.

Fight the Good Fight

In yesterday's lesson we explored Paul's instructions to young Timothy on issues of concern for a young pastor leading a church (1 Timothy 1–3). Now we give consideration to Paul's final instructions to Timothy in this letter.

Begin by reading 1 Timothy 4–6. As you read, keep in mind that the Word of God brings spiritual maturity (1 Corinthians 3:1-2; Hebrews 5:12-14).

Chronological marker. Paul wrote 1 Timothy in AD 64.

Overview of Today's Scripture Reading

1 Timothy 4. Paul advised Timothy on some issues that false teachers had addressed, including marriage, food, and exercise. Paul urged Timothy to watch his doctrine closely. Just as good doctrine leads to a healthy spirituality, so bad doctrine can be spiritually injurious. Paul indicated to Timothy that the best way to combat error is to constantly engage in a simple exposition of God's Word. Teaching God's Word and living God's Word punches a big hole in false doctrine.

1 Timothy 5. Paul advised Timothy on how he, as a young pastor, ought to treat people in the church (verses 1-2), focusing specifically on widows (verses 3-16) and elders (verses 17-20). Paul's underlying idea was that Timothy ought to treat other people as he would his own family. Paul is careful to clarify what type of widow should be cared for in the church. For example, she must be a Christian, have no family to take care of her, and be at least 60 years old. Young women (who should marry), idle women, gossipers, and busybodies are ineligible for church handouts.

1 Timothy 6. Paul closed with a warning about the unbiblical idea that godliness results in material blessing. The pastor ought to focus on godliness while being content with what he has (6:3-16). The man of God specifically—and all Christians generally—ought to crave godliness and not money.

Today's Big Ideas

- Apostasy will increase in the latter times (4:1-5).
- Be a committed servant of Christ (4:6-16).
- Godliness with contentment is great gain (6:2-10).
- Fight the good fight of faith (6:11-21).

Insights on Difficult Verses

1 Timothy 5:21. The "elect angels" are angels who kept their first estate and did not sin against God when Lucifer led an angelic rebellion (Isaiah 14:12-14; Ezekiel 28:11-19). They are called elect because following the rebellion, God intervened to permanently confirm (elect) them in their holiness so there would be no possibility of future sin on their part.

1 Timothy 5:23. Then as now, people sometimes got sick by drinking water that was not purified. Wine was often mixed with water to purify the water. Apparently Paul advised Timothy to drink a little wine because of his perpetual stomach problems.

Scripture provides principles relevant to the question, "Should I drink wine?"

- "'All things are lawful for me,' but not all things are helpful. 'All things are lawful for me,' but I will not be dominated by anything" (1 Corinthians 6:12).

- "It is good not to eat meat or drink wine or do anything that causes your brother to stumble" (Romans 14:21).

- "So, whether you eat or drink, or whatever you do, do all to the glory of God" (1 Corinthians 10:31).

Major Themes

The danger of materialism (1 Timothy 6:9). Paul stated that "those who desire to be rich fall into...many senseless and harmful desires that plunge people into ruin and destruction." Jesus warned His followers, "Take care, and be on your guard against all covetousness" (Luke 12:15). It is better to lay up treasures in heaven (Matthew 6:19-20).

The glory of God/Jesus (1 Timothy 6:16). The word "glory," when used of God, refers to the luminous manifestation of His person. Brilliant light consistently accompanies the divine manifestation in His glory (Matthew 17:2-3; Revelation 1:16). God "dwells in unapproachable light" (1 Timothy 6:16). The word "glory" is often linked with verbs of seeing (Exodus 16:7; 33:18).

Digging Deeper with Cross-References

Contentment (1 Timothy 6:6-10)—Psalm 37:16; Proverbs 15:13; 30:8; 19:23; Ecclesiastes 3:12-13; 5:10; Philippians 4:11-12; Hebrews 13:5

The fight of faith (1 Timothy 6:11-21)—1 Kings 2:2; 2 Chronicles 15:7; Isaiah 35:4; Haggai 2:4; Zechariah 8:9; 1 Corinthians 16:13; Ephesians 6:10

Life Lessons

Beware of being deceived (1 Timothy 4:1-5). God's people can be deceived. Jesus warned His followers to beware of false prophets (Matthew 7:15-16). Paul warned the Ephesian elders that "fierce wolves" would not spare the flock (Acts 20:28-30). Paul also referred to the possibility of Christians being led astray by Satan (2 Corinthians 11:2-3). A word to the wise: Stay anchored in the Word of God (2 Timothy 3:15-17).

Godliness with contentment (1 Timothy 6:6). Paul knew that external things don't bring contentment, but our relationship with God does. Paul affirmed in Philippians 4:11-13, "I have learned in whatever situation I am to be content. I know how to be brought low, and I know how to abound. In any and every circumstance, I have learned the secret of facing plenty and hunger, abundance and need. I can do all things through him who strengthens me."

Verses to Remember

- "Godliness with contentment is great gain, for we brought nothing into the world, and we cannot take anything out of the world" (1 Timothy 6:6-7).

- "Those who desire to be rich fall into temptation, into a snare, into many senseless and harmful desires that plunge people into ruin and destruction" (1 Timothy 6:9).

Questions for Reflection and Discussion

1. Why do you think Paul made such a big deal about pursuing correct doctrine?

2. Are you a contented Christian? If not, what have you learned today that might help you?

3. Do you desire to be rich? Has today's lesson altered your attitude toward personal wealth?

My Father, it is sobering to ponder that I did not bring anything into this world and cannot take anything out of this world. Please work in my life so I can fully experience godliness with contentment. That's the kind of Christian I want to be. In Jesus's name, amen.

Stand for the Truth

Yesterday we considered Paul's final instructions to Timothy in their first letter (1 Timothy 4–6). Today we will focus on the importance of standing for truth.

Begin by reading through 2 Timothy. Read with the anticipation that the Holy Spirit has something important to teach you today (see Psalm 119:105).

Chronological marker. Three years after writing 1 Timothy, Paul needed to give yet more advice to his young coworker. He wrote 2 Timothy in AD 67.

Introduction to 2 Timothy

Author: the apostle Paul

Fast facts:

- When Paul wrote 2 Timothy, he was in prison and expected to be executed shortly (1:16; 2:9).

- Paul encouraged Timothy to maintain the faith, hold on to sound doctrine, be faithful in ministry, and preach the gospel relentlessly (1:6,13-14; 3:15–4:5).

Key words in 2 Timothy (and the number of times they appear):

faith (8)	abide (3)
endure (5)	be diligent (3)
ashamed/unashamed (4)	gospel (3)
doctrine (4)	

Overview of Today's Scripture Reading

2 Timothy 1. Paul encouraged Timothy to stand firm in the power of the gospel and not give way to fear, intimidation, or shame. Persecution will come, but God sustains His servants.

2 Timothy 2. Paul encouraged Timothy to disciple and teach others (verses 1-2), be single-minded in serving the Lord (verses 3-5), patiently endure all things (verses 6-13), work diligently for the Lord (verses 14-19), pursue righteousness and avoid youthful lusts (verses 20-23), and be gentle as a servant of God (verses 24-26).

2 Timothy 3. Paul warned Timothy of an impending time of apostasy. People will increasingly fall prey to empty religiosity and false teaching (verses 1-9). There will be increased arrogance, godlessness, deception, and persecution. Timothy must therefore stand strong in his defense of the Word of God (verses 10-17). Paul reminded Timothy that all Scripture is inspired by God and sufficient to equip people for the work of ministry.

2 Timothy 4:1-5. Paul exhorted Timothy to be ready to preach the word in season and out of season. Many will abandon sound doctrine, but Timothy was to do the work of an evangelist and fulfill his ministry.

2 Timothy 4:6-22. Paul revealed that the time of his departure (death) was near. He was content, having fought the good fight, finished the race, and kept the faith. He expressed his desire to see Timothy again (verses 9,21) .

Today's Big Ideas

- Timothy is to boldly testify to the truth (1:3-18).
- Timothy is to be a good soldier of Jesus (2:1-18).
- Timothy is to be a worker approved by God (2:14-26).
- There will be godlessness in the end times (3:1-9).
- All Scripture is inspired by God (3:10-17).
- Timothy is to preach the Word (4:1-8).

Insights on Difficult Verses

2 Timothy 1:10. Officially, death has already been abolished. But this will not become an actual reality until the rapture, at which time "death is swallowed up in victory" (1 Corinthians 15:54).

2 Timothy 3:8. There is no Old Testament text that informs us about Jannes and Jambres. Paul wrote under the direct inspiration of the Holy Spirit.

2 Timothy 3:16. The term "Scripture" here refers not just to the Old Testament but also to as many New Testament books as had been written up till the time 2 Timothy was written (see 1 Timothy 5:18; 2 Peter 3:16).

Major Themes

Warnings of apostasy (2 Timothy 4:3-4). The word "apostasy" comes from the Greek word *apostasia,* meaning "falling away." The word refers to a determined, willful defection from the faith, or an abandonment of the faith (see 1 Timothy 4:1-2).

God's Word is fully sufficient (2 Timothy 3:15-17). A primary emphasis in 2 Timothy is that God's Word is fully sufficient for salvation and the Christian life. All the revelation God desired us to have is found in the Bible.

Digging Deeper with Cross-References

Examples of evil times (2 Timothy 3:1-2)—Genesis 6:12; 1 Kings 19:10; Psalm 12:1; Isaiah 59:14; Jeremiah 5:1; Micah 7:2; Ephesians 5:16

Last days (2 Timothy 3:1–4:5)—1 Timothy 4:1; James 5:3; 2 Peter 3:3; Jude 18

Life Lessons

God's Word is like... (2 Timothy 3:15-17). The Bible is like a manufacturer's handbook that instructs us how to operate our lives. It is like an eyeglass that helps us see spiritual realities. It is like a lamp that sheds light on our path (Psalm 119:105). It is like an anchor that prevents us from being swept away when adversity comes. It is like food because it gives us spiritual nourishment (Hebrews 5:12; 1 Peter 2:2). It is like a love letter, telling us about God's love for us (John 3:16-17).

Flee youthful passions (2 Timothy 2:22). Paul instructs Timothy to "flee youthful passions and pursue righteousness." First Corinthians 6:18 exhorts, "Flee from sexual immorality." This is illustrated in the life of Joseph. Potiphar's wife tried to seduce him, but he "fled and got out of the house" (Genesis 39:12). Joseph is a good example to all Christians today.

Verses to Remember

- "Do your best to present yourself to God as one approved, a worker who has no need to be ashamed, rightly handling the word of truth" (2 Timothy 2:15).

- "All Scripture is breathed out by God and profitable for teaching, for reproof, for correction, and for training in righteousness, that the man of God may be complete, equipped for every good work" (2 Timothy 3:16-17).

Questions for Reflection and Discussion

1. How much time do you spend in God's Word each week? How does that compare with the time you spend watching TV? Do you want to pursue more balance in your life?

2. Do you make it a habit to flee temptations as soon as they surface in your mind?

3. Review 2 Timothy 2:14-19. What do you need to do to become a worker approved by God?

My Father, I want to spend time in Your Word every day. My spiritual health depends on it. Please enable me to prioritize my time rightly so that I do not allow the urgent to crowd out the important. In Jesus's name, amen.

Day 79

Beware of False Teachers

Yesterday we gave attention to the importance of standing for truth (2 Timothy). Today we turn our attention to false teachers and the need to stay rooted in the Word of God.

Begin by reading through 2 Peter and Jude. As you read, never forget that you can trust everything that is recorded in the Word of God (Matthew 5:18; John 10:35).

Chronological marker. Second Peter and Jude were written not long after 2 Timothy—around AD 67–68.

2 PETER

Introduction to 2 Peter
Author: the apostle Peter
Fast facts:

- Some mystics had placed more weight on their own spiritual experiences than on the revelations from prophets and apostles that Jesus would come again.

- Peter rebuked these ideas, emphasizing that since Jesus will in fact return, one had better live in righteousness.

Key words in 2 Peter (and the number of times they appear):

know/knowledge (8)	promise (4)
destroy (5)	diligent (3)

Overview of Today's Scripture Reading

2 Peter 1. Christians are recipients of great and precious promises (verses 1-4). Accordingly, believers ought to divorce themselves from the corruption of the world and pursue Christian virtues instead (verses 5-11).

Peter knew his death was near. He urged his readers to hold fast to the truth and never forget the riches of their position in Christ (verses 12-21). He knew what he was talking about, for he was an eyewitness of Christ's glory (verses 16-18) and knew that Scripture was inspired by God (verse 21).

2 Peter 2. Knowing that his time was short, Peter spoke against false teachers who put the flock in danger (verses 1-3). They rejected authority, sought self-gratification, denied the Lord by the way they lived, and exploited others for profit. Dire punishment awaits them from God (verses 4-22).

2 Peter 3. Christ's future return is certain, but many unbelievers will scoff at the idea (verses 1-7). If God delays the second coming, it is only because He wants plenty of time for people to be saved (verses 8-10). The reality of Christ's future coming should motivate Christians to righteous living (verses 11-18).

Today's Big Ideas

- Live as God desires you to live (1:3-15).

- The truth about Jesus is based on eyewitness testimony (1:16-21).

- Beware of false teachers (2).

- Because the day of the Lord is coming, we should pursue holiness (3:1-13).

Insights on Difficult Verses

2 Peter 1:20. The prophecies did not come from the prophets themselves, but from God.

2 Peter 2:9. The wicked dead are condemned prisoners, awaiting sentencing at the great white throne judgment.

JUDE

Introduction to Jude
Author: Jude
Fast facts:
- Jude was a younger brother of Jesus and James.
- He earlier rejected Jesus as the Messiah (John 7:1-9). Following Jesus's resurrection, he and his brothers converted (Acts 1:14).
- He became a church leader in Jerusalem.

Key words in Jude (and the number of times they appear):
ungodly (6)
beloved (3)
everlasting (3)
judgment (3)

Overview of Today's Scripture Reading

Jude 1-4. Jude exhorted his readers to contend for the faith once for all delivered to the saints. "The faith" refers to the body of Christian truth handed down by the apostles.

Jude 5-16. False teachers denied that Jesus was the Son of God and were turning Christian grace and liberty into a license to sin. Jude thus urged Christians to anchor themselves to the truth. He reminded his readers of God's past dealings with those who felt free to sin—including unbelieving Israelites, the wicked people of Sodom and Gomorrah, and the wicked angels (5-7).

Jude 17-25. The apostles had warned that such false teachers would emerge (17-19). Jude thus encouraged his readers to guard against apostasy (20-21). As they mature in the Christian faith, they will be able to rescue others from false doctrine (22-23).

Today's Big Ideas

- False teachers will be judged (3-16).
- Christians are to persevere in the truth (17-23).

Insights on Difficult Verses

Jude 14. Jude's citation of the book of Enoch does not mean the book of Enoch belongs in the Bible. It simply means Enoch included a truth that was worthy of inclusion in Jude.

Major Themes

False prophets (2 Peter 2; Jude 3-16). False prophets give predictions that do not come true (Deuteronomy 18:21-22), promote false gods (Exodus 20:3-4; Deuteronomy 13:1-3), deny Christ's deity (Colossians 2:8-9), and promote immorality (Jude 4-7) and legalism (Colossians 2:16-23).

Scoffers (2 Peter 3:3-4). Unbelief will predominate as the second coming of Christ approaches. There will be many scoffers (Jude 18).

Digging Deeper with Cross-References

> *False teachers (2 Peter 2; Jude 3-16)*—Matthew 5:19; 15:9; 1 Timothy 1:7; 4:2; 6:3; 2 Timothy 4:3; Titus 1:11
>
> *The day of the Lord (2 Peter 3:1-13)*—Malachi 4:5; 1 Corinthians 5:5; 2 Corinthians 1:14; 1 Thessalonians 5:2; 2 Peter 3:10

Life Lessons

Testing truth claims (Jude 3). Scripture is our barometer of truth against which we test all other truth claims (2 Timothy 3:15-17). When we know true doctrine, we are more likely to recognize false doctrine. We should follow Paul's exhortation: "Test everything; hold fast what is good" (1 Thessalonians 5:21; see Acts 17:11).

Living in light of Christ's return (2 Peter 3:4). Biblical prophecies are often found side by side with exhortations to righteousness (Romans 13:11-14; Titus 2:11-13; 1 John 3:2-3). Belief in Christ's soon return removes complacency.

Verses to Remember

- "Keep yourselves in the love of God, waiting for the mercy of our Lord Jesus Christ that leads to eternal life" (Jude 21).

- "The Lord knows how to rescue the godly from trials" (2 Peter 2:9).

Questions for Reflection and Discussion

1. Have scoffers ever mocked your beliefs about biblical prophecy?

2. Can you think of some examples of famous false teachers today?

3. Are you contending for the faith once for all handed down to believers (Jude 3)?

My Father, I want to be ready when Christ comes again. I do not want to be found in a life of spiritual complacency when He arrives. Please empower me by Your Spirit to be consistent in living a life that is pleasing to You. In Jesus's name, amen.

The Supremacy of Christ

In the previous lesson we discussed false teachers and the need to stay rooted in the Word of God (2 Peter and Jude). Today we explore the supremacy of Jesus Christ and the salvation He provides.

Begin by reading Hebrews 1:1–4:13. As you read, remember that the Word of God is alive and working in you (Hebrews 4:12).

Chronological marker. Hebrews was written in AD 68, just two years before Jerusalem and the temple were overrun by Rome in AD 70.

Introduction to Hebrews

Author: unknown, but possibly the apostle Paul, Apollos, or Barnabas

Fast facts:

- Jews who converted to Christ in the first century were branded as apostates and blemishes to the Jewish nation. They were expelled from the synagogue. Their children were denied attending school at the synagogue. They lost their jobs. They were sometimes thrown in jail (10:33-34). These circumstances caused some of these Jewish believers to wane in their outward commitment to Christ.

- These converts didn't renounce Christ, but to avoid persecution, they considered participating in the outward observances of Judaism, including rituals, ceremonies, and sacrifices (6:1-2).

- The author emphasized that Jesus is the ultimate fulfillment of the Old Testament and is greater than all Old Testament personalities and institutions (1:5–7:28). To step back into Judaism was unacceptable. The author called his Jewish readers to move on to maturity in the Christian faith (6:1).

Key words in Hebrews (and the number of times they appear):

faith/faithful (37)	better (13)
high priest/priesthood (34)	once/once for all (11)
covenant (17)	perfect (9)
angels (13)	

Overview of Today's Scripture Reading

Hebrews 1. To help these Jewish believers move on to Christian maturity rather than reverting to the external practices of Judaism, the author laid out convincing evidence that Christ is superior in every way to the old Jewish system. Jesus is superior to the prophets (verses 1-3). He is also superior to angels, through whom revelations were delivered (verses 4-14). Jesus is God's Son and is absolute deity. He created and sustains the world and is seated at the Father's right hand.

Hebrews 2. Because Jesus is superior, we ought not neglect the salvation message we have received from Him. We must not drift away from His new teachings in favor of the legalistic rituals of Judaism. If people were punished in Old Testament times for ignoring the Law mediated through angels, how much more will people be punished for ignoring Christ and His work of salvation.

Hebrews 3:1–4:13. Jesus is also superior to Moses, the lawgiver and the hero of Jewish people. Moses was a great servant of God, but Jesus is God's Son! Moreover, those who followed Moses in the wilderness had unbelieving hearts and sinned against God. As a result, they did not enter rest in the Promised Land. The writer of Hebrews therefore urged his readers not to harden their hearts in unbelief and fail to enter God's spiritual rest.

Today's Big Ideas

- Jesus is supreme (1).

- One must not drift away from salvation in Jesus (2).
- Jesus is even greater than Moses (3).
- Don't miss the spiritual rest available in Jesus (4:1-13).

Insights on Difficult Verses

Hebrews 1:2. Jesus was a perfect revelation of God's awesome power (John 3:2), incredible wisdom (1 Corinthians 1:24), boundless love (1 John 3:16), and unfathomable grace (2 Thessalonians 1:12).

Hebrews 1:3. Jesus is the "exact imprint" of God's nature—an absolutely authentic representation of God's being (see John 14:9). Jesus is truly God!

Major Themes

God reveals (Hebrews 1:1-2). God has always taken the initiative in providing revelation to humans. God's ultimate revelation came in the person of Jesus Christ (John 1:18; Hebrews 1:2; Revelation 1:1).

The Trinity and creation (Hebrews 1:2). Creation is attributed to the Father (Psalm 102:25), the Son (John 1:3; Colossians 1:16; Hebrews 1:2), and the Holy Spirit (Job 26:13; 33:4; Isaiah 40:12-13). The Father planned it, the Son executed it, and the Holy Spirit gave it life (Psalm 104:30; 1 Corinthians 8:6).

Digging Deeper with Cross-References

Angels (Hebrews 1:4-14)—2 Kings 6:17; Psalm 91:11; Matthew 25:31; Luke 15:7-10; Colossians 1:16; Hebrews 13:2

God is grieved by human sin (Hebrews 3:7-13)—Deuteronomy 5:29; 32:29; Psalms 78:40; 81:13; Isaiah 48:18; 63:10; Ezekiel 33:11; Luke 19:41-42; Ephesians 4:30

Life Lessons

Calloused hearts (Hebrews 3:8; 4:7). Scripture warns that Christians' hearts can become calloused (Psalm 95:8). Just as calloused skin is insensitive, so a calloused heart is insensitive to the things of God. The best remedy is regular exposure to God's Word (Psalm 119), obedience

(John 14:21; 1 John 5:3), and immediate repentance when one falls into sin (Acts 3:19).

Be aware of your mortality (Hebrews 2:14-15). Humans fear death. None of us knows when the day will come (Genesis 27:2; Ecclesiastes 9:12). The psalmist wisely prayed, "O Lord, make me know my end and what is the measure of my days; let me know how fleeting I am!" (Psalm 39:4).

Verses to Remember

- "We must pay much closer attention to what we have heard, lest we drift away from it" (Hebrews 2:1).

- "Today, if you hear his voice, do not harden your hearts" (Hebrews 3:7-8).

Questions for Reflection and Discussion

1. Do you sometimes pay too little attention to God's Word?

2. On a scale of 1 to 10, how do you rate your sensitivity to the things of God?

3. Do you consider Christ supreme over all things in your life?

My Father, I fear that I am sometimes not as sensitive as I should be to Your Word. It seems all too easy to lapse in my daily spiritual growth. Please motivate my heart to desire spiritual maturity. In Jesus's name, amen.

Moving On to Maturity

Yesterday we focused on the supremacy of Jesus Christ and the salvation He provides (Hebrews 1:1–4:13). Today we zero in on moving from spiritual immaturity to spiritual maturity in Jesus Christ, our faithful High Priest.

Begin by reading Hebrews 4:14–7:28. As you read, remember that those who obey the Word of God are truly blessed (Psalm 119:2; Luke 11:28; Revelation 1:3).

Chronological marker. Hebrews was written in AD 68.

Overview of Today's Scripture Reading

Hebrews 4:14–5:10. Just as Jesus was shown to be superior to the Old Testament prophets, the angels, and Moses, so now Christ's priesthood is shown to be superior to the Levitical priesthood. The Levitical priesthood involved many priests; Christ is our single High Priest. Levitical priests were tainted by sin; Christ was without sin. Levitical priests offered animal sacrifices; Christ offered Himself as a once-for-all sacrifice. Levitical priests died; Christ lives on forever.

Hebrews 5:11–6:12. These Jewish believers had it tough. As we saw in yesterday's reading, when Jews became Christians in the first century, the high priest persecuted them. This caused some of the Jewish Christians to become gun-shy in their Christian lives. They weren't as open about their Christian faith. Perhaps they thought that if they kept quiet about their faith and withdrew from external involvement in Christian affairs (such as church attendance), the high priest would lighten up on them. The author of Hebrews countered by instructing them to "go on to maturity" and render absolute commitment to the faithful High Priest, Jesus Christ (6:1).

Hebrews 6:13–7:28. God's promises are trustworthy, so the salvation of the Jewish believers is sure and steadfast. After all, Christ's priesthood is eternal, and He removed sin forever by His one sacrifice at Calvary.

Christ is a priest after the order of Melchizedek, whose name is made up of two words meaning "king" and "righteous." Melchizedek foreshadows Christ, our righteous King-Priest. We are also told that Melchizedek was the king of Salem, a word that means "peace." This points forward to Christ as a righteous King-Priest of peace.

Today's Big Ideas

- Jesus is our faithful High Priest (4:14–5:10; 7).
- Do not spiritually stagnate (5:11-14).
- Move on to spiritual maturity in Jesus Christ (6).

Insights on Difficult Verses

Hebrews 5:8. Jesus "learned obedience" not in terms of His divine nature but in terms of His human nature in the Incarnation.

Hebrews 6:4-6. The context of Hebrews 6:4-6 is set for us in verses 1-3—"Go on to maturity." The Jewish readers of Hebrews had failed to mature spiritually. They had spiritually stagnated because of persecution from the high priest. Despite such persecution, they are encouraged to plow on to maturity. Such temporal persecution does not compare with the eternal joy of salvation brought by Jesus Christ, our faithful High Priest.

Hebrews 7:25. Christ became a man *and* a High Priest, both of which make it fitting that He pray and intercede.

Major Themes

Eternal security (Hebrews 6:4). Some believe Hebrews 6:1-4 means Christians can lose salvation. Ephesians 4:30, however, promises that believers are permanently sealed by the Holy Spirit, guaranteeing they will be brought into full redemption (see also John 10:28-30; Romans 8:29-39). Hebrews 6:1-4 warns against falling away from maturity, not from salvation.

Melchizedek (Hebrews 7:3). This verse says Melchizedek is *like* the Son of God, not that he *is* the Son of God (Hebrews 7:3). Melchizedek was a historical person who served as a type of Christ, prefiguring Christ as a righteous King-Priest. Melchizedek was not the preincarnate Christ.

Digging Deeper with Cross-References

Christ's ascension (Hebrews 4:14)—Mark 16:19; Luke 24:51; John 6:62; 20:17; Acts 1:9; Ephesians 4:8; Hebrews 9:24; 1 Peter 3:22

Spiritual maturity (Hebrews 5:14; 6:4)—1 Corinthians 13:11; 14:20; Ephesians 4:13,15; Philippians 1:27-30; 4:12; 2 Thessalonians 1:3; 2 Timothy 2:22; 3:16-17; 1 Peter 5:10; 2 Peter 3:18; 1 John 2:14

Life Lessons

The throne of grace (Hebrews 4:16). You and I are privileged to approach God's throne of grace, where we receive grace and mercy in time of need (literally, "for timely help"). Are you in need of timely help? What are you waiting for?

Christians and tithing (Hebrews 5:7). The word "tithe" literally means "a tenth" (see Genesis 28:22). God's Old Testament people gave a tenth back to God, acknowledging that He ultimately owns all things (Psalm 24:1). The New Testament emphasizes "grace giving" rather than tithing. We are to freely give as we have freely received (2 Corinthians 8:12). For some, this will mean less than 10 percent. Others can afford more than 10 percent. Foundationally, we must first give ourselves to the Lord (2 Corinthians 8:5).

Verses to Remember

- "We do not have a high priest who is unable to sympathize with our weaknesses, but one who in every respect has been tempted as we are, yet without sin. Let us then with confidence draw near to the throne of grace, that we may receive mercy and find grace to help in time of need" (Hebrews 4:15-16).

- "He is able to save to the uttermost those who draw near to God through him, since he always lives to make intercession for them" (Hebrews 7:25).

Questions for Reflection and Discussion

1. What are some specific areas in your life where you may need some "timely help"? Take them immediately to God's throne of grace and mercy.

2. What does it mean to you personally that Jesus is a *sympathetic* High Priest, having been tempted just as we are tempted?

3. What is your attitude toward tithing?

My Father, I am so appreciative that Jesus is my sympathetic High Priest, who thoroughly understands what it is like to be tempted. It touches me deeply that He prays and intercedes for me. On top of all that, I am privileged to bring my personal needs to Your throne of grace and mercy. What a blessing! In Jesus's name, amen.

Day 82

A Better Covenant

In yesterday's lesson we explored the necessity of moving from spiritual immaturity to spiritual maturity in Jesus Christ (Hebrews 4:14–7:28). Now we consider the better covenant instituted by our better High Priest, Jesus Christ.

Begin by reading Hebrews 8:1–10:18. As you read, keep in mind that just as we eat food for physical nourishment, so we need the Word of God for spiritual nourishment (1 Corinthians 3:2; Hebrews 5:12; 1 Peter 2:2).

Chronological marker. Hebrews was written in AD 68.

Overview of Today's Scripture Reading

Hebrews 8. Jesus Christ—with His superior priesthood (verses 1-5)—has brought about a new covenant, which is clearly superior to the old covenant (verses 6-13). This superior covenant is based on a single, final sacrifice for sin, with a High Priest who is enthroned at the right hand of God and who ministers in a true heavenly sanctuary on our behalf. Best of all, the new covenant does what the old covenant could not do—it brings about the true forgiveness of sins and yields a personal relationship with God.

Hebrews 9:1–10:18. Christ's superior covenant is based on His superior sacrifice. The earthly tabernacle provided only limited access to God and necessitated the continual offering of sacrifices, year after year. Since the continual sacrifice of animals could not truly take away sin, a worshipper in the old system could not be fully restored to God. The old system was inadequate. How much better is Christ's once-for-all sacrifice, which enabled Him to completely remove sin and attain eternal redemption for all God's people. Because He has brought about the forgiveness of sins once for all, there is no longer any need for an offering for sin. By His superior sacrifice, Jesus has enacted the new covenant prophesied by Jeremiah (31:31-34).

Having said all this, here is the primary point for the Jewish Christians reading this epistle: Because Christ is superior (in His person as God and in His priesthood), and because He has brought about a superior covenant, it would be sheer folly for these Jewish believers to stagnate as Christians, choosing instead to continue flirting with the external observances of Judaism in a misguided effort to placate the Jewish high priest. It is better to move on to maturity as Christians.

Today's Big Ideas

- Jesus is the High Priest of a better covenant (8).
- The better covenant is based on the once-for-all sacrifice of Christ on the cross of Calvary (9:1–10:18).

Insights on Difficult Verses

Hebrews 8:5. Some interpreters argue against the idea that there is actually a tabernacle in heaven from which the earthly version was copied. They suggest that the earthly tabernacle was an adequate symbolic representation of heavenly realities. It seems more accurate to say that the earthly tabernacle points to a literal heavenly archetypal tabernacle, which is why God warned Moses to make it "after the pattern" (Exodus 25:40) and "according to the plan" (Exodus 26:30).

Hebrews 9:28. The word "many" is intended as a contrast to Christ's "one" sacrifice. Christ actually died for all human beings (John 3:16-17; 4:42; Romans 5:6,18; 1 Timothy 4:10; Hebrews 2:9; 1 John 2:2).

Major Themes

Christ's sacrifice (Hebrews 9:12; 10:1-19). Christ accomplished our salvation "by means of his own blood, thus securing an eternal redemption." Christ the divine Lamb of God was utterly unblemished (1 Peter 1:19). Our sin was imputed to Him, and He was our sacrificial substitute (2 Corinthians 5:21). Christ's sacrifice was once for all—a key feature of the new and better covenant.

Anticipating the second coming (Hebrews 9:28). Christians eagerly await Christ's second coming. Indeed, we are "waiting for our blessed hope, the appearing of the glory of our great God and Savior Jesus Christ" (Titus 2:13). The crown of righteousness is promised to all those "who have loved his appearing" (2 Timothy 4:8).

Digging Deeper with Cross-References

Death follows life (Hebrews 9:27)—Psalms 23:4; 116:15; Ecclesiastes 3:1-2; 7:2; 8:8; Isaiah 25:8; Ezekiel 33:11; Romans 14:8; 1 Corinthians 15:26; Philippians 1:21; Revelation 21:3-4

Redemption through the blood of Christ (Hebrews 9)—Acts 20:28; Romans 5:9; Colossians 1:14,20; 1 John 1:7; Revelation 1:5; 5:9

Life Lessons

Jesus is our High Priest (Hebrews 8:1-6). As our divine High Priest, Jesus represents God the Father to us and represents us to God the Father. Jesus is our go-between. He is the bridge between God and us. "There is one God, and there is one mediator between God and men, the man Christ Jesus" (1 Timothy 2:5).

God forgets our sins (Hebrews 8:12). God not only forgives sin but "will remember their sins no more." This reminds us of the description of the new covenant in Jeremiah 31:34: "I will forgive their iniquity, and I will remember their sin no more." How marvelously wondrous is such forgiveness!

Verses to Remember

- "He is the mediator of a new covenant, so that those who are called may receive the promised eternal inheritance" (Hebrews 9:15).

- "This is the covenant that I will make with them after those days, declares the Lord: I will put my laws on their hearts, and write them on their minds...I will remember their sins and their lawless deeds no more" (Hebrews 10:16-17).

Questions for Reflection and Discussion

1. Does the fact that "it is appointed" for you to die affect the way you choose to live your life?

2. What does it mean to you personally that because of Jesus's sacrifice, God no longer remembers your sins? Does this motivate you to pursue righteousness?

3. Have you ever thought about how Jesus's death for your sins relates to John 15:13?

My Father, what a wonder is Jesus—my bridge to a relationship with You. What a wonder is Jesus—my High Priest, who prays for me. What a wonder is Jesus—who shed His blood for me and brought me salvation. What a wonder is Jesus—who instituted a better covenant on my behalf. I am in awe. It is in His name I pray, amen.

Day 83

The Assurance of Faith

Yesterday we considered the better covenant instituted by our better High Priest, Jesus Christ (Hebrews 8:1–10:18). Today we will focus on the need for faith in Him.

Begin by reading Hebrews 10:19–13:25. As you read, remember that storing God's Word in your heart can help you to avoid sinning (Psalm 119:9,11).

Chronological marker. Hebrews was written in AD 68.

Overview of Today's Scripture Reading

Hebrews 10:19-39. Christ alone is our hope and our Savior. We need nothing more. Jesus has completed the work of salvation on our behalf, and it remains for us only to trust in Him. We can now draw near to God with a full assurance of faith. The writer of Hebrews affirms to his Jewish readers that despite persecutions from the high priest, there should be no more doubt and no more wavering. Hold fast to your confession. Encourage each other as the day of judgment for the Jews and their temple draws near. (Jerusalem and the temple were destroyed in AD 70, two years after Hebrews was written.)

Hebrews 11. The author defines the nature of faith (verses 1-3) and then provides many examples of faith (verses 4-40). These examples ought to be a strong encouragement to these discouraged, weak-kneed Jewish Christians. The chapter implies that only a weak faith will succumb to the pressures put on them by the Jewish high priest. A strong faith, by contrast, will resist the temptation to succumb, knowing that a better country (heaven) lies directly ahead.

Hebrews 12. Believers ought to fix their eyes not on the Jewish high priest but on Jesus Himself. They ought to keep their gaze on Jesus, just as a runner fixes his gaze on the finish line. As a runner runs with endurance and lets go of all that weighs him down, believers ought to run with endurance to the finish line of heaven, letting go of all sins and distractions that weigh them down.

Hebrews 13. How we live matters. Our faith should show itself in the way we live our lives.

Today's Big Ideas

- Faith gives us assurance in God's promises (Hebrews 10).
- Faith is the assurance of things hoped for, the conviction of things not seen (Hebrews 11).
- Jesus is the Author and Perfecter of our faith (Hebrews 12).
- Let your faith show itself in how you live (Hebrews 13).

Insights on Difficult Verses

Hebrews 10:25. Hebrews was written in AD 68. The "Day drawing near" is apparently the judgment that fell on Jerusalem and the temple in AD 70.

Hebrews 12:7-11. God's motive for discipline is love. God loves us far too much to allow us to remain in unrepentant sin. His desire is to take some things away (related to sin) so that He can replace them with something better (holiness).

Hebrews 13:2. Angels are by nature incorporeal (nonmaterial) and invisible, but they can nevertheless appear as men (Matthew 1:20; Luke 1:26; John 20:12).

Major Themes

A better country (Hebrews 11:13-16). Heaven is "a better country." Eighteenth-century Bible expositor John Gill contemplates how the heavenly country is "full of light and glory; having the delightful breezes of divine love, and the comfortable gales of the blessed Spirit."[5] There is no more sin, disease, death, temptation, sorrow, affliction, or Satan in the heavenly country.

Christ as Shepherd (Hebrews 13:20). Jesus is the Good Shepherd, for He cares for and watches over His sheep (believers) (John 10:1-16). Jesus is the Great Shepherd, for He brought us peace with God through His blood (Hebrews 13:20). Jesus is the Chief Shepherd, who will one day come again (1 Peter 5:4).

Digging Deeper with Cross-References

The living God (Hebrews 10:31)—Joshua 3:10; 1 Samuel 17:26; Psalm 42:2; Isaiah 37:17; Jeremiah 23:36; Daniel 6:26; Matthew 26:63; Acts 14:15; 1 Thessalonians 1:9

Acceptable worship (Hebrews 12:28)—Exodus 20:3-5; 1 Samuel 15:22-23; Psalms 29:2; 95:6; 100:2; Isaiah 29:13; Revelation 14:7

Life Lessons

Walk by faith and not by sight (Hebrews 11). Even when things seem at their most hopeless, the God of miracles can come through in ways that we would never have fathomed. That's why it's important to maintain faith. Examples include Daniel's rescue in the lion's den (Daniel 6) and David's victory over Goliath (1 Samuel 17). Keep your faith in God strong (Psalm 40:4; Proverbs 3:5; Jeremiah 17:7; Matthew 15:28; Luke 17:5-6; Romans 10:17; 2 Corinthians 5:7; 1 Timothy 1:19; 1 Peter 1:7).

Helping people (Hebrews 13:16). We are all called to be people helpers. Philippians 2:4 instructs, "Let each of you look not only to his own interests, but also to the interests of others." In 1 John 3:17 we are asked, "If anyone has the world's goods and sees his brother in need, yet closes his heart against him, how does God's love abide in him?" Check out Jesus's words in Matthew 25:35-40.

Verses to Remember

- "Without faith it is impossible to please him, for whoever would draw near to God must believe that he exists and that he rewards those who seek him" (Hebrews 11:6).

- "Since we are surrounded by so great a cloud of witnesses, let us also lay aside every weight, and sin which clings so closely,

and let us run with endurance the race that is set before us"
(Hebrews 12:1).

Questions for Reflection and Discussion

1. Do any particular sins seem to cling to you? What have you
   learned in this lesson that might help you?

2. Are you presently facing any trials that require you to keep
   your faith in God strong?

3. Do you consider yourself a people helper? What steps could
   you take this week to improve in this area?

*My Father, thank You for Your patience with me. I sometimes feel enslaved
to certain sins, but I do not want to passively surrender to them. Enable me,
by the power of Your Spirit, to shake loose from them and cling instead to
You. Please strengthen my faith. In Jesus's name, amen.*

Day 84

Fellowship with God and with One Another

Yesterday we gave attention to the need for faith in our faithful High Priest, Jesus Christ (Hebrews 10:19–13:2). Today we turn our attention to fellowship with God and with each other, walking in the light, and not being tainted by the world system.

Begin by reading through 1, 2, and 3 John. As you read, trust God to open your eyes so you can discover wondrous things from His Word (Psalm 119:18).

Chronological marker. John wrote 1, 2, and 3 John around AD 90, after some heresies had emerged in the early church.

Introduction to 1, 2, and 3 John

Author: the apostle John

Fast facts:

- By the time the aging apostle John wrote his letters, Christianity had been around for more than 50 years. Plenty of time had passed for spiritual and doctrinal errors to develop.

- The primary heretical system John faced was an early strain of Gnosticism. (See Major Themes.)

Key words (and the number of times they appear):

1 John	truth (15)	abide (3)
love (45)		walk (3)
know (39)	*2 John*	
sin (27)	love (4)	*3 John*
abide (23)	commandment(4)	truth (6)
world (23)	truth (4)	witness (5)

1 JOHN

Overview of Today's Scripture Reading

1 John 1:1–2:27. John wanted his readers to experience fellowship with Christ (1:1-4). A prime condition is that one must walk in the light (1:5-7). Christians must confess their sin to God so that fellowship can be restored (1:8-10). Meanwhile, Christ pleads our case with the Father (2:1-2).

John reveals what walking in the light looks like. Christians must be obedient to God (2:3-6), love others (2:7-14), not love the world (2:15-16), and avoid false ideas about Jesus (2:18-27).

1 John 2:28–5:3. Genuine fellowship with God shows itself in one's life. Characteristics include moral purity (2:28–3:3), righteousness (3:4-12), loving others (3:13–4:21), and obedience to God's commandments (5:1-3).

1 John 5:4-21. When we fellowship with God, we gain victory over the world (verses 4-5), assurance of salvation (verses 6-13), confidence in prayer (verses 14-17), and freedom from habitual sin (5:18-21).

Today's Big Ideas

- Life is found in Jesus Christ (1:1-4; 5:6-12).
- Christians are to walk in the light (1:5-19).
- Christians are to love one another (2:7-17; 3:11-24; 4:7-21).

Insights on Difficult Verses

1 John 3:9. Christians do not *habitually* sin, or make a regular practice of sinning.

1 John 5:6-8. The false teacher Cerinthus taught that a cosmic Christ spirit came upon a human Jesus after His baptism but departed before His crucifixion. John refutes this heresy. "Water" refers to Jesus's baptism. "Blood" refers to His crucifixion. They are metaphorical witnesses that Jesus Christ experienced baptism and crucifixion.

1 John 5:16. This refers to any sin that is repeatedly committed, drawing one progressively deeper into the world's death-producing system.

2 JOHN

Overview of Today's Scripture Reading

2 John 1-6. John wrote to "the elect lady and her children." This could be a literal woman and her children, or it could be a metaphorical reference to a church and its members.

2 John 7-13. Gnostic false teachers said that Jesus couldn't have taken on a material human body because matter is evil. (See Major Themes.) John rebukes this attack against Christ's humanity.

Insights on Difficult Verses

2 John 10. In Bible times, churches met in people's houses (Romans 6:15; 1 Corinthians 16:19; Colossians 4:15). John warns against allowing a false teacher into one's house-church and giving him a platform from which to teach.

3 JOHN

Overview of Today's Scripture Reading

3 John 1-8. Gaius was a godly (2-4) and generous (5-8) man.

3 John 9-14. By contrast, Diotrephes was full of pride and ambition (9-11). John hopes to visit his readers soon (13-14).

Insights on Difficult Verses

3 John 2. This does not mean God desires Christians to be financially prosperous. The Greek word translated "prosper" (NASB) means "to go well with someone." This was a standard form of greeting.

Major Themes

Gnosticism (1 John 4:1-6). Gnosticism taught that spirit is good but matter is evil. This means Christ could not have become human because a human body would be evil. In this line of thought, a spiritual Christ entered into the body of a human Jesus after His baptism and left the body of the human Jesus before the crucifixion. This scenario avoids the idea that the good Christ became material.

Beware of false Christs (1 John 4:1-6). Jesus warned about false Christs (Matthew 24:5). The apostle Paul warned of a different Jesus (2 Corinthians 11:4). The concern is obvious: A counterfeit Christ who preaches a counterfeit gospel can yield only a counterfeit salvation.

Digging Deeper with Cross-References

Characteristics of the believer's walk (1 John 1:7; 2:6)—Romans 6:4; 2 Corinthians 5:7; Galatians 5:16; Ephesians 4:1; 5:2,15

Separation from the world (1 John 2:15-17)—Isaiah 52:11; John 15:19; Acts 2:40; 2 Corinthians 6:17; Ephesians 5:11; 2 Thessalonians 3:6

Life Lessons

Love for others (1 John 3:11-24). Our vertical relationship with God should affect our horizontal relationships with other people (1 John 2:7-17; 4:7-21).

Don't love the world (1 John 2:15-17). Christians should not love the world. The word "world" here refers not to the physical earth but to an anti-God system that Satan has promoted and that conforms to his ideals, aims, and methods.

Verses to Remember

- "We have an advocate with the Father, Jesus Christ the righteous" (1 John 2:1).

- "This is the love of God, that we keep his commandments" (1 John 5:3).

Questions for Reflection and Discussion

1. How would you characterize your struggle with the desires of the flesh, the desires of the eyes, and the pride of life?

2. How would you assess your ability to concretely express love to others?

3. Is anything in your life presently hindering you from walking in the light?

My Father, how I desire to walk in the light. How I desire to be consistent in resisting the desires of the flesh, the desires of the eyes, and the pride of life. Please mold me. In Jesus's name, amen.

Jesus Christ—the Lord of the Churches

In the previous lesson we discussed John's epistles and learned about fellowshipping with God and with each other (1, 2, and 3 John). In the present chapter, we begin study of the book of Revelation and will explore Jesus's assessment of the seven churches.

Begin by reading Revelation 1–4. As you read, allow the Word of God to bring revival to your soul (Psalm 119:25,93,107).

Chronological marker. John wrote the last book of the New Testament, Revelation, around AD 95.

Introduction to the Book of Revelation

Author: the apostle John

Fast facts:

- Revelation is the only apocalyptic book in the New Testament.

- The apostle John had been exiled on the isle of Patmos in the Aegean Sea for his evangelistic activities (1:9). It was on this island that John received the "revelation."

- The recipients of the book were undergoing severe persecution—some even being killed. John wrote this book to give his readers a strong hope that would help them patiently endure in the midst of suffering.

Key words in Revelation (and the number of times they appear):

God (98)	lamb (29)	judge/judgment (16)
angel (75)	Spirit (23)	wrath (16)
throne (46)	church (20)	plague (15)
beast (38)	overcome (17)	Jesus (14)

Overview of Today's Scripture Reading

Revelation 1. The word "revelation" carries the idea of "uncovering" or "revealing." This book uncovers and reveals prophetic truth (1:1). Notice the exalted language used of Jesus (1:5,7-8,17-18).

Revelation 1:19 provides an outline for the book: John writes about what he had seen (Revelation 1), the things "that are" (Revelation 2–3), and the things that "take place after this" (Revelation 4–22).

Revelation 2. Christ commends the churches where He can (2:2-3, 6,9,13,19) but also rebukes them where He must (2:4-5,14-16,20-23). In each case, He calls for repentance. He loves His people but will not turn a blind eye toward sinful behavior or spiritual lethargy. Jesus is not only a loving Savior but also an advocate of tough love.

Revelation 3. Christ continues His policy of commending the churches where He can (3:4,8) but also rebuking them where He must (3:1-3,15-20). He continues to call for repentance. He promises to bless the faithful (3:5,10-12,21). We learn from Christ's interactions with the churches that tough circumstances on earth (such as persecution) are no excuse for a compromised spiritual life.

Revelation 4. John witnessed God on the throne, indicating His absolute sovereignty (see Isaiah 14:24; 46:10). The scene is resplendent and glorious. John speaks of jewels in an attempt to portray the matchless beauty of the throne room. Lightning and thunder around the throne point to God's glory (Revelation 4:5). The floor is like a glistening crystal (Revelation 4:6; see Exodus 24:10). The throne is surrounded by various creatures who worship the Creator (4:10-11).

Today's Big Ideas

- Jesus is the Lord of glory (1:9-20).
- Jesus commends the churches when possible (2:2-3,6,9,13,19; 3:4,8).
- Jesus rebukes the churches when necessary (2:4-5,14-16,20-23; 3:1-3;15-20).
- Jesus promises blessings to the faithful (2:7,10-11,17,26-28; 3:5,10-12,21).

Insights on Difficult Verses

Revelation 1:4. "The seven spirits" is apparently a reference to the Holy Spirit (see Isaiah 11:2).

Revelation 3:5. This is not a threat but instead an assurance that saved peoples' names will always be in the book of life.

Revelation 3:14. Jesus is the "beginning" or Creator of all things (see John 1:3; Colossians 1:16).

Major Themes

God reveals (Revelation 1:1). God has always been the aggressor in revealing Himself and His will (Hebrews 1:1-2). All the revelation God wants us to have is in the Bible (see Psalm 119; 2 Timothy 3:15-17).

The glory of Jesus (Revelation 1:12-16). Brilliant light consistently accompanies the manifestation of His divine glory (Matthew 17:2-3; 1 Timothy 6:16). Philippians 2:5-11 indicates that Jesus veiled His pre-incarnate glory during His time on earth.

Digging Deeper with Cross-References

The importance of correct doctrine (Revelation 2–3)—Romans 16:17; Ephesians 4:14; 1 Timothy 1:10; 4:1; 6:3; 2 Timothy 4:3-4; Titus 1:9; 2:1

Praise and worship (Revelation 4:10)—Exodus 20:3-5; 1 Samuel 15:22-23; Psalms 29:2; 95:6; 100:2; Hebrews 12:28;

Life Lessons

Trusting God with the future (Revelation 1:1-3). We don't know every detail of what the future holds, but we do know the One who does (Isaiah 46:9-10). It therefore makes great sense to trust God with our futures (Psalm 37:5; Proverbs 3:5-6).

A failure to repent brings discipline (Revelation 2:4-5,14-16,20-23). A failure to repent of sin always brings God's discipline in the life of a believer. That's what happened to David following his sin with Bathsheba (see Psalms 32:3-5; 51). It can happen to us today too (Hebrews 12:5-11). It therefore makes good sense to have a lifestyle of repentance before God. As 1 Corinthians 11:31 puts it, "If we judged ourselves truly, we would not be judged."

Verses to Remember

- "You have abandoned the love you had at first. Remember therefore from where you have fallen; repent, and do the works you did at first" (Revelation 2:4-5).

- "I know your works: you are neither cold nor hot. Would that you were either cold or hot! So, because you are lukewarm, and neither hot nor cold, I will spit you out of my mouth" (Revelation 3:15-16).

Questions for Reflection and Discussion

1. Does false doctrine bother you? Do you ever feel tempted to turn a blind eye toward false doctrine in order to avoid conflict with others?

2. Just as Christ knows all that goes on in the churches, so He knows all that goes on in each of our lives. Does that reality please you or scare you?

3. On a spectrum that runs from cold to hot, where would you place your own spiritual life?

My Father, it is clear to me that You are calling me to a life of complete commitment and obedience. Partial obedience is unacceptable to You. Please enable me by the power of the Holy Spirit to consistently live in a way that pleases You. In Jesus's name, amen.

Judgment Falls from the Lord of Glory

In yesterday's lesson, we gained insights on Jesus's assessment of the seven churches in Asia Minor (Revelation 1–4). Today we zero in on the outbreak of God's judgments on a fallen world.

Begin by reading Revelation 5–8. As you read, never forget that God urges you to quickly obey His Word in all things (Psalm 119:60).

Chronological marker. John wrote Revelation in about AD 95.

Overview of Today's Scripture Reading

Revelation 5. The scroll contains the seven seal judgments to be unleashed during the tribulation period. Only Jesus, the divine Messiah and Lamb of God, is worthy to open it. The seven horns of Christ symbolize His complete power and might. Christ takes the scroll from the enthroned Father, and appropriately, all heaven worships Him. A new song erupts that anticipates final redemption through Christ (see John 3:16-17; Romans 5:8; 1 Peter 1:18-19).

Revelation 6. As Jesus breaks each seal, a new divine judgment is unleashed on earth. Those on earth recognize that the wrath of God is falling upon them. These seal judgments bring about the rise of the antichrist, bloodshed and war, famine and extreme deprivation, death, the martyrdom of believers, and a powerful earthquake with worldwide and cosmic consequences.

Revelation 7. John now witnesses two groups of people—one on earth, one in heaven. God's 144,000 Jewish witnesses on earth are supernaturally sealed for their protection. They will apparently seek to fulfill God's original mandate for the Jewish people to share the good news of salvation with all nations (Isaiah 42:6; 43:10). The second group is a multitude of believers in heaven who either died or were martyred (see Matthew 24:21). They praise God for their salvation.

Revelation 8. The seventh seal judgment brings seven new trumpet judgments, four of which are described in Revelation 8. All of heaven becomes silent—soberly aware of what now lies ahead. These judgments bring hail and fire on the earth, a "fiery mountain" striking and poisoning the sea, a star (perhaps large meteor) with a near-extinction-level deep impact of the earth, and cosmic disturbances.

Today's Big Ideas

- Only the Lamb is worthy to open the scroll and its seven seals (5).
- The seal judgments are unleashed on earth (6).
- The 144,000 Jewish witnesses are sealed (7).
- The first four trumpet judgments are unleashed on earth (8).

Insights on Difficult Verses

Revelation 6:9-10. When believers die, their souls go to heaven and are conscious in the presence of God.

Revelation 7:4. The tribes of Dan and Ephraim were omitted from this list of Jewish tribes because both became guilty of idolatry and paganized worship (Leviticus 24:11; Judges 18:1,30; see also Judges 17; 1 Kings 12:28-29; Hosea 4:17).

Revelation 7:4. Levi was included in this list of Jewish tribes (even though excluded in Old Testament lists) because the Levitical priesthood was fulfilled in Christ (Hebrews 7–10). There was no further need for the services of the tribe of Levi as priests, so they were included in the tribal listing.

Major Themes

God the Judge of all people (Revelation 6). God is a God of love, grace, mercy...and judgment (see Matthew 21:43; Acts 5; 12:21; 1 Corinthians 11:29-32; 1 John 5:16). In the future, Christians will face the judgment seat of Christ (1 Corinthians 3:12-15; 2 Corinthians 5:10). Unbelievers will face the great white throne judgment (Revelation 20:11-15).

Angels execute judgments (Revelation 8:2). Angels both announce and execute judgments (see Acts 12:22-23). This is nowhere clearer than in the book of Revelation. For example, the angels unleash the seven trumpet judgments on humankind (Revelation 8; see also 16:1).

Digging Deeper with Cross-References

Worship and singing (Revelation 7:11-12)—Exodus 15:1-21; Judges 5:1-12; Psalms 33:3; 40:3; Isaiah 27:2; 42:10-11; 44:23; Ephesians 5:19; Colossians 3:16

War as a judgment from God (Revelation 6:4)—Leviticus 26:25,33; Deuteronomy 28:22; Isaiah 1:20; Jeremiah 5:17; 6:25; Ezekiel 21:12; 32:11

End-time cosmic disturbances (Revelation 6:12-13)—Isaiah 13:10; 24:23; Ezekiel 32:7; Joel 2:10,31; 3:15; Amos 5:20; 8:9; Zephaniah 1:15; Acts 2:20

Life Lessons

Don't worry—trust God (Revelation 5:13). God remains on the throne, bringing about His eternal purposes, even when the world around us seems tumultuous. A great antidote to fear is to meditate on Bible verses that speak of God's absolute control of all things, such as Deuteronomy 10:14; 1 Chronicles 29:12; 2 Chronicles 20:6; Job 42:2; Psalms 33:8-11; 47:2; Isaiah 46:10; Ephesians 1:20-22; and John 14:1-3.

Angels are among us (Revelation 8:2). The angels do some scary things related to judgment in the book of Revelation. We must keep all this in perspective. Don't forget the good things angels do for us. They are our guardians (2 Kings 6:17; Psalm 91:9-11). They are sometimes used by God in answering our prayers (Acts 12:5-10). They escort us into heaven following death (Luke 16:22). They minister to us in many ways (Hebrews 2:14).

Verses to Remember

- "Salvation belongs to our God who sits on the throne, and to the Lamb" (Revelation 7:10).

- "The Lamb in the midst of the throne will be their shepherd, and he will guide them to springs of living water, and God will wipe away every tear from their eyes" (Revelation 7:17).

Questions for Reflection and Discussion

1. Can you think of any recent answers to prayer that move you to exult, "Worthy are you, O Lord"?

2. If it ever came to it, would you give your life as a martyr rather than deny Jesus?

3. Do you think you've ever been rescued by an angel?

My Father, salvation truly does belong to You and to the Lamb, Jesus Christ, who died for me. I praise You for the salvation You have provided for me. And I marvel that Jesus is my personal Shepherd. I yearn for the day when I will be face-to-face with You and You will wipe away every tear. I am thankful for You. In Jesus's blessed name, amen.

God's Two Witnesses

In yesterday's lesson we explored the outbreak of God's judgments (Revelation 5–8). Today we continue our study of God's judgments but also consider the little scroll, God's two prophetic witnesses, and the outbreak of satanic persecution.

Begin by reading Revelation 9–12. As you read, ask God to help you understand His Word (Psalm 119:73).

Chronological marker. John wrote Revelation in about AD 95.

Overview of Today's Scripture Reading

Revelation 9. Things get even worse on earth when the fifth trumpet judgment is unleashed, causing locust-like demonic spirits to be released from spirit prison so they can torment humans for five months. Then, with the unleashing of the sixth trumpet judgment, four powerful fallen angels lead an army of 200 million demonic spirits, who use three plagues to cause mass murder among humans.

Revelation 10. Earlier God's martyrs in heaven asked, "How long?" Now an angel affirms there will be no further delay (10:6). As soon as the seventh angel sounds the seventh trumpet (11:15), the seven bowl judgments will be unleashed in rapid-fire manner (Revelation 16).

Revelation 11. Meanwhile, God's two prophetic witnesses testify to the true God with miraculous acts for the first half of the tribulation period. Anyone who tries to harm them comes to a fiery end. Once their ministry is complete, God withdraws His providential protection, and the antichrist kills them. Three days later, they are resurrected and ascend into heaven in full view of everyone.

The seventh trumpet judgment is then unleashed, which includes the seven bowl judgments. Woe unto those still alive on earth!

Revelation 12. The woman in our text represents Israel (Isaiah 54:5-6; Jeremiah 3:6-8; 31:32). That the woman (or Jewish nation) is pregnant and in pain likely refers to the harsh treatment the Jewish nation experienced as she awaited the eventual birth of her Messiah. The dragon is Satan, who desired to kill the promised Messiah at birth. Under God's providence, Satan was unsuccessful. Jesus ascended into heaven following His resurrection (Acts 1:9; 2:33; Hebrews 1:1-3; 12:2).

War now erupts in heaven between God's holy angels and the evil angels. Satan and his fallen angels are no match for God's heavenly host. Once ousted from heaven, Satan persecutes the Jews, from whose lineage the Messiah was born. But the Jews providentially find refuge in the wilderness.

Today's Big Ideas

- Increasingly worse judgments are unleashed on earth (Revelation 9).

- God's two prophetic witnesses give a powerful testimony of the true God (11).

- War breaks out on earth (12:1-6,13-17) and in heaven (12:7-12).

Insights on Difficult Verses

Revelation 10:1. The angel's face was like the sun not because he was a deity but because he had just been in the glorious presence of God (much like Moses—see Exodus 34:29).

Revelation 10:3-4. God's voice is often compared to or associated with thunder (Job 26:14; 37:5; Psalm 29; John 12:28-29).

Revelation 12:4. The word "stars" is sometimes used of angels in the Bible (Job 38:7). Lucifer apparently drew a third of the angelic realm after him in this rebellion.

Major Themes

Violation of God's commandments (Revelation 9:20-21). People during the tribulation will worship pagan idols, thereby breaking God's first and second commandments (Exodus 20:3-6). As murderers (Revelation 9:21; 21:8; 22:15), they will violate God's sixth commandment (Exodus 20:13). As thieves (Revelation 9:21), they will break the eighth commandment (Exodus 20:15). These will be evil times.

Authority (Revelation 8:3). God gave His two witnesses authority. Death and Hades will be given authority over a fourth of the earth (Revelation 6:8). Satan will give authority to the antichrist (Revelation 13:2,4). The false prophet, too, will be given authority (13:12).

Digging Deeper with Cross-References

Two witnesses (Revelation 11:1-14)—Deuteronomy 17:6; 19:15; Matthew 18:16; John 8:17; Hebrews 10:28

War on the saints (Revelation 6:9-11)—Daniel 7:25; Revelation 7:9-14; 13:7,10; 20:4-5; compare with Job 1:9-11; 2:6-7; 1 Peter 5:8

Life Lessons

Withstanding persecution (Revelation 11:5). We may not die for our faith as the two witnesses do, but we will all likely be persecuted in one way or another. Scripture reveals that the wicked despise the godly (Proverbs 29:27) and the godly should expect persecution (2 Timothy 3:12; 1 John 3:13). However, those who are persecuted for righteousness are blessed (Matthew 5:10-11) and ought to rejoice in being counted worthy to suffer (Acts 5:41).

Fear God (Revelation 11:18). As Christians, we are called to live in reverent fear of God (1 Samuel 12:14,24; 2 Chronicles 19:9; Acts 10:35; 1 Peter 1:17; 2:17). Fear of the Lord motivates obedience to God (Deuteronomy 5:29; Ecclesiastes 12:13) and the desire to serve Him (Deuteronomy 6:13).

Verses to Remember

I heard a loud voice in heaven, saying, "Now the salvation and the power and the kingdom of our God and the authority of his Christ have come, for the accuser of our brothers has been thrown down, who accuses them day and night before our God. And they have conquered him by the blood of the Lamb and by the word of their testimony, for they loved not their lives even unto death. Therefore, rejoice, O heavens and you who dwell in them!" (Revelation 12:10-12).

Questions for Reflection and Discussion

1. Self-examination is healthy. Ask yourself, "Am I in complete submission to the authority of God in all areas of my life? Am I holding anything back?"

2. Does your lifestyle at home and at work consistently show that you have reverence for the Lord?

3. Would you say you are comfortable or uncomfortable in giving your testimony to others?

My Father, sometimes I sense I may not have a proper level of reverent fear for You. Sometimes I sin all too easily, with little resistance. As I continue to study Your Word, please enable me to increasingly gain the kind of reverent fear that motivates consistent obedience. And if I ever slip out of proper reverence for You, please allow the Holy Spirit to bring it to my attention. I thank You in Jesus's name. Amen.

Day 88

The Antichrist and the False Prophet

Yesterday we considered the little scroll, God's two prophetic witnesses, and satanic persecution (Revelation 9–12). Today we will focus on the rise of the antichrist and the false prophet, the outpouring of the bowl judgments, and the emergence of a global false religion.

Begin by reading Revelation 13–17. As you read, remember that God's Word is the true source of hope (Psalm 119:81).

Chronological marker. John wrote Revelation in about AD 95.

Overview of Today's Scripture Reading

Revelation 13. The term "antichrist" can mean "against Christ" or "instead of Christ." Energized by Satan, the antichrist will attain global dominion. He will appear to be killed and resurrected, thereby motivating the world to worship him. The antichrist's right-hand man will be the miracle-working false prophet, whose goal will be to promote the worship of the antichrist.

Revelation 14. This chapter provides a preview of what takes place at the end of the tribulation period. Jesus will stand on Mount Zion with the 144,000 Jewish witnesses, who will be invited into Christ's millennial kingdom (verses 1-5). The fall of Babylon (verses 6-8) and the punishment of the wicked (verses 9-13) are foreseen. Verses 14-20 provide a preview of Armageddon.

Revelation 15. Heaven now prepares for the final plagues—the bowl judgments—that will be unleashed on earth. These judgments represent the climax of God's holy wrath against God-rejecting humankind, the antichrist, and the false prophet.

Revelation 16. The seven judgments escalate from bad to worse:

1. Painful sores break out on worshippers of the antichrist.

2. The sea becomes like blood.

3. The rivers and springs turn to blood.

4. The sun's heat scorches the earth.

5. Darkness falls on the earth.

6. The Euphrates is dried up, making it easier for the kings of the east to assemble in preparation for Armageddon.

7. Lightning, thunder, and a catastrophic earthquake wreak havoc.

Revelation 17. The antichrist initially utilized the false religious system to bring unity to the world's people. Once he has accomplished this purpose, he no longer needs the false religion. He will dispose of it with the help of his ten sub-commanders. The antichrist now wants to be the sole object of worship.

Today's Big Ideas

- The antichrist will attain global dominion (13:1-10).

- The false prophet will motivate the world to worship the antichrist (13:11-18).

- God will pour out His wrath in the bowl judgments (15–16).

- The false religious system will be destroyed (17).

Insights on Difficult Verses

Revelation 13:18. Some suggest the number 666 points to a counterfeit Trinity—the antichrist, the false prophet, and Satan. Others suggest it may point to a specific (though yet unknown) man who will one day arise.

Revelation 14:9-11. The wicked are eternally tormented. The Greek word translated "torment" means "to vex with grievous pain." It carries the idea of torture. This torment is never ending (verse 11).

Revelation 16:14. Can demons perform miracles? Theologians suggest that they can apparently do grade-B supernormal signs but not grade-A supernatural miracles, which only Almighty God can do. God is infinite in power (omnipotent); the devil and the demons are finite creatures and are limited.

Major Themes

The antichrist mimics Christ (Revelation 13:3). Christ is God (John 1:1-2; 10:36); the antichrist will claim to be (2 Thessalonians 2:4). Christ performed miracles (Matthew 9:32-33; Mark 6:2); the antichrist will mimic miracles (Matthew 24:24; 2 Thessalonians 2:9). Christ is crowned with many crowns (Revelation 19:12); the antichrist is crowned with ten crowns (Revelation 13:1).

Satan energizes the antichrist (Revelation 13:8). The antichrist takes on the character of the one who energizes him (Satan). Just as Lucifer (Satan) sought godhood and exaltation (Isaiah 14:13-14), so does the antichrist (2 Thessalonians 2:4).

Digging Deeper with Cross-References

Blasphemy (Revelation 13:6)—Exodus 20:7; Leviticus 19:12; 22:32; Deuteronomy 5:11; Matthew 12:31-32; 2 Thessalonians 2:4

Satan's power (Revelation 12:9)—Job 1:12; Luke 4:6; Acts 26:18; Ephesians 6:12; 2 Thessalonians 2:9

Life Lessons

Satan's attack against Christians (Revelation 12:12). Satan will attack God's people during the future tribulation period, and he spiritually attacks Christians today. But we are not defenseless. God provides us with spiritual armor and encourages us to stand firm (Ephesians 6:11-18). We are instructed, "Resist the devil, and he will flee from you" (James 4:7). We are to depend on the Holy Spirit, remembering that "he who is in you is greater than he who is in the world" (1 John 4:4).

Following Jesus (Revelation 14:4). Like the 144,000, you and I are called to follow the Lamb regardless of the cost. "If anyone would come after me, let him deny himself and take up his cross and follow me" (Matthew 16:24). "If anyone serves me, he must follow me" (John 12:26; see 14:15).

Verses to Remember

- "'Blessed are the dead who die in the Lord from now on.' 'Blessed indeed,' says the Spirit, 'that they may rest from their labors, for their deeds follow them!'" (Revelation 14:13).

- "Great and amazing are your deeds, O Lord God the Almighty! Just and true are your ways, O King of the nations! Who will not fear, O Lord, and glorify your name? For you alone are holy. All nations will come and worship you, for your righteous acts have been revealed" (Revelation 15:3-4).

Questions for Reflection and Discussion

1. Have you ever been so awestruck at how the Lord came through for you that you were moved to ask, "Who is like you, O Lord?" (Exodus 15:11).

2. Do you think you could ever be deceived by false doctrine? Why or why not? (See Acts 17:11; 1 Thessalonians 5:21.)

3. If you were ever accused of being a Christian, would there be enough evidence to convict you?

My Father, it can be frightening to ponder what lies ahead for humanity. Despite the horror of what is to come, however, You have told us not to fear, but to peacefully rest in Your sovereign oversight of our lives. Please enable me to keep my attention focused on You and not be sidetracked by the distractions of this world. In Jesus's name, amen.

Day 89

The Second Coming

Yesterday we gave attention to the antichrist, the false prophet, the bowl judgments, and the global false religion (Revelation 13–17). Today we turn our attention to the fall of Babylon, the second coming of Christ, Christ's millennial kingdom, and the great white throne judgment.

Begin by reading Revelation 18–20. As you read, remember that great spiritual wisdom comes from studying God's Word (Psalm 119:98-104).

Chronological marker. John wrote Revelation in about AD 95.

Overview of Today's Scripture Reading

Revelation 18. Political Babylon will be destroyed as a direct, decisive judgment from the hand of God. God will settle the score for Babylon's long history of standing against His people of Israel. Just as Babylon showed no mercy in its oppression against Israel in the past, so God will now show no mercy to Babylon during the tribulation. This judgment will apparently occur at the very end of the seven-year period. The collapse of Babylon will indicate to the rulers of the world that the luxurious empire of the antichrist is utterly doomed.

Revelation 19. Babylon's destruction leads to a great outbreak of praise in heaven. Heaven's inhabitants are now invited to rejoice and exult over the imminent marriage of the Lamb (see Matthew 9:15; 22:2-14; 25:1-13; Mark 2:19-20; Luke 5:34-35; 14:15-24; John 3:29).

The description of Christ's second coming is majestic. Christ rides a white horse, fitting for the glorious Commander in Chief of heaven's armies. He is called Faithful and True, returning to earth just as He promised (Matthew 24:27-31). On His head are many diadems, representing total sovereignty and royal kingship. He comes as the "King of kings and Lord of lords" (1 Timothy 6:15).

Revelation 20. Satan is now imprisoned in the bottomless pit (see Luke 8:31; 2 Peter 2:4). There he remains for the duration of Christ's millennial kingdom on earth. Christ's millennial kingdom will feature an enhanced physical environment, plenty of food for all, harmony with the animal kingdom, longevity among humans, physical health, prosperity, and joy.

At the end of Christ's millennial kingdom, Satan will be loosed and lead one final rebellion (verses 7-9). Fire instantly destroys the rebels (verse 9). Satan is cast into the lake of fire. The wicked dead are then resurrected and judged at the great white throne judgment.

Today's Big Ideas

- Political/economical Babylon falls (18).
- The marriage of the Lamb has come (19:6-10).
- Christ's second coming is glorious (19:11-21).
- Christ reigns during the millennial kingdom (20:1-10).
- The wicked are judged at the great white throne judgment (20:11-15).

Insights on Difficult Verses

Revelation 18:9. Just as a prostitute seduces a man into sexual immorality, so commercial/political Babylon seduces the unbelieving world into anti-God materialism. This materialistic system will crash and burn.

Revelation 20:11-15. The great white throne judgment takes place after the millennial kingdom and is a judgment of only the wicked dead. Once before the divine Judge, they are evaluated according to their works not only to justify their condemnation but also to determine the degree to which each person should be punished throughout eternity in hell.

Major Themes

Sudden destruction (Revelation 18:8). Sudden destruction often falls on the wicked. Proverbs 6:15 warns, "Calamity will come upon him suddenly." Proverbs 24:22 warns that disaster "will rise suddenly." God affirms in Jeremiah 15:8, "I have made anguish and terror fall upon them suddenly."

Christ the King (Revelation 19:16). Genesis 49:10 prophesied that the Messiah would come from Judah's tribe and reign as king. The Davidic covenant promised a Messiah who would have an eternal throne (2 Samuel 7:16; Luke 1:32-33). Psalm 110 affirms that the Messiah will rule over all.

Digging Deeper with Cross-References

The Old Testament basis for the millennial kingdom (Revelation 20:2-3)—Psalm 2:6-9; Isaiah 65:18-23; Jeremiah 31:12-14,31-37; Ezekiel 34:25-29; 37:1-13; 40–48; Daniel 2:35; 7:13-14; Joel 2:21-27; Amos 9:13-14; Micah 4:1-7; Zephaniah 3:9-20

The judgment of the wicked (Revelation 20:11-15)—Psalm 62:12; Proverbs 24:12; Matthew 16:27; Romans 2:6; 2 Corinthians 5:10; Revelation 2:23

Life Lessons

Betrothed to Christ (Revelation 19:6-10). The church is betrothed, or engaged, to Jesus Christ. Just as betrothed brides in Bible times kept themselves pure and faithful prior to the marriage ceremony, so you and I as members of the church ought to seek purity and faithfulness as we await our divine Bridegroom from heaven (see John 14:1-6; 1 Thessalonians 4:13-18, Titus 2:13-14).

Jesus is King of kings and Lord of lords (Revelation 19:16). Christ sovereignly oversees all that comes into our lives. No matter what we may encounter, and no matter how much we may fail to understand why certain things happen in life, the knowledge that our sovereign King of kings is in control anchors us in the midst of life's storms. Because Christ is sovereign, we are never victims of our circumstances.

Verses to Remember

- "Hallelujah! Salvation and glory and power belong to our God, for his judgments are true and just" (Revelation 19:1-2).

- "Then I saw heaven opened, and behold, a white horse! The one sitting on it is called Faithful and True, and in righteousness he judges and makes war. His eyes are like a flame of fire, and on his head are many diadems, and he has a name written that no one knows but himself. He is clothed in a robe dipped in blood, and the name by which he is called is The Word of God" (Revelation 19:11-13).

Questions for Reflection and Discussion

1. Do you think you live more like a citizen of earth or like a citizen of heaven?

2. Is your lifestyle befitting a bride who is awaiting the soon appearance of her Bridegroom?

3. Are you facing any difficult circumstances that you would like to entrust to the King of kings, the Lord Jesus Christ?

My Father, I fear that the attractions of this world sometimes sidetrack me so that I live more like a citizen of this world than a citizen of heaven. Please enable me, Father, to take my heavenly citizenship more seriously. I love You. In Jesus's name, amen.

Day 90

The Eternal State

In the previous lesson we discussed the fall of Babylon, the second coming of Christ, Christ's millennial kingdom, and the great white throne judgment (Revelation 18–20). Today we explore the new heavens and the new earth, the New Jerusalem, and Jesus's closing exhortation.

Begin by reading Revelation 21–22. As you read, remember that reading Scripture can strengthen your faith in God (Romans 10:17).

Chronological marker. John wrote Revelation in about AD 95.

Overview of Today's Scripture Reading

Revelation 21. Before the eternal kingdom can be made manifest, God must deal with this present earth, which has been tainted by sin and Satan (see Genesis 3:17-18; Romans 8:20-22). The present (old) heavens and earth will pass away (Psalm 102:25-26; Isaiah 51:6; Matthew 24:35), and God will create new heavens and a new earth.

The New Jerusalem is the eternal city that you and I will one day inhabit on the new earth. Christ Himself created it (John 14:1-3). God will now live directly with redeemed humankind (see Leviticus 26:11-12; Deuteronomy 12:5). Here at last we find unfettered companionship between the Creator and His creation. The words John chooses to describe the eternal city no doubt represent a feeble human attempt to describe the utterly indescribable.

Revelation 22. The New Jerusalem features the river of the water of life and the tree of life. The pure river of life, though it may be a real and material river, is likely also symbolic of the abundance of spiritual life that will characterize those who live in the eternal city. The tree of life—first seen in the Garden of Eden—is a tree that bestows continuing life (see Genesis 2:9,17; 3:1-24). The crowning feature of heaven will be seeing God face-to-face (Revelation 22:4; see also Psalm 17:15; 1 Corinthians 13:12; 1 John 3:2). The prophecies in this book are "trustworthy and true." They come from the One who is called Faithful and True (Revelation 19:11).

Today's Big Ideas

- God will create new heavens and a new earth (21:1-8).

- The New Jerusalem is the eternal city of the redeemed that will rest on the new earth (21:9-27).

- The city will feature the river of the water of life and the tree of life (22:1-5).

- Christ is coming soon (22:6-21).

Insights on Difficult Verses

Revelation 22:12. Some believe Jesus is coming soon from the divine perspective (see Hebrews 1:2; James 5:3). Others suggest He is coming soon from the vantage point of those living during the time of the tribulation described in Revelation.

Revelation 22:16. "The bright morning star" is a messianic title from Numbers 24:17—"A star shall come out of Jacob."

Major Themes

God dwelling among us (Revelation 22:4). In the Garden of Eden, God walked with Adam and Eve (Genesis 3:8-10). Once sin entered the world, God dwelt among the Israelites through the Jewish tabernacle (Exodus 40:34), and later the temple (2 Samuel 22:7). In New Testament times, God dwelt (or "tabernacled") among us in the person of Jesus (John 1:14). Today, Christians are the temple of the Holy Spirit (1 Corinthians 3:16; 6:19). In the New Jerusalem, God will dwell with His people face-to-face.

A city and a country (Revelation 22:2,14,19). Heaven is not only a city but also "a better country" (Hebrews 11:13-15). Such words indicate that heaven is a real, physical place where we'll dwell forever.

Digging Deeper with Cross-References

The inheritance awaiting Christians in heaven (Revelation 21:1-4)—Matthew 5:5; 19:29; 25:34; 1 Corinthians 6:9-10; Hebrews 1:14; 9:15; 1 Peter 1:4; 3:9; 1 John 5:5

Worship of God (Revelation 22:3)—Exodus 20:3-5; Deuteronomy 5:7; Psalms 29:2; 95:6; 100:2; Hebrews 12:28

Life Lessons

Happiness in heaven, suffering in hell (Revelation 21:4). Some theologians believe God may purge our memories so that they do not retain memories of those now in hell. "Behold, I will create new heavens and a new earth. The former things will not be remembered, nor will they come to mind" (Isaiah 65:17-19).

Recognition in heaven (Revelation 21–22). We will recognize our Christian loved ones in the New Jerusalem! The Thessalonian Christians were concerned about their Christian loved ones who had died. Paul tells them they'll be reunited in heaven—implying they'll recognize each other (1 Thessalonians 4:13-17). David knew he'd be reunited with his deceased son in heaven and had no doubt about recognizing him (2 Samuel 12:23). The rich man, Lazarus, and Abraham all recognized each other in the afterlife (Luke 16:19-31).

Verses to Remember

I heard a loud voice from the throne saying, "Behold, the dwelling place of God is with man. He will dwell with them, and they will be his people, and God himself will be with them as their God. He will wipe away every tear from their eyes, and death shall be no more, neither shall there be mourning, nor crying, nor pain anymore, for the former things have passed away." And he who was seated on the throne said, "Behold, I am making all things new" (Revelation 21:3-5).

Questions for Reflection and Discussion

1. Do you make a habit of maintaining a top-down perspective—that is, a heavenly one?

2. Scripture reveals that if we are faithful in this life, Christ will entrust us with more opportunities to serve Him in the next (Luke 19:11-26). Does this reality bless you, scare you, or maybe a little of both?

3. Think about some of your Christian loved ones who are now in heaven. Does your future reunion with them put wind in your spiritual sails?

My Father, how I yearn to be with You in the New Jerusalem, dwelling face-to-face with You for all eternity. I yearn for the day when there will be no more tears, mourning, or death. And all of this is made possible because of the salvation Jesus attained for me at the cross. How thankful I am for Jesus! In Jesus's name, amen.

Jesus—the Heart of the New Testament

Now that you have gone through the entire New Testament, I'm sure you have noticed that Jesus is the very heart of it. In fact, all the major New Testament doctrines—including those of God, man, salvation, the church, angels, and the afterlife—are tied directly to the person of Jesus Christ. He is the thread that runs through all these doctrines. He ties the whole New Testament (and even the Old Testament) together. Consider these eight brief nuggets of truth.

Jesus is God. Jesus is referred to in the New Testament as both God (Hebrews 1:8) and Lord (Matthew 22:43-45). Jesus has all the attributes (or characteristics) of God. For example, He's all-powerful (Matthew 28:18) and all-knowing (John 1:48). Jesus does things only God can do, such as creating the entire universe (John 1:3) and raising people from the dead (John 11:43-44). Moreover, Jesus was worshipped as God by those who came to know Him (as in Matthew 14:33).

Jesus is the Creator. The Old Testament presents God Almighty as the Creator of the universe (Isaiah 44:24). But in the New Testament, Jesus is portrayed as the agent of creation (John 1:3; Colossians 1:16; Hebrews 1:2). This points to the reality that Jesus Himself is God. When we look at the universe around us, we see the handiwork of Jesus. He's the one who made it. We catch a glimpse of His majesty and glory as we look at the starry sky above.

Jesus is the ultimate revelation of God. God has revealed Himself to humankind in numerous ways. For example, God reveals His majesty and glory in the universe around us (Psalm 19; Romans 1:19-20). And since Christ Himself created the universe, the revelation in the universe is His doing.

God has also revealed Himself through the mouths of the prophets. First Peter 1:11 tells us that the Spirit of Christ spoke through all the prophets in biblical times. So the revelation that came through them is Christ's doing.

Scripture reveals that the ultimate revelation of God was Jesus Himself in the Incarnation. Jesus—as eternal God—took on human flesh so He could be God's fullest revelation to humankind (Hebrews 1:2-3). Jesus was a revelation of God not just in His person (as God) but in His life and teachings as well. By observing the things Jesus did and said, we learn a great deal about God, including...

- His awesome power (John 3:2)
- His incredible wisdom (1 Corinthians 1:24)
- His boundless love (1 John 3:16)
- His unfathomable grace (2 Thessalonians 1:12)

All this serves as the backdrop as to why Jesus told a group of Pharisees, "Whoever believes in me, believes not in me but in him who sent me. And whoever sees me sees him who sent me" (John 12:44-45).

Jesus is the divine Savior. Humanity's sin against God posed a problem for God. How could God remain holy and just and at the same time forgive sinners and allow them into His presence? God's ineffable purity cannot tolerate sin. He is of purer eyes than to behold evil. How, then, can the righteous God deal in a just way with the sinner and at the same time satisfy His own compassion and love in saving him from doom? The answer is found in Jesus. Jesus came as our beloved Savior and died on the cross on our behalf (Matthew 20:28). Jesus our Savior "gave himself as a ransom for all" (1 Timothy 2:6). The New Testament says that In Christ, we are...

saved (Hebrews 7:25)
forgiven (Ephesians 1:6-7)
justified (1 Corinthians 6:11)
reconciled (Colossians 1:20)
redeemed (Ephesians 1:7)

made alive (Romans 6:11)
brought near (Ephesians 2:13)
given eternal life (Romans 5:21)

How great a salvation we have in Christ!

The Holy Spirit glorifies Jesus. Just before His crucifixion, Jesus met with the disciples in the upper room and gave them some final words of encouragement. One of the things He spoke to them about involved the coming of the Holy Spirit. A primary ministry of the Holy Spirit is to glorify Christ and to make known the things of Christ (John 14:26). The Spirit testifies about Christ (John 15:26). The Spirit does not make Himself prominent but rather exalts Jesus Christ.

Jesus is the head of the church. The church is a company of people who have one Lord and who share together in one gift of salvation in the Lord Jesus Christ (Titus 1:4). In Matthew 16:18, Jesus affirmed to Peter, "I will build my church." The church is not the result of a pastor or priest or body of elders. It is not owned by a denomination. Christ Himself builds and owns the church (see Acts 20:28). The church is His alone. Christ not only owns the church—He is the head of it. Ephesians 5:23 tells us that Christ is the head of the church, His body, even as the husband is the head of the wife.

The angels worship and serve Jesus. Jesus created the angels (Colossians 1:16). An angel announced Jesus's birth to Mary (Luke 1:26-28) and to Joseph (Matthew 1:20). Angels proclaimed Jesus's birth to the shepherds in the field (Luke 2:9). Angels ministered to Jesus during His infancy (Matthew 2:13-18), during His three-year ministry (Matthew 4:1-11), and just before the crucifixion (Luke 22:43). An angel rolled away the stone following Jesus's resurrection from the dead (Matthew 28:1-6). Angels appeared when Jesus ascended back into heaven (Acts 1:9-11). When Jesus comes again, He will be accompanied by angels (Matthew 16:27). The angels will worship and exalt Jesus for all eternity (Revelation 5:11-14).

Jesus made it possible for us to live with Him forever. Those who believe in Jesus receive eternal life and will live with Him forever (John 3:16-17; Acts 16:31). What an awesome gift and privilege Jesus has provided for us!

Can anything be more sublime and more utterly satisfying for the Christian than to enjoy the sheer delight of unobstructed, unbroken fellowship with Christ in heaven (2 Corinthians 5:6-8)? We will see our beloved Lord face-to-face in all His splendor and glory. We will gaze on His countenance and behold His resplendent beauty forever. And in His presence, we will find fullness of joy and pleasures forevermore (Psalm 16:11).

Do you now see what I mean when I say Jesus is a thread that runs through the entire New Testament? Now that you have studied through the New Testament, it is appropriate that we close our time together by reflecting on the wonder that is Jesus Christ. What a wondrous Savior we have in Jesus! Lift your hands in praise. I urge you to do it now.

> To him who loves us
> and has freed us from our sins by his blood
> and made us a kingdom,
> priests to his God and Father,
> to him be glory and dominion forever and ever.
> Amen (Revelation 1:5-6).

Bibliography

Alexander, David, and Pat Alexander. *Zondervan Handbook to the Bible*. Grand Rapids: Zondervan, 2011.

Boa, Kenneth, and Karen Boa. *Handbook to Scripture: Integrating the Bible into Everyday Life*. Grand Rapids: Zondervan, 2011.

Cox, Steven L., and Kendell H. Easley. *HCSB Harmony of the Gospels*. Nashville: B&H Publishing Group, 2007.

Geisler, Norman L. *A Popular Survey of the New Testament*. Grand Rapids: Baker, 2008.

George, Jim. *The Bare Bones Bible Handbook*. Eugene: Harvest House, 2006.

Halley, Henry H. *Halley's Bible Handbook*. Grand Rapids: Zondervan, 1961.

Hays, J. Daniel, and J. Scott Duvall, eds. *The Baker Illustrated Bible Handbook*. Grand Rapids: Baker, 2011.

Hoehner, Harold W. *Chronological Aspects of the Life of Christ*. Grand Rapids: Zondervan, 1978.

Holman Illustrated Bible Handbook. Nashville: Broadman and Holman, 2005.

MacArthur, John. *The MacArthur Bible Handbook*. Nashville: Thomas Nelson, 2003.

Mears, Henrietta. *What the Bible Is All About*. Grand Rapids: Zondervan, 2011.

Miller, Stephen. *The Complete Guide to the Bible*. Uhrichsville: Barbour, 2007.

Pentecost, J. Dwight. *The Words and Works of Jesus Christ: A Study of the Life of Christ*. Grand Rapids: Zondervan, 1981.

Robertson, A.T. *A Harmony of the Gospels for Students of the Life of Christ*. New York: Harper & Row, 1950.

Scroggie, W. Graham. *A Guide to the Gospels: A Comprehensive Analysis of the Four Gospels*. Grand Rapids: Kregel, 2010.

Tenney, Merrill C. *New Testament Survey*. Grand Rapids: Eerdmans, 1985.

Thomas, Robert L., and Stanley N. Gundry. *A Harmony of the Gospels: New American Standard Edition*. San Francisco: HarperOne, 1986.

Unger, Merrill F. *The New Unger's Bible Handbook*. Chicago: Moody, 2005.

Wiersbe, Warren. *With the Word Commentary*. Nashville: Thomas Nelson, 1991.

Willmington, Harold L. *Willmington's Guide to the Bible*. Wheaton: Tyndale House, 2011.

Notes

1. *The Chronological Life Application Study Bible* (Carol Stream: Tyndale House, 2012), p. A17.
2. *The Chronological Study Bible: NIV* (Nashville: Thomas Nelson, 2014), p. xi.
3. *The Chronological Study Bible: New King James Version* (Nashville: Thomas Nelson, 2008), p. xiv.
4. Robert Thomas and Robert Gundry, *The NIV Harmony of the Gospels* (New York: HarperOne, 1988), p. 294.
5. *John Gill's Exposition of the Bible*, q.v. Hebrews 11:16. Available online at www.biblestudytools.com/commentaries/gills-exposition-of-the-bible/hebrews-11-16.html.

Daily Reading Index

14.	Parables of the Kingdom, Part 2	Matthew 8:23-34; 13:31-52; Mark 4:30–5:20; Luke 8:22-39; 13:18-21
15.	Healing a Woman and Raising a Dead Girl	Matthew 9:18-34; 13:53-58; Mark 5:21–6:6; Luke 4:16-30; 8:40-56
16.	Jesus Sends Out 12 Apostles	Matthew 9:35–10:42; 14:3-12; Mark 6:6-13,17-29; Luke 9:1-6
17.	Feeding 5000 and Walking on Water	Matthew 14:1-2,13-33; Mark 6:14-16, 30-52; Luke 9:7-17; John 6:1-21
18.	The Bread of Life	Matthew 14:34–15:20; Mark 6:53–7:23; and John 6:22-71
19.	Miraculous Proofs of Christ's Identity	Matthew 15:21–16:20; Mark 7:24–8:30; Luke 9:18-21
20.	The Transfiguration	Matthew 16:21–17:20; Mark 8:31–9:29; Luke 9:22-43
21.	Restoration and Forgiveness	Matthew 17:22–18:35; Mark 9:30-50; Luke 9:43-50; John 7:1-9
22.	Counting the Cost	Matthew 8:18-22; 19:1-2; Mark 10:1; Luke 9:51-62; John 7:10–8:20
23.	The Good Samaritan	Luke 10; John 8:21-59
24.	Prayer, Anxiety, and Watchfulness	Luke 11:1-13,33-54; 12:1-48
25.	The Good Shepherd	Luke 12:49–13:17; John 9:1–10:21
26.	The Narrow Door	Matthew 23:37-39; Luke 13:22–15:10; John 10:22-42
27.	The Prodigal Son	Luke 15:11–17:10
28.	The Resurrection and the Life	Luke 17:11-37; John 11
29.	Prayer, Humility, Wealth, and Marriage	Matthew 19:3-30; Mark 10:2-31; Luke 18:1-30
30.	Bartimaeus and Zacchaeus	Matthew 20; Mark 10:32-52; Luke 18:31–19:10
31.	The Triumphal Entry	Matthew 21:1-11; 26:6-13; Mark 11:1-11; 14:3-9; Luke 19:11-40; John 12:1-19

Other Great Harvest House Books
by Ron Rhodes

BOOKS ABOUT THE BIBLE

40 Days Through Genesis
The Big Book of Bible Answers
Bite-Size Bible® Answers
Bite-Size Bible® Charts
Bite-Size Bible® Definitions
Bite-Size Bible® Handbook
Commonly Misunderstood Bible Verses
The Complete Guide to Bible Translations
Find It Fast in the Bible
The Popular Dictionary of Bible Prophecy
Understanding the Bible from A to Z
What Does the Bible Say About...?

BOOKS ABOUT THE END TIMES

8 Great Debates of Bible Prophecy
40 Days Through Revelation
Cyber Meltdown
The End Times in Chronological Order
Northern Storm Rising
Unmasking the Antichrist

BOOKS ABOUT OTHER IMPORTANT TOPICS

5-Minute Apologetics for Today
1001 Unforgettable Quotes About God, Faith, and the Bible
Answering the Objections of Atheists,
Agnostics, and Skeptics
Christianity According to the Bible
The Complete Guide to Christian Denominations
Conversations with Jehovah's Witnesses
Find It Quick Handbook on Cults and New Religions
The Truth Behind Ghosts, Mediums, and Psychic Phenomena
Secret Life of Angels
What Happens After Life?
Why Do Bad Things Happen If God Is Good?
Wonder of Heaven

To learn more about Harvest House books and
to read sample chapters, visit our website:

www.harvesthousepublishers.com

HARVEST HOUSE PUBLISHERS
EUGENE, OREGON